Silenced Witnesses *Vol. II*

The Parents' Story
The Denial of Vaccine Damage by Government, Corporations and the Media

written by the parents
edited by Martin J Walker

SLINGSHOT PUBLICATIONS
London
2009

Silenced Witnesses Vol. II

The Parents' Story: The denial of vaccine damage by government, corporations and the media.

Written by the parents
Edited by Martin J Walker

© Slingshot Publications

Slingshot Publications,
BM Box 8314, London, England
www.slingshotpublications.com

First Published November 2009

ISBN: 978-0-9519646-6-8

Type set by Viviana Guinarte
In Palatino and Apple Chancery

Cover design and photo lay-out: Andy Dark

Printed in Italy

CRYSHAME
PO BOX 677
BURY ST EDMUNDS
IP33 9WZ

TO ORDER MORE COPIES
CHEQUES PAYABLE TO CRYSHAME
PLEASE SEND TO THE ABOVE
ADDRESS WITH YOUR DETAILS

OR TEL: 01359 232772

Acknowledgements and Dedication

Thanks to all the contributors who worked hard on their chapters
and who took criticism and editorial advice
in good faith and the will to learn.
Thanks to Alan Golding whose film *Selective Hearing*
makes an exceptional contribution to this second volume.
Thanks to Carol and Viviana for their review
of the contributions and their corrections. Thanks to the
'Fondazione Hans Ruesch per una medicina senza vivisezione',
Switzerland, for their funding contribution to the parents' cause.
Finally, my thanks as editor for the support I have received from
my family, the parents of vaccine damaged children, as well as
those intimate strangers who have supported me and the book
with substantial funding but wish to remain anonymous.

Like the first book, this volume is dedicated to all
the children adversely affected by vaccines and the parents
who care for them. It is also dedicated to the three
doctors still appearing before the General Medical Council,
who have consistently sided with the parents.

It seems, in principle, self evident that no free enterprise can expect only to share the profit of their products without also taking responsibility for any damage caused by them. It is preposterous to assume that the drug industry can be allowed to prosper when their results are positive, but refrain from paying damages and pass the burden of responsibility on to society when something goes wrong with their products.

Henning Sjostrom and Robert Nilsson,
Thalidomide and the Power of the Drug Companies.
A Penguin Special, 1972.

While it is illogical and unscientific to assume that *all* serious health problems following vaccination *are* causally related, it is more illogical and even less scientific to assume that *all* serious health problem following vaccination are *not* causally related.

Barbara Loe Fisher,
Silenced Witnesses: The Parents' Story. Vol. II
Slingshot Publications, 2009.

C O N T E N T S

v

The Eye of the Storm

When Carol Stott and I wrote our separate parts of the introduction to the first *Silenced Witnesses*, we tried to describe very generally the climate of the campaign against Dr Andrew Wakefield. Now, with this second volume, published near the end of the two-year GMC fitness-to-practise hearing against Dr Wakefield, Professor Murch and Professor Walker-Smith, Carol has added an objective view from outside the GMC, looking mainly at the way that most British journalists have avoided the hearing. After attending almost every single day of the two-year hearing, I have followed this with a relatively detailed view of the charges mounted by the GMC prosecution and then at the end of the introduction I have introduced each of the book's chapters and looked at its focus.

Part One

For those who come new to this story, there follows a summary of what happened to Dr Wakefield in the years leading up to the General Medical Council Fitness to Practice hearing.

In 1993, Dr Andrew Wakefield, a well-respected academic gastroenterologist, working at the Royal Free Hospital in Hampstead, London, began writing to Dr David Salisbury, head of vaccination and immunology for the NHS. Dr Wakefield made clear in a number of letters and telephone calls, that he was concerned about the possibility of a public health crisis consequent upon the continued use of the mumps, measles and rubella (MMR) vaccination. Dr Wakefield told Dr Salisbury that research at the Royal Free was indicating that some children had suffered serious adverse reactions from MMR. Wakefield was given no credence by Salisbury, and over the next decade Salisbury managed to attend only one short meeting with the doctor.

In February 1998, the *Lancet* published a case review paper authored by Dr Wakefield and twelve others, which showed clearly that in 12 children consecutively referred to the Royal Free Hospital, regressive autism had occurred together with inflammatory bowel disease (IBD); in eight of the twelve children, it had also been noted, either by the child's parent or the GP, that onset followed exposure to a measles containing vaccine. The paper suggested that the measles virus – or this in conjunction with other viruses – might act as a trigger for this new syndrome. Three peer-reviewers for the *Lancet*, and the editor of the *Lancet*, together with the 12 authors, all agreed the paper for publication.

In 2004, the *Sunday Times* ran a long article by pro vaccine journalist Brian Deer, which amounted to a sustained character assassination of Dr Wakefield. In the decade prior to the article, Deer had specialised in trying to cast doubt on the parents of children who had made claims for vaccine damage. He had apparently been helped in carrying out his 'investigation' into Wakefield, by Medico-Legal Investigations, a private inquiry company almost wholly subsidised at that time by the Association of the British Pharmaceutical Industry.

In the *Sunday Times* article, the then Minister of Health, John Reid, ordered that Deer's 'findings' should be immediately tendered as a complaint, to the General Medical Council. Consequently, based on a complaint by a single journalist whose views seemed to coincide with those of the vaccine manufacturers, the GMC prosecution process began to assemble a case against Dr

Wakefield and two of his colleagues, Professor Murch and Professor Walker-Smith, one of the most respected paediatric gastroenterologists in Europe.[i] The prosecution itself began in October 2007. It has continued, in and out of session, for over two years, and is not due to conclude, with or without significant findings, until 2010.

Deer's *Sunday Times* article and a later Channel 4 *Dispatches* programme *MMR: What They Didn't Tell You*, a farrago of selective truths, serious errors and bias, that might have been a better science fiction drama than a documentary, were not the only blows struck against Dr Wakefield in 2004. What was then the Legal Aid Board (LAB), but became the Legal Services Commission (LSC), withdrew legal aid from a large group of parents of vaccine damaged children whose case against three pharmaceutical companies had been continuing over a ten-year period. Dr Wakefield was the most important expert witness retained by lawyers for these parents.

Deer's article, followed by his complaint to the GMC and the aborting of the claim against the three pharmaceutical companies, signalled the end of any possibility that Dr Wakefield's research would be acted upon by the government, or that parents would ever see justice for their vaccine damaged children. At this time, four years ago, it looked as though New Labour and the pharmaceutical companies were getting away with the biggest public health fraud in the history of Britain's National Health Service (NHS).

Prior to and during the General Medical Council (GMC) fitness-to-practice hearing against Dr Wakefield, the GMC frequently denied that Brian Deer had tendered the main contents of his *Sunday Times* article as a complaint to the GMC.

However, it is now clear that the GMC acted both on the Health Minister's instruction, and on the substance of Deer's article, which he offered to the GMC in the form of a complaint.

One of the reasons why the GMC denied accepting a complaint from Brian Deer, was probably that their lawyers could see quite clearly that his article was desperately insufficient to convert on its own into a full-blown legal prosecution. Pressed as they were, however, by the government and the ABPI, they appear to have decided to make the best of a bad job.

A Tale of Two Cities

For me Carol, and I think for the campaign, 2007 and 2008 was the best of times in Austin, Texas, but the worst of times in London, England. We saw the seasons unfold at the GMC, and we saw them come around again. In London, Spring turned to Summer, Summer turned to Autumn, Autumn turned to Winter and the whole cycle began again. This being England, the weather stayed much the same throughout; gloomy, grey, damp; resigned to cloud cover but with the occasional burst of brilliant sunshine. It reflected the autism community here: struggling on, with a non-seeing, non-hearing government awaiting only the outcome of its kangaroo court.

In Austin, Texas, the sun shone almost daily – with only the occasional cloud. News came in from Washington that Hannah Poling and Bailey Banks won their autism-MMR cases and three presidents elect promised to research the vaccine-autism link, obviously having been advised by senior Whitehouse officials that the numbers affected were now big enough for this to be a vote-catching issue. The 'Green Our Vaccines' US rally attracted thousands of concerned and angry parents and the US Institutes of Medicine confirmed that vaccines were 'still on the table' as a possible cause of autistic-like regression.

Within the walls of the GMC theatre – impervious to real life, and to the suffering of children with ASD and gastro-intestinal pathology – the case against the three doctors began to unravel. As each took the stand in turn, counsel for the prosecution fell, sometimes literally, on its face and still the children remained unseen. Known only by numbers, their illness, presented by prosecution counsel as a Wakefield delusion, continued relentlessly and their hidden faces provided a virtual backdrop to the stage-play. The gallery for the play comprised the parents, who in most other cases would have sought to witness the fruits of their complaint, but in this case sought only to come together in continuous support of the doctors who dared to help their children. The gallery also comprised other journalists, writers, colleagues, friends and family, and the original complainant.

For many of us, the beginning of the GMC hearing brought the uncomfortable sitting, for the first time, with Brian Deer. As the evidence unfolded, he sat on the periphery, a sole and impassive physical specter with the appearance, uncannily like the case itself, of being cobbled together from a disparate selection of spare parts.

There are many aspects to this hearing and the more general issue: genuine concern for public health, and the fight against infectious disease; health-care dogma founded on an untested vaccine schedule and pharmaceutical dictate; academic dogma founded on ineptitude and cowardice. But perhaps a key factor is how the British press has handled the case.

The media machine first kicked in during the late 1990s with the now infamous *Lancet* paper the publication of which was followed by a press briefing. In the briefing, Dr Wakefield advised caution, and suggested a return to single-vaccines to protect against measles, mumps and rubella until more was learned about the safety of the combined MMR vaccine. The *Lancet* paper itself had claimed not to have proven any causal association between MMR and autism, but the authors reported a number of parental concerns in this regard.

But this was news, a good story, and in true British journalistic tradition, why let the facts get in the way? As far as the British press was concerned the statement *'we did not prove an association between measles, mumps, and rubella vaccine and the syndrome described'* (p. 641) meant that Wakefield claimed *'MMR causes autism'* and here began the journey into testing the wrong hypothesis. Since that time the 'wrong hypothesis' has been tested time, after time, after time (unlike the cumulative vaccine schedule, which remains untested to this day), and this 'wrong hypothesis' has been found to be, well… wrong.

Even the esteemed Ben Goldacre, *doctor-cum-journalist*, or *journalist-cum-doctor* depending on what day it is – has gone halfway to setting the record straight. He berates the British press for making so much of the MMR-autism hypothesis, and pats Wakefield on the back with a condescending 'ah, well, we can't always get it right, not your fault mate' sort of attitude. What Ben fails to grasp is that it wasn't Wakefield that either framed or tested the 'wrong hypothesis'. On the contrary it was Ben's colleagues (the press ones) who framed it, and his other colleagues (the medical ones) who tested it. Of course, had this gone on in the silly circles of a *Guardian* blog it might not be terribly important. But it didn't and it *is* terribly important.

It's terribly important because whilst the Goldacre clones and half-thinking epidemiologists spent the last decade following the wrong path, naively and happily, and with no real understanding of the science, more sinister forces, who understood only too well, had spotted their vehicle and moved in.

Wakefield had to be stopped. Not because of anything he *personally* or *scientifically* claimed, but because of what the popular media *claimed* he *claimed*; and because in doing so, they had got it half right. Children with autism were appearing in unprecedented numbers on all parts of the planet where records were kept, and where a schedule for mass childhood vaccination had been introduced.

In the UK, where incidentally, children were treated to four years of exposure to an MMR brand *known* to cause problems, children regressed into autistic-like behaviour and started to become seriously ill. Unsurprisingly, their parents could not be persuaded by the UK Department of Health to ignore the evidence before their eyes. It was early in the 21st century and scientific dogma was failing. Time to go for the man.

Brian Deer made his original allegations against Dr. Wakefield in the London *Sunday Times* on Feb. 22nd 2004. Whilst he has consistently denied being the complainant in the case (a denial curiously upheld by the GMC themselves), a letter from Deer to the GMC on Feb 25th 2004 reads as follows:

Following an extensive enquiry for the *Sunday Times* into the origins of the public panic over MMR *I write to ask your permission to lay before you an outline of evidence that you may consider worthy of evaluation with respect of the possibility of serious professional misconduct on the part of the above named medical practitioners.*

The *'above named medical practitioners'* appear on the letter as *'2733564 Andrew Jeremy Wakefield, 1700583 John Angus Walker-Smith and 2540201 Simon Harry Murch.'*

Quite how this letter does *not* constitute a letter of complaint is unclear. But whatever it is, it undoubtedly set a number of wheels in motion; and the rest is history – or will be at some unspecified time in the future.

In the early stages of the GMC hearing, prosecution counsel called several 'witnesses-to-fact' who variously seemed reluctant, confused and unable to clearly recall events of ten years before. More disturbing still, as the hearing reaches its end, key witnesses, whose statements were considered central to the prosecution case have themselves become the subject of a formal complaint in which the accuracy of their statements has been seriously questioned.

The complaint has been served by Mr Jim Moody, US Attorney, and director of the US charities Safe Minds and the National Autistic Association. He authored the complaint on behalf of thirteen US and British autism charities, naming four major establishment figures called by the GMC prosecution as witnesses to 'fact': Dr Richard Horton, Professor Arie Zuckerman, Dr Michael Pegg and Professor David Salisbury.

Dr Richard Horton, editor of the *Lancet* testified on oath to the GMC that he had no knowledge of Dr Wakefield's involvement with solicitors representing parents in MMR litigation at the time the 1998 paper was published. However, evidence presented to the hearing clearly demonstrates that Dr. Horton had been in receipt of information stating Dr Wakefield's involvement, a full year before the publication of the paper. Dr Horton has claimed publicly that, had he known about Dr Wakefield's involvement in MMR related litigation, the 1998 paper would not have been published. Further he has claimed that Wakefield's failure to declare his involvement meant that the paper was 'fatally flawed'. Horton's oft cited claims have seriously undermined both Dr Wakefield's position in the scientific community and the validity of the *Lancet* paper and have contributed to a lack of faith in the reported findings. Should such claims prove inaccurate, and there is a great deal of documentary evidence to suggest that they are, one might justifiably lay responsibility for serious misrepresentation at Dr Horton's door, potentially making his position as editor of the *Lancet* untenable.

Professor Arie Zuckermann was Dean of the Royal Free Medical School at the time of the publication of the *Lancet* paper. Professor Zuckerman told the GMC hearing that, at a press briefing called immediately after publication of the paper in 1998, he was taken completely by surprise when Dr Wakefield recommended the use of single vaccines, in preference to MMR, until further studies were carried out into the safety of the triple jab. The GMC panel was shown correspondence between the Dean and Dr Wakefield that casts serious doubt on Zuckerman's right to 'surprise'. In the

correspondence, Professor Zuckerman urges Dr Wakefield to state
·his support for use of the *monovalent* (single) *vaccine* if asked to
comment at the press briefing. In the GMC hearing, when Professor
Zuckerman was asked to read aloud from the correspondence, he
countered the evidence by claiming that his apparent reference to
the monovalent vaccine must have been a typographic error, made
by his secretary. As the reference appeared on more than one occasion, one can only assume that the same typographic error was
made repeatedly.

Michael Pegg was Chairman of the Ethics Committee overseeing
research at the Royal Free Hospital in 1998. In his evidence to the
GMC Dr. Pegg told the panel that the Ethics Committee had
received no protocol seeking approval to carry out research on the
children whose cases were reported in the *Lancet* paper.
Documentary evidence refuting this claim was submitted to the
GMC by Professor Walker-Smith.

Finally, Dr David Salisbury has been asked to explain why he told
the GMC that the MMR vaccine has an exemplary safety record,
when no placebo controlled trials have been undertaken into its
safety. The complaint alleges specifically that: 'Dr Salisbury gave
misleading testimony regarding the safety of the MMR vaccine, and
concealed information material to its safety from the public.'

Mr Moody's complaint, which should force the GMC to
investigate whether the four witnesses have lied under oath could
result in a perjury prosecution against each of them. And so, as I
write, the hearing draws to a close. The children have not been
visible, their parents have not been heard; reference to their
collective suffering has been evaded, and its very existence denied.
Evidence for the prosecution has been seriously contested;
witnesses to fact have appeared to support the defense position.
And Mr Deer has remained impassive.

The hearing has been lengthy and complex but as the
prosecution's best attempts have failed to dent the compelling

defenses of each of the doctors, a growing thought has occurred to me; that it is so often the simpler things that are the most revealing. So much of the information 'unearthed' by Brian Deer has now been shown, without a shadow of a doubt, to be contrived, selective and essentially false; yet Deer hasn't once appeared surprised, or even concerned.

Surely in such a scenario a real investigative journalist, of the caliber of say, John Pilger, would have begun to question his sources? Surely, despite any position previously undertaken, an investigative journalist worthy of his profession would have become curious as to how he could have got at least some things so desperately wrong? In the end, it isn't the force of his venom, or the occasionally unhinged nature of his writing, that is suggestive of Deer's complicity. What ultimately gives the game away is his failure to show even one scrap of interest in the evidence.

In the words of T. D. Allman, provided as a jacket note to John Pilger's 'Tell Me No Lies':

> Genuine objective journalism not only gets the facts right, it gets the meaning of events right. It is compelling not only today, but stands the test of time. It is validated not only by 'reliable sources', but by the unfolding of history. It is journalism that ten, twenty, fifty years after the fact still holds up a true and intelligent mirror to events.

We shall see. Today brilliant sunshine has broken through the clouds here in London. Polly Tommey and Oliver Jones, representing the Autism Trust, have met with the UK Prime Minister Gordon Brown and in a huge leap forward for the UK Autism community, Polly has been asked to work with the government in bringing major autism groups together. The sun is also shining in Texas and the future suddenly looks a little brighter.

But as far as the GMC hearing is concerned there can be no winners. Whatever the outcome, the real issues will remain unaddressed until the scientific community has the courage to stand where these three men have stood, and ask the questions that have yet to be answered.

I am Martin Walker. I write and investigate medical issues usually related to pharmaceutical companies. Around five years ago, I began writing about and became involved in the case of Dr Wakefield. When the GMC fitness to practice case began, along with all the other parties I was told that the hearing against Dr Wakefield, Professor Murch and Professor Walker-Smith would last around three months. Now, in the summer of 2009, the hearing is coming to the end of its second year. Although evidence has gradually emerged that makes a collusion between New Labour, the drug companies, Brian Deer and the General Medical Council appear perfunctory, in my mind the simple fact that a major British regulatory body can so mismanage a hearing that it runs now twenty one months over its scheduled timetable is a leading reason for sacking all senior staff and reorganising the GMC.

Shifting allegations [ii]

At present the medical corps retains the power to define health and to determine which methods of care deserve public financing. It rules against heretical opinions and can deprive those who apply them of public support, if not of the right to practise.[iii]

Looking at the allegations in Deer's *Sunday Times* article, we can see that the case made against Dr Wakefield was, even at its beginning, easy to dispute and without substance. The GMC allegations are similar to Deer's. However, he has never revealed to *Sunday Times* readers his role in furnishing the GMC with the allegations. In effect, complainants, whatever their motivation, can make damaging charges against doctors under a veil of anonymity; whether they be patients or representatives of the pharmaceutical industry.

Deer's allegations concerned research and clinical work carried out by the gastrointestinal unit at the Royal Free Hospital (RFH) in the mid- to late-1990s, and in particular to the by-now notorious paper authored by twelve doctors and published in the *Lancet* in February 1998. The accusations against Wakefield alone included conflict of interest issues relating to research in support of autistic children seeking damages from MMR/MR manufacturers, and issues centring on his suggestion that clinicians should prescribe an experimental treatment, Transfer Factor (from the smallest molecule in colostrums, derived from breast milk), to one of the children attending the RFH.

The following rebuttal draws on information in the public domain, and has been drafted ahead of the conclusions that the GMC's fitness to practise hearing will reach in 2009. Deer made the following claims, which have been replicated by the GMC:

- In 1998, the *Lancet* published a paper by Wakefield et al, which claimed that MMR causes autism and bowel disease (AJ Wakefield et al, 'Ileal-lymphoid-nodular hyperplasia, non-specific colitis, and pervasive developmental disorder in children', *Lancet*, Vol. 351, 28 February 1998).
- Wakefield did not disclose in the *Lancet* his work on behalf of autistic child claimants litigating against MMR manufacturers.
- Wakefield and the Royal Free started a scare that MMR causes autism and bowel disease.
- Dr Wakefield advocates the use of single vaccines instead of MMR, against government policy.
- The 1998 *Lancet* paper was methodologically flawed.
- Wakefield used invasive procedures, involving scopes of the children's bowels and lumbar punctures.

Claim 1: Brian Deer states incorrectly that Wakefield et al's 1998 *Lancet* article claims MMR is linked to autism and bowel disease. It does not. Rather, the article identifies an association between bowel disease and regressive autism – an entirely different finding.

His article in the *Sunday Times* of 22 February 2004 contains several paragraphs that refer to:

'the alleged link between measles, mumps and rubella vaccine and autism in young children' as the *Lancet* paper's 'findings' (para 2); 'research claiming a link with autism' (para 3); 'findings linking MMR and autism' (para 4).

In fact, the abstract summarising the paper's main findings does not mention an MMR-autism link. Instead it says: 'We identified associated gastrointestinal disease and developmental regression in a group of previously normal children, which was generally associated in time with possible environmental triggers' (p. 637).

The main purpose of the paper was to report the presence of bowel disease in 12 autistic children. The mention of an MMR-autism link is a subsidiary part of the paper and is expressly treated in hypothetical terms requiring 'further investigations' (p. 641). For example, it summarises the prior environmental exposures that the parents and children's doctors reported as associated with the onset of autism.

In eight out of 12 children this environmental exposure was MMR. For the other four children, parents/doctors of two referred to measles and otitis media, and two were unable to identify any exposure. The summary is simply what the parents reported, which the researchers were duty bound to report, given the paper's terms of reference. Such temporal association between autism and MMR is not presented as causal. The paper clearly states that it 'did not prove an association between measles, mumps, and rubella vaccine and the syndrome described' (p. 641).

The distinction between the principal factual findings (the presence of bowel disease in the autistic children) and a subsidiary hypothesis requiring further research (a putative link between MMR, bowel disease and autism) is fundamental to the paper (as it is to other scientific papers recommending further research into hypotheses beyond published findings). Deer does not refer to the principal purpose of the 1998 paper, i.e., to show findings of bowel disease in autistic children, and elevates a subsidiary hypothesis – for which no evidence is given – to the principal finding.

Despite the authors' express denial of a proven link, Deer goes on to make a judgement of the paper, that it 'contained no scientific evidence of a link with MMR, only the "association" made by parents' (para 13). That is precisely what the paper said; yet Deer treats this finding as his revelation, in the face of his misreading of the paper that it claimed a link between autism and MMR.

Although the *Sunday Times* articles repeatedly refer to the editor of the *Lancet*, Richard Horton, as stating when interviewed on 21 February, 2004, that the 1998 paper was 'fatally flawed', they never quote the editors of the *Lancet*'s more temperate statement, issued on Friday 20 February – ahead of the *Sunday Times*' first article on 22 February – that 'we do not judge that there was any intention to conceal information or deceive editors, reviewers, or readers about the ethical justification for this work and the nature of patient referral'. Nor were Horton's relatively confusing statements in his book *MMR: Science and Fiction – exploring the vaccine crisis*, also published in 2004, ever referred to:

'The findings on physical examination of the children remained unquestioned. The hypothesis that formed the principal conclusion of the paper – that a new syndrome of bowel disease and an autistic-like behavioural disorder had been discovered – was intact, although it still remained a subject of continuing investigation'. [iv]

Claim 2: On 22 February 2004, Deer claimed in the *Sunday Times* that '*Andrew Wakefield, the doctor who champions the alleged link between measles, mumps and rubella vaccine and autism in young children, stands discredited for misleading his medical colleagues and the Lancet, the professional journal that published his findings. The investigation has found that when he warned parents to avoid MMR, and published research claiming a link with autism, he did not disclose he was* *being funded through solicitors seeking evidence to use against the vaccine manufacturers'* (paras 2 & 3).

'*The Sunday Times has now established that four, probably five, of these children were covered by the legal aid study. And Wakefield himself had been awarded up to £55,000 to assist their case by finding scientific evidence of the link*' (para 9).

The *Lancet* paper was an 'Early Report' case study based on clinical findings from 12 children treated by the RFH between 1996 and 1997 who were diagnosed with autism and symptoms of bowel disease. Whatever hypothesis the authors held about a link between autism and MMR, the paper does not present this hypothesis as fact.

For the authors, the paper's express purpose was to present findings of an autism-bowel disease link that justified further research, presumably with larger samples and controls. Its purpose lay outside Wakefield's own interest in advising claimants in the MMR litigation. Presumably, in the light of the paper's principal findings of an autism-bowel disease link, Wakefield did not disclose his other interests when submitting it to the *Lancet*.

This would have been a matter for his judgment. The GMC, on the other hand, insists that it should have been clear to Wakefield that others would have perceived the paper as involving a conflict of interest. But this can only be claimed if the subsidiary hypothesis is elevated to the main purpose of the paper and the principal findings of an autism-bowel disease link ignored.

However, even though his receipt of legal aid had been made public in the year prior to the paper being published in the *Lancet*, and although Horton was actually aware of this matter as the paper was being prepared for publication, just to ensure that the record was set straight Wakefield revealed his involvement in litigation research by letter in the *Lancet* on 2 May 1998. Deer does not mention this.

While Deer obsesses about Wakefield's failure to disclose in the February 1998 article, he ignores the convention at the time for medical scientists rarely to disclose *potential* conflicting interests. Even in the early 2000s, such disclosure was rare. Between 2000 and February 2004, when Deer first published his allegation, there was not, as far as we have been able to discover, a single disclosure among all the publications we have found by the 32 expert witnesses for the defendant manufacturers in the MMR litigation. Nor does Deer address the extent to which medical scientists conducting parallel research for pharmaceutical companies fail to disclose their financial links to industry in papers published in academic journals.

Deer further suggests that, at the time of publication, one-third of the children in the *Lancet* paper were litigants in the action against MMR manufacturers. However, he failed to publish in the *Sunday Times* the dates when each of the children started litigation in relation to dates they were selected for the study. The children were patients at the Royal Free in 1996, when they were enrolled in the research. The research was given ethical approval in December 1996, and analysis of data began in 1997. The children were selected by Professor John Walker-Smith, the most senior clinician, who stated to the *Lancet*, following Deer's *Sunday Times* report, that the children were selected on a chronological basis, i.e., the first to be admitted as patients were the first to be selected – a conventional method of selection for small case studies. The paper says that the children were 'consecutively referred to the department of paediatric gastroenterology'.

The fact that some of the parents of the 12 children went on to start litigation against MMR manufacturers after their children were admitted to the RFH, was a decision entirely for them, and not one about which they were duty bound to inform the *Lancet* study. There is an important issue of human rights that Deer and the GMC ignore: the right of parents of severely disabled children, who suspect that their children were damaged by MMR, to seek compensation through the courts. The parents have an entitlement

– even a duty – to protect their children's interests in the face of a lifelong condition for which there is no cure.

The temporal link between MMR and autism and other symptoms was the basis for a legitimate suspicion that required scientific research to establish the validity and nature of the link – a link in time to which many parents of autistic children, not only the 1,500 litigant parents, attest. In the absence of clinical research financed by government, the task of establishing the link lay with the litigant parents themselves. Would Deer have them delay litigation for several years until after the research is published, so denying themselves their right to litigate, or that Wakefield should remove all litigants from his *Lancet* research? Deer's (and the GMC's) view of medical research appears to be that research subjects should be powerless political subjects – a view that is questionable and certainly inappropriate in the case of children who, because of severe disabilities, have good reason to pursue their rights.

All of the above claims would have more relevance if it were true that (a) the *Lancet* paper had made specific claims about the causal nature of the MMR vaccine, or (b) that at the time Dr Wakefield researched biopsy material from these children, not only did he know whether or not they were in receipt of legal aid funding, but he himself had actually by then received the funding that Deer says he had. In fact, the first £55,000 paid out by the Legal Aid Board for research went not to Dr Wakefield for his central study for the LAB, but to another researcher, who was identifying and isolating viruses. This money was anyway paid to this worker on the understanding that it had come, not from the Legal Aid Board, but from the Royal Free Trustees.

Claim 3: Dr Wakefield and the Royal Free Hospital started a scare that the MMR vaccine caused autism and bowel disease, as a result of Wakefield publishing the 1998 *Lancet* paper, and of the Royal Free's press conference on the paper, both in February 1998.

'*Dispatches* reveals what parents were never told. How a major London teaching hospital and Dr Andrew Wakefield launched a health scare which questioned the three in one MMR vaccine.' [v]

In fact, the fall in MMR take-up began a year after it was introduced in the UK in 1988. In 1989/90, the numbers of children who completed the primary series of vaccination was 1,396,000. This number fell to 1,069,000 in 1990/91, and to 561,000 in 1996/97.[vi] The uptake of primary MMR had fallen by 60% before the Wakefield paper was published in 1998.

One public 'scare' that contributed to a fall in MMR take-up was concern over the Urabe mumps strain in the early 1990s, whereby a number of children in the UK contracted meningitis from the mumps component of the Pluserix and Immravax brands of MMR available at the time. In fact, months before the UK vaccine authorities decided to introduce Pluserix and Immravax in 1988, the Canadian government had already withdrawn them because of the dangers associated with the Urabe strain.

The minutes of the UK Joint Committee on Vaccination and Immunisation (JCVI) for May 1987 show that the decision to introduce MMR in 1988 was made in the full knowledge of this. In 2006, parents in Japan won an action against the government for damages caused to their children by the mumps component of the MMR vaccine.[vii]

Claim 4: At the Royal Free press conference to launch the *Lancet* paper, Dr Wakefield advocated the use of single vaccines instead of the MMR vaccine.

Andrew Wakefield is quoted as saying, ' *"the single vaccines in this context is safer… giving the measles vaccine on its own reduced the risk of this particular syndrome developing." Dr Wakefield believes that the MMR should be broken up into single vaccines.'* [viii]

Dr Wakefield gave this reply to a question from a journalist at the press conference held by the Royal Free Hospital in February 1998, to dispel suggestions that the paper was anti-vaccine.

In 1998, the government was providing free on the NHS, both single vaccines for mumps, measles and rubella, and the combined MMR vaccine. The government removed access to the former in 1999, having provided a choice between the multivalent and single-valent vaccines since MMR was introduced in 1988. Dr Wakefield was therefore voicing a viewpoint clearly within the scope of government's policy to provide choice of combined MMR or single vaccines.

Claim 5: Because the 1998 *Lancet* paper used a small sample of 12 child patients, its findings are unreliable.

'In Feb 1998, Dr Wakefield and his colleagues published their findings in a leading medical journal. Described as an "Early Report", the study was tiny, just 12 case histories and Dr Wakefield claimed that in just eight cases, parents had blamed MMR. Despite shortcomings in the paper…' [ix]

The study of 12 children was published under the *Lancet*'s 'Early Report' section, and was therefore based on a small sample not intended as representative, which the *Lancet*'s readership would have understood. The paper was subject to rigorous peer-review by anonymous experts.

The children were part of a case series and, according to the paper, 'consecutively referred to the department of paediatric gastroenterology' at the Royal Free Hospital (p. 637). They were not part of a random sample. As an 'Early Report', the paper makes clear that the findings reported are not conclusive, but subject to further research.

Wakefield and colleagues went on to publish further papers using much larger samples. The publication of a small case series study is a legitimate part of developing research leading to larger comparative studies.

Claim 6: Wakefield used unnecessary invasive procedures in his research – i.e., bowel scopes and lumbar punctures – on the child patients.

Parents of the child patients in the *Lancet* paper have reported the extent of their children's gastric symptoms, reflecting the wider experience of autistic children with bowel disease. The symptoms include constipation alternating with diarrhoea, faecal impaction, intestinal dysmotility and abdominal pain. The use of endoscopy was based on clinical need. Likewise, the use of lumbar punctures for some of the children was dictated by their neurological symptoms. These tests were used to support diagnosis and treatment, and the findings contributed to the *Lancet* paper.

The suggestion that these investigative procedures are not necessary is part of wider attempt to diminish the seriousness of the children's symptoms and to deny or withdraw treatment. More needs to be said about these serious medical developments.

Claim 7: Dr Wakefield peddled quack remedy: pregnant goat's milk.

In Channel 4's *Dispatches* programme, Brian Deer claims that Dr Wakefield lodged at the Patents Office, patents for a treatment based on 'transfer factor' (TF), which Deer presents as an alternative, and indeed competing, vaccine to the MMR.

In fact this whole assertion was wrong. Any money the remedy made, if it proved useful, was destined to go to the Royal Free, and it was not an alternative to MMR, but a prophylactic remedy for children who suffered immediate adverse reactions to MMR.

TF has immunological properties that have been known of for several decades. It is transferred from a mother to her child after birth, and is assumed to provide resistance to illnesses in the young baby. The question for research, which has not been settled, is whether or not these properties can be used for children who lack immunities to disease. It is a legitimate question for research in the case of autistic children with bowel disease where there is evidence that the auto-immune system is not functioning normally.

While in Mr Deer's hands the 'pregnant goat's milk' theory is treated with ridicule, it is a plausible hypothesis for scientific investigation in a condition where there are no known cures.

Although Deer solicits expert medical opinion on the patents, it appears in the programme that the experts give their instant and not considered opinions of a patent document of which they had not had advanced sight.

Conclusion

We hope, for the doctors' own sake, that the GMC does not find against Wakefield and his two colleagues, Professors Simon Murch and John Walker-Smith. However, it is also worth considering the possible outcome for autistic children if the *Sunday Times* and Deer's campaign is successful and the GMC Panel finds against the doctors.

Wakefield's research programme of investigating the role of MMR in autism and associated enterocolitis will end.

Doctors and scientists in the UK could be discouraged from doing research that might lead to questioning the safety of other vaccines, or indeed many pharmaceutical products. In effect parents deciding whether or not to vaccinate their children would have only the safety claims of manufactures and government to rely upon. There would be no alternative, independent scientific assessment of vaccine safety.

An important area of independent medical research could end. The core ethic of independent science would be damaged by government and GMC inference on a scale rarely seen in Western democracies.

Autistic children exhibiting symptoms of bowel disease – e.g. constipation alternating with diarrhoea, faecal impaction, intestinal dysmotility and abdominal pain – may no longer receive treatment. Many children are already denied treatment.

Instead of conducting clinical research to replicate or disprove Wakefield's findings, the UK government and medical establishment have engaged in personal attacks and produced epidemiological research that fails to address Wakefield et al's clinical evidence. Without precedent in medical history, Prime Minister Tony Blair and John Reid, then Secretary of State for Health, personally criticised Wakefield in February 2004, with Reid, as we have seen, encouraging the General Medical Council to prosecute Wakefield.

Medicine has a strange history of accusing and prosecuting its own number for unorthodox research and claims. This doesn't tend to happen in many other fields of professional endeavour. Engineering, the law and even mathematics, although they are all based on conservative constructs and look askance at Young Turks, do not immediately put into chains such radicals and dissidents, and throw them into a dungeon as might the guardians of medical orthodoxy.

This kind of conflict is happening increasingly in medicine, owing to the gulf that has opened up over the past century between honest physicians and the profit-motivated corporations that supply medicines. As Ivan Illich pointed out in the 1970s, the doctor has increasingly become only a conduit for the distribution of pharmaceutical medicines to the public.

What is most startling, when we look at the chronology of the Wakefield affair, is that he first began to make waves around 1995, writing with others the now infamous paper in 1998, and yet his 'trial' had still not ended over ten years after the paper was published in the *Lancet*.

The choice of the General Medical Council to end, or at least to put on hold, the career of a well-respected doctor, is interesting. Although the GMC always claims that it is not censorious of different, novel, or alternative diagnoses or therapies, and that its prosecutions are always based upon the protection of patients and mainly relating to ethics or perhaps the accountability of science, a search through its records seems to suggest something slightly different.

Many radical alternative thinkers and practitioners have been brought before the GMC on charges that, although disguised, amount to little more than accusations of heresy. In the MMR debacle, what better prosecuting agency could there have been than the GMC. Here was a body eager to do the bidding of the New Labour government. It was involved in a long-standing row with the BMA, the doctors professional association, who at an early stage had offered advice in support of Dr Wakefield to Dr Wakefield's Head of School. It was, furthermore, desperate to redeem a tarnished reputation following a public display of its impotence in the matter of Britain's most productive serial killer, Dr Harold Shipman, and has a history of mounting prosecutions processed through its offices by the UK drugs industry.

Of course there was, in the early days, a real need for a professional regulatory body – some authority had to keep recalcitrant doctors in line. Robert Bell was one of those great independent doctors who felt it was his life's duty to educate ordinary people to deal with their own health, so avoiding medical doctors, whom he described in the late 1900s as 'a set of ignorant, avaricious, narrow minded and selfish men, whose first care is their own interests'. In 1890, Bell wrote *The Deputy Physician*, so that people reading it might get to know their own bodies and treat themselves for common ailments. This he thought was a good alternative to being treated by one of only two kinds of doctor, who, quipped a French satirist of the time, either kill their patients or allow them to die. Inevitably, Bell's sense of independence saw him brought before the General Medical Council in a fitness-to-practice hearing.

As European society has gradually escaped from the grip of unified economic, political and religious organisations, it has been increasingly the case in medicine that patients and groups of patients have wanted to go their own way, usually with 'their own' doctors and especially in fields such as cancer, where the drugs industry has kept an unremitting grip on what they laughably call the 'ethics' of their drug-based treatments.

For the first time in the history of medicine, the past thirty years or so have seen numerous public demonstrations by patients in support of 'their' doctors, most of whom have offered sympathetic, original and often more effective treatments than the pharmaceutical companies.

Inevitably, at the forefront of these public battles have been alternative medical practitioners. The war against these and their therapies has been an easy one for Big Pharma to wage, by means of total control of information, by censoring the results of studies, by giving massive publicity to the occasional mishap, by the prosecution of practitioners and the suppliers of their remedies, often with criminal charges. Little wonder that, in Europe and North America, alternative and nutritional medicine have become beleaguered – or that the users and recipients of these therapeutic processes have been at the forefront of the battles brought to 'their' practitioners.

More importantly to the case of Dr Wakefield, this war has not stopped at the boundaries of alternative and complementary medicine, but has, on many occasions, lapped over to contest the original ideas of well-trained doctors and scientists whose treatment of patients in a number of fields has proved successful.

However, the GMC was always a body created to protect the good name of its own members, and not necessarily to protect the health of the patient population. With the post-modern period has come a concern among patients, that they should have a say in how their doctors treat them. Bell would have been proud of these patients who increasingly feel the need to demonstrate on their own behalf, and on behalf of their honest and ethical doctors who are out of tune with orthodoxy.

Inevitably, we have to question any system that, critical of particular doctors, provokes demonstrations by the laity in those doctors' support. The case of Dr Wakefield is not, of course, the first case where the patients have gone to the bar in defence of their doctor. On 12 April 2005, her 70th birthday, Professor Wendy Savage retired from the General Medical Council. Twenty years earlier, few of her supporters or patients would have imagined that she would have even been allowed to join their ranks. In the mid-1980s, Dr Savage stood up for women's rights to choose how their babies were delivered, against a male medical establishment that assumed not only that it knew best, but that it had the right to exert power over women's choice.

In 1985-6, Dr Savage came under fire for her management of five obstetrics cases. Her determined belief that women should be allowed to choose their method of treatment and delivery opposed the views of conservative theory, that of 'doctor knows best'. She was charged with incompetence and suspended from clinical work and teaching. Some of her obstetrical colleagues who disagreed with her management fought, often behind the scenes, to remove her from the London Hospital, where she worked.

But the debate was much broader. 'I knew I was not incompetent, and that my differences with my colleagues stemmed from a difference in approach and attitude,' she wrote in 1986 in her book, *A Savage Enquiry: Who Controls Childbirth?* She and others raised questions of power and choice: how much say should doctor versus patient have in clinical management? [x]

An article in the *BMJ* fails to mention the street demonstration organised by women's and libertarian political groups in East London.

The most significant cases where patients show committed support for their doctors who are attacked by their own profession or regulators, tend to be in illnesses where orthodoxy has no answers. Despite the illnesses in Dr Wakefield's case being created by vaccine damage, if orthodoxy had admitted to them and then researched treatments, Wakefield would still be respected within his profession.

Quite rightly, patients get quickly disillusioned with doctors who either hand out treatments in which they themselves have no faith, or pretend that their patients have insufficient intelligence to recognise when there is something wrong. Over the past half-century this question has arisen time and again in relation to the treatment of cancer. [xi]

The circumstances of the late Italian Professor Luigi Di Bella are exemplary although not idiosyncratic. Di Bella, a marvellously ethical and sympathetic doctor, worked inside the system, with a cancer cure he had developed in the 1970s. By the mid-1990s he was curing hundreds of people in the north of Italy. It wasn't long before the State, in the form of the Department of Health and various local authorities, were engaged in a full-scale campaign to shut his practice down. Di Bella was a massive problem to the Italian medical establishment and the drug companies, for not only could he cure cancer, but also he was a leading figure within orthodox oncology, and, most startlingly, he refused to accept payment for treating people.

A look at the war that he had to endure with the Health establishment is instructive on many levels,[xii] but most interesting is the considerable coalition of forces that came out onto the streets to demonstrate on the Professor's behalf when the battle between him and the Ministry of Health was at its height. Here in this context we saw cured cancer sufferers and their families, out on the street demonstrating their right to freedom of choice in medicine. This politicisation even forced, ultimately, the Italian high court to rule that local health authorities acted illegally in withholding the Di Bella treatment from cancer sufferers.

The steadfast commitment of parents of vaccine damaged children to the cause of Dr Wakefield is perhaps the most exhilarating fact about the whole 'Wakefield affair'. These, after all, are parents living out a terrible tragedy, who have had to take on a massive temporal, emotional and financial commitment to their children and their future, but who can still find the time and the funds to travel across the country and demonstrate in support of their doctors.

By ignoring these parents, the General Medical Council shows its true colours. Against the wishes of these parents, the GMC has assumed a right to care for their children, basing a whole prosecution on their own perverted code of ethics. When we examine this situation logically, not only does it cast the GMC in an unbelievably patronising light and the parents in the position of being deemed somehow ignorant and corrupted in their respect for Wakefield, but it raises the most fundamental question of *who is the victim?*

The case doesn't even come close to representing a crime without a victim: not only is there no victim but there is no crime. This can only be described as an 'inverted' judicial process: those who are bringing the prosecution are the ones whose vanity, hubris and profits are highlighted by Dr Wakefield's transparent honesty and regard for the children. When seen in this light, it is clear that the prosecution is the worst kind of corruption, driven by those who feel their sectional and personal interests to have been damaged.

Besides Deer, the New Labour government and the *Sunday Times*, another link in the prosecution chain was probably constituted by the drugs industry private inquiry agency, Medico-Legal Investigations, an agency that had spent the previous decade arranging and managing complaints to the GMC against doctors who presented a competitive threat to the industry.[xiii]

Cases that have originated with MLI are different in a number of ways from the run-of-the-mill cases brought to the GMC by patient complainants against individual doctors. The pharmaceutical industry, and particularly its biggest companies such as Wellcome (which has over the past ten years lost its name and become part of GlaxoSmithKline), desperately need a way to regulate doctors whose practices or research on crucial issues do not support the competitiveness of the industry. The GMC provided a perfect vehicle to 'try' such people.

According to Richard Horton, the editor of the *Lancet*, in his book, *MMR: Science and Fiction, exploring the vaccine crisis*, the GMC had no idea in this case, how they might act upon the Minister's instructions and bring a prosecution against Dr Wakefield. Horton, whose online manager at the *Lancet* is a non-executive director of GlaxoSmithKline,[xiv] says that he himself suggested ways in which they could progress the prosecution.

However, although Horton probably finessed the schedule of the prosecution, turning aspects of Deer's unremittingly crude accusations into a more slippery prose, there can be no doubt that this most substantial blow to Dr Wakefield and his high-quality scientific research originated and was pressed forward by Deer and those he was working with.

In fact, no juridical process could be more overtly unfair than that which has prosecuted Dr Wakefield and his two colleagues.

Most of the matters prosecuted took place between 1995 and 1998, between ten and fifteen years ago. The complaint as proffered to the GMC by Brian Deer was constructed with the help of Medico-Legal Investigations, an agency subsidised by the ABPI. The GMC's further construction of the prosecution does not seem to have been overseen by any independent body. The GMC chose the prosecuting counsel, and the GMC chose the jury – or the 'panel' as it is called in fitness-to-practice cases.

The GMC has determined the whole timetable of the hearings. Apart from the complete domination of this prosecution by agencies that favoured it, and on whose behalf it is taking place, other abuses of process can be clearly seen in the timetable of the prosecution. Over nine years between the preparation and publication of the *Lancet* paper and the beginning of the fitness-to-practice hearing; almost four years between the submission of Brian Deer's complaint and the start of the prosecution; a 'trial' that drags out for a period of over two years; a 'trial' that scape-goats three doctors with exemplary records in the place of a whole hospital and medical school department, 14 years after clinicians have seen the children involved; and finally and most telling of all, a 'trial' that is totally opposed by the parents of the children who are the subject of the prosecution and who would be in favour of politicians and government advisors being on trial. There are no damaged patients in this scenario, only angry ones who have to deal with both the vaccine damage of their children and the deceit of all those who deny their malfeasance.

Part Two

This volume of *Silenced Witnesses* has taken longer to produce than the first. In some ways this is a measure of the growing concern around MMR and vaccination generally in Britain. Both Carol Stott and myself, together with some of the contributors, have hardly had time to breathe so intense has the work become over the last year. Despite the lateness of the book, the energy with which the chapters were written by parents, themselves with so little time to spare, has not ceased to surprise us.

I have always believed in the ability of lay people to write if ground rules are explained and they are given the necessary support. The other ingredient, of having something deeply affecting and important to write about, is inevitably the case for all the parents of vaccine damaged children. Confirmed with these chapters was the fact that however insecure some people were about writing their chapter initially, hard work, concentration and a willingness to learn have again produced some exceptionally moving and well-written pieces.

I hope that I will be forgiven by contributors and readers for introducing some slight humour into these introductions. While in one overriding sense, the chapters show a soaring and heroic spirit there is no doubt that some of the stories are profoundly upsetting, not only because of the tragic circumstances in which parents find themselves, but also because of the crass and criminal behaviour of the authorities faced with what is becoming a national and international scandal. I'm sure that all the contributors will allow me to fend off the angst and sorrow that affects an editor working on such stories with the magic of a little humour.

As with the first book, there were those contributors whose expressed insecurity was simply a wave to the crowd while passing at speed. A contributor would say 'Well I don't know, I've never really written anything before and don't think I could write 10,000 words', then turn in 15,000 words in an almost faultless prose. I have come to see these individuals like indigenous people in far flung countries who when asked if they can speak English shrug their shoulder and say in their idiom 'a little', then proceeding to discuss Einstein's theory of relativity in better English than many indigenous Brits could muster.

The intense personal and emotional experience at the heart of each of these chapters has led some contributors into the recounting of personal experiences that in theory lies beyond the discipline of the book; for an editor this is a serious challenge. For the first time writer, writing about such a subject as their vaccine damaged child opened the page to accounts from everything from the shopping habits, local friends, and shortcomings of their partners! Perhaps the one thing that really surprised me, this time as with the first time, was the willingness of some contributors to slip in comments about their partners not because such things were important to the narrative about their children but because, 'This has been on my mind for a long time and it's very important'. It is, of course, difficult to persuade a first time writer that focus is paramount and some things are best not brought up in *this* chapter.

When it comes to the introductory chapters for both volumes we have been extraordinarily fortunate in having Rosemary Fox write for the first volume and Barbara Loe Fisher, co-founder & President of the National Vaccine Information Center, write for the second. These two energetic and cultured women played a similar and ongoing transatlantic part in the vaccine damage movement. To be honest I was more than a little frightened of approaching Barbara, as anyone would be when approaching someone who has contributed to the most important book on vaccination with the most consequential twentieth century writer on medical history and sociology, Harrison L. Coulter. [xv]

In the event, despite incidental distractions such as moving the office of one of the world's biggest vaccine campaign group and getting married, like a consummate professional Barbara got back to me more or less immediately to agree her chapter and then delivered it within the time schedule.

Of course, I never had any fears about the substance or the quality of Barbara's chapter and in the event she turned in a US introduction that mirrored the feelings, facts and events of Rosemary Fox's first volume's introduction. However, it is clear from Barbara's chapter that many distinct factors that have influenced the growth and continuity of the US campaign are not present in Britain. The US campaign against unsafe vaccination and vaccine damage has progressed in a variety of ways down avenues that have not opened up in Britain.

Perhaps the first thing that might be said about the mass campaign in the US and the rather mired and sometimes nullified campaign in the UK is that the US is a more open, diverse and less 'secret' society. Its size and diversity of political opinions allow a 'coming together' that is missing in Britain and while the battle in Britain seems often to revert to individual actions, in the US a mass movement has developed.

However, the individual stories of British parents and children in this and the first volume are inevitably similar to those of parents in the US. The rising of individual consciousness of parents with vaccine damaged children, in the face of obstructive vested interests, is probably similar throughout the world. In the US the beginnings of scientific and legal advances can clearly be seen, while in the UK, the approach of Britain's 'one party state' has plunged the families of vaccine damaged children into an apparently unwinnable battle. In the UK corporate and government interests lie, cheat and deny parents social benefits that would be given automatically in any developing society.

When it comes to introducing Heather Edwards, the author of the second chapter I am stuck for words and worried that I might not be able to present her as she deserves. Heather and her husband Nick have found themselves in as Kafkaesque a situation as modern Britain can present. In brief, Josh Edwards developed normally as a baby but was damaged by the MMR vaccination and its booster. He developed inflammatory bowel disease and a concomitant regressive autistic disorder. No one could treat these conditions or alleviate them. Eventually doctors felt the need to remove the whole of Josh's lower bowel and colon. Now fifteen, Josh and Heather's life is governed by a colonoscopy bag, he is often in pain, cannot speak, is unable to eat solid foods and could be in a similar state all his life. Heather has by necessity spent the last twelve years of her life totally immersed in caring and seeking treatment for her son.

If there was ever a case where government ministers and civil servants should be charged with criminal offences in relation to causing damage to a child and psychologically and physically assaulting a mother, this is it. In no other case, apart from those where death by vaccination has occurred, is the case against the vaccine damage deniers stronger.

Being human it is tempting to cry for Josh, Heather and Nick, but crying will do no one any good. While we are waiting over the next couple of decades for the pharmaceutical war crimes tribunals, which have to come, it is in cases like this one that communities have to come together and build supportive environments for those damaged by vaccines. When the State refuses to carry out its duties, obligations and responsibilities, the people themselves must take action. The Edwards family clearly needs co-operative support from their community and building this in cases of vaccine damage and autism is just as important as battling with the government for welfare provision, appropriate medical care and the funding of research into the causes of Autism Spectrum Disorders (ASD).

What has happened to the Edwards family is the consequence of a deeply dysfunctional political society, a society in which a psychotic political leadership has ditched any sense of moral honesty. In finding ways to understand, help and support the cases outlined in this book, we need to look not only for medical, political and financial solutions to growing rates of environmentally caused autism but new ways of living that might, even temporarily, give support to people like Josh and the Edwards family.

In this second volume we have introduced an inter-generational account of caring for a vaccine damaged child. David Nash, now a young man in his late teens has been cared for by his grandparents and his parents. The chapter *Our Children's Children*, written by Iris and Derek Noakes, brings a number of things into focus such as the advantages of an extended family in caring for a family member with a disability. The grandparents reflect on the seminal problem of how private and government interests simply refuse to sustain care for vaccine damaged children.

The Noakes grandparents are also able to introduce a note of history into our understanding of the vaccine damage situation. They comment on the radical changes over the last 40 years both in the authorities approach to infectious disease and the extended family responsibility in caring for children.

Our Children's Children and other chapters draw attention to the terrible hypocrisy of the British government. In an age when government agencies seem to be obsessed with child safety, frequently claiming that parents are the weak link in this safety, the British government sanctions experimentation by vaccination on children while refusing to vouchsafe for those damaged by this experimentation.

Celia Forrest brought her autistic son Adam to this volume when we put out a call for a contributor to step in at the last minute to replace someone who had dropped out. Not only did Celia step in and then finish her chapter in a very short time but she wrote like an angel. Her chapter *Adam* is redolent with good prose, intellectual discovery and sneaky atmospheric feelings. Celia speaks of Adam in terms of lost dreams and a confused sense of what might have been. She is also one of the parents in this volume who have fought a relentless legal battle to get proper educational provision for her son.

Celia's chapter inevitably raises the issue, that while *outside* autism seemingly every help and support is given to parents by all kinds of individuals, organisations and groups, *inside* autism and even deeper, *within vaccine damage autism*, support is rare, principally because along with support would have to come the admittance of possible environmental damage.

As someone who has worked as a para-legal worker for most of my life, helping people fight court cases without professional representation, I feel an immense respect for those parents who have single-handedly fought legal battles. The learning of a new language, the 'out of the box' thinking necessary as well as the temporal effort, make legal battles stressful, draining and often confidence eroding. The search for advice from sympathetic lawyers and advisors; the endless research, the strategic decision making, all these things take their toll.

Legal professionals with their sibling medical professionals are perhaps the least sympathetic of all professionals when it comes to aiding those who lack power. While lawyers in the big companies polish their nails on around £1,000 an hour and talk energetically about pro bono work for NGOs, they most decidedly turn their well suited backs on the real legally needy and particularly those in Britain suffering any kind of environmental illness or those involved in grass roots campaigns against government or corporation policies.

Deborah Heather is one of the women who claimed not to be able to write and began her chapter suggesting that she would have immense difficulty in stringing more than a few words together. Looking back now on the evolution of Deborah's chapter *Being the Voice of my Child*, I can see just how a lack of confidence can put off even the most talented of lay people. I was convinced that I was going to have an unbelievable struggle in getting anything even vaguely readable from Deborah for she had given me that impression. However, not only is her chapter about her son Andrew concise and readable, she has introduced a tone of rhetorical familiarity to it that creates a very personal style. How much this has to do with the fact that Deborah was born within the sound of Bow bells and like any other cockney has story telling built in, I don't know.

Deborah's story recounts how Andrew is loved both despite and because of his disability, while pursuing a seemingly endless mission to get a diagnosis and treatment for him. Deborah struggles to share what is left of her life with her husband and other son. There is more than an element of Kafka in Deborah and Colin's quest to get a doctor, any doctor, to admit that Andrew is suffering from Inflammatory Bowel Disease, a journey of endless meetings that seem to take her case no further forward.

I was inevitably struck while editing Deborah's chapter with the surreal similarities in her personal account of doctors' intransigence and the whole pastiche of the Deer's-GMC account of the children's illnesses. Brian Deer and the GMC constantly claim that the *Lancet* paper children only had constipation and, or, diarrhoea and did not suffer from anything resembling the new syndrome detailed by Dr Wakefield and his gastrointestinal team at the Royal Free. In fact, Deborah's chapter documents the retreat into unreason by the regime that replaced this team once Wakefield had been forced into exile and the rest of the team intimidated into leaving the hospital or pursuing other work.

Bill Marchant is one of the drollest parents on the autism circuit, he can tell a funny semantic joke with an acerbic use of few words, as he did recently in an email quoting the Crown Prosecution Service as the Crown Prostitution Service. However, when it comes to writing, Bill finds it difficult to tell the story of the struggle faced by him and his wife Pat on behalf of their daughter Jodie. In encountering this difficulty to analyse simply, sharply and chronologically the story of his daughter's vaccine damage Bill is in the company of many other parents.

The role of an advocate who can professionally resolve confusions in the stories of those who are up against more powerful adversaries, is one of the roles that the parents of vaccine damaged children really need. Of course, good lawyers do this every day, but not so good lawyers tend to either shy away from such cases or confuse them even more with their lack of statement taking skills. As a consequence of the real difficulties Bill found in relating the story for his chapter it is very short. I feel deeply for him in his search for both legal and medical professionals who can give him support in pursuing Jodie's case.

Bill and Pat together with pictures of Jodie feature in Alan Golding's brilliant documentary *Selective Hearing*,[xvi] a copy of which is given away with this book. In the film, Bill tells an anecdote about Brian Deer and his Channel 4 camera crew. They were filming Jodie when she suffered a fit, vomiting over herself and the floor. While Bill and his wife made steps to reassure Jodie and clean her up, Deer, after he had stopped giggling, asked if they could film Jodie playing in the vomit. In *Selective Hearing*, Bill shows his perchance for spontaneous humour, saying: 'I said to Deer, "no, you play in it, we're going home"'.

Polly Tommey, founder and editor of *The Autism File*, was the first person to return her chapter for Volume II. Like Allison Edwards writing for the first book, she seemed to write her chapter in a kind of trance with only the occasional need for correction; her story begins, has a middle and then ends exactly as it should do. After reading her chapter, I came to think of Polly as being to autism and vaccine damage what Steve McQueen was to the sixties: an icon of cool. After her chapter, but completely unrelated to it, we all learnt that she was the woman who had body modelled for Charlotte Rampling. Perhaps more importantly she is the woman who spent half a million pounds of other people's PR company money putting up posters all over London asking Gordon Brown to ring her and got a reply from him. Above and beyond all this, Polly is the Boadicea Mother of Billy, an autistic boy, whose case she fights twenty-four seven.

In her chapter *Futures for Billy* Polly tells a story about her breaking point in the early years of dealing with her son; it's a common story. She took her son to the park, and let him run; however, like many autistic children, given the chance to run, Billy ran and ran oblivious to Polly's increasingly frantic screams for him to turn and come back. Breaking down in the car after eventually retrieving Billy, Polly decided to start campaigning.

Her story is a well-written account of what might be described metaphorically as the battle to end her son's obsessive mania for forcing the family to turn left out of the house on every trip regardless of where they are going.

Chapter Eight, *Disgusterous!*, reads like an adventure story and in case your wondering what disgusterous means, the word is one of the apposite words created by Richard and Jan Crean's autistic son, Thomas. The use of this great word as the title for the chapter raised in my mind the whole issue of the positive aspect of some types of ASD. Clearly this creation and acceptance of new and fitting words and language with their humour and surreal intelligence is an aspect of autism which could well be introduced to children who do not have ASDs of any type.

When I first read Richard Crean's chapter, which is dedicated to the memory of a good and supportive friend Rene Wijers, whom they met when they first went to a Dutch hospital seeking a diagnosis for Thomas, I wondered not just at what people *would* do for their children, but simply at what people *could* do. Being an artist, I'm not much good when it comes to the practical issues of modern life. Put me down on a desert island and I would be able to build a shelter, and probably be reasonably happy for the rest of my life, but put me down broke in South London, without a phone and I'd die of exposure and starvation in a couple of days. And when it comes to the higher reaches of civilised behaviour such as talking to bank employees, you might as well forget it. Add to all this that I'm pretty inflexible in my personal habits and you will be able to see why the story of Richard and Jan Crean *Disgusterous!* awed me.

When Thomas first became vaccine damaged and then suffered from ASD, his parents changed life and direction seemingly without a second's thought. Richard Crean changed jobs to work locally on half his previous salary while Jan left her job and turned to home educating her child. They sold the property they lived in and bought a relatively cheap one that needed rebuilding. Basically they began life again ploughing everything into the care and education of their son. I have nothing but respect for people who treat the difficulties of contemporary life as if they were nothing more than the last third of the finger past the knuckle, something that responds implicitly to thought and commands.

In fact, the Crean's chapter depressed me slightly, not this time because it told a sad and horrendous story but because it made me feel profoundly inadequate. The Crean family appear to have accomplish these changes naturally and by the time that Thomas was fifteen they not only had a home schooled son, proficient in minor building skills and working with others, but were resident in a beautiful holiday settlement, The Thomas Centre, they had created so that autistic people of all kinds could holiday together with non-autistic family and friends.

Our politicians have deserted us. Our doctors are owned by the pharmaceutical industry. Our sociologists, psychologists and medical researchers are no longer interested in the down to earth intellectual problem solving of previous generations. Those skilled in media have lost the ability to communicate and can only preen themselves. Perhaps it is time now for the people to be more positive about assuming power over their own lives; increasingly, especially amongst the vaccine damaged, we are all we have.

Endnotes

i. Deer claimed from the time that he wrote his *Sunday Times* 'exposé' that he was asked to submit his evidence to the GMC. But in Alan Golding's documentary film, *Selective Hearing*, a letter is shown, sent from Deer to the GMC two days after the *Sunday Times* article, asking approval for him to tender any evidence that he has gathered as a complaint against Dr Wakefield.

ii. This section that looks in detail at the allegations made by Brian Deer was written originally in rough draft by the parent of a vaccine damaged child.

iii. Illich, Ivan. *Medical Nemesis: The expropriation of health*. Calder and Boyer. London 1975.

iv. In his evidence for the prosecution at the GMC hearing in October 2007, Horton went even further than he had before claiming that Wakefield's description of the new syndrome was a classic piece of science. He compared the paper's case review to those that validated AIDS-related illnesses in the mid-eighties.

v. *Dispatches - MMR: what they didn't tell you*, Channel 4, Thursday 18 November 2004.

vi. NHS Immunisation Statistics, England: 1997-98, Dept. of Health, Table 5 Completed Primary Course, 1989 to 1997-98, p.9.

vii. Walker M.J. The Urabe Farrago - A Recent Historical Example of Corporations and Governments Hiding Vaccine Damage for the Greater Good. *Medical Veritas*, 2009; 6(1): 2125-2146.

viii. Op. cit.

ix. Op. cit.

x. *BMJ* 2005; 331: 256 (30 July), doi: 10.1136/bmj. 331.7511.256 [http://bmj.bmjjournals.com/cgi/content/full/331/7511/256]

xi. See, for example: Lynes, Barry. *The Cancer Conspiracy*. Elsmere Press. NY 2000. Morris, Nat. *The Cancer Blackout*. Regent House 1959-1977.

xii. Brancatisano, Vincezo. *Di Bella: The man, the cure, a hope for all*. Quartet, London 1998. Brancatisano, Vincenzo. *Di Bella: Un po' di verita sulla terapia*. Travel Factory. Rome, Italy 1999.

xiii. There can be no doubt that some of these cases were prosecuted for the common good in circumstances where orthodox drugs companies, trial procedures and ethical practices had been ignored or broken down. Others, however, represent simple competitive marketing strategies, such as this case that stifles evidence of adverse reactions to vaccines.

xiv. See the first volume of *Silenced Witnesses*. It was reported originally by John Stone that the High Court Judge Sir Nigel Davis who turned down the appeal against the decision to withdraw Legal Aid from the parents' claim, had a brother, Sir Crispin Davis. Crispin Davis is an executive director and manager of the publishing company that owns the *Lancet*, in effect Richard Horton's manager, as well as being since 2003, a non-executive director of GlaxoSmithKline.

xv. Coulter, Harris L. and Loe Fisher, Barbara. *DPT: A shot in the dark*. Harcourt Brace Jovanovich. USA 1985.

xvi. Golding, Alan. *Selective Hearing: Brian Deer and the GMC*. www.cryshame.com

CHAPTER ONE

The Vaccine Safety and Informed Consent Movement in America

I am the mother of a son, my first-born, who was brain injured in 1980 by his fourth DPT shot at the age of two and a half in 1980. In 1982, I joined with parents of vaccine injured children in the Washington, D.C. area and co-founded a non-profit organization known today as the National Vaccine Information Center (NVIC). Since then I have been working to prevent vaccine injuries and deaths and protect informed consent to vaccination through public education.

The daughter of an officer in the U.S. Army, I was born in 1947 and grew up in the 1950's and 60's attending many different schools in North America and abroad. I am old enough to remember the way it used to be when there was no need for self contained special education classrooms to cope with large numbers of learning disabled, hyperactive, autistic, developmentally delayed and emotionally fragile children suffering with immune and brain dysfunction.

I remember when the biggest disciplinary problem was boys smoking behind the gym or drag racing in the parking lot after school, not boys punching walls or shooting kids in the library.

When I went to school, children didn't need Ritalin to concentrate or Prozac to combat depression or inhalers to cope with asthma attacks. Autism was a word nobody knew because, back then, autism was so very rare there were no autistic children in schools.

A few children took longer to learn to read or master the multiplication tables but, with a little extra help after school, they did. And the college entrance test scores were rising, not falling, because most children did not have a problem focusing and learning.

In the 1950's and 60's, there was a fair amount of air and water pollution in the U.S. because the Clean Air Act and other environmental protection legislation had not yet limited toxic exposures. Pregnant women and children were exposed to routine spraying of neighborhoods and beaches with bug killing DDT; chemical and other toxic waste was being dumped into rivers and streams serving as sources of drinking water; unregulated car exhaust and industrial waste emissions filled the air; and there was lead in paint and asbestos in floors and ceilings of homes and schools.

Back in the 40's, 50's and 60's, there were no childbirth classes at which pregnant women could learn about the dangers of anesthetics. So often our mothers were heavily drugged through their labor and many of their babies delivered with forceps. Breast feeding was out of fashion so most of us were bottle fed with formula that had minimum nutrition standards.

Lots of kids got their tonsils yanked out but very few had chronic ear infections and nobody had ever heard of banning peanut butter sandwiches to protect classmates from life threatening peanut allergies. Antibiotics were new so most of us got through respiratory infections with chicken noodle soup, lots of fruit juice and bed-rest.

Television was also new. But once most American families got a black and white television set in the late 1950's, we couldn't get enough of watching TV. On Saturdays, there were cartoons, cow-boy shows, science fiction thrillers and old movies from dawn to dusk. After school, there was the Mickey Mouse Club and more cartoons. We probably sat around watching too much TV, just like today's kids do, and we ate an awful lot of candy, ice cream, hamburgers, fries and milkshakes at movie theaters and roadside diners in the days before McDonald's.

Like me, most American children born in the 1940's who grew up in the 1950's and 60's experienced routine childhood infectious diseases because, until 1955, the only vaccines we got were smallpox and DPT (diphtheria, pertussis, tetanus) vaccines. In 1949, there were 625,281 cases of measles, 69,479 cases of pertussis. Cases of rubella, mumps, and chicken pox numbered in the tens of thousands but were not routinely reported to the government.

Coming down with the measles or chicken pox was an excuse to stay home from school for a few days or even a week. Most of us got measles before we were six. Counting the number of red spots on our faces was a game and during our illness, we wore sunglasses indoors because the light hurt our eyes.

Chicken pox was undoubtedly itchy and our mothers put pink calamine lotion on us, gave us lukewarm baths with Epsom salts and warned that if we scratched the pox lesions, it would leave scars on our skin. Mumps made us look like blowfish and it was hard to swallow for a few days.

However, ninety nine percent of us, who came down with these infectious childhood diseases, were left with nothing more than the memory of enjoying some extra attention from our parents while we recovered. Then we went back to school and had no problem graduating from high school and scoring well enough on our college pre-admission tests to be accepted. And for ninety nine percent of us, having those childhood diseases gave us a qualitatively superior immunity that usually persisted throughout life so we didn't have to think about getting measles, chickenpox or mumps again.

Along with the rest of my generation in 1955, when there were nearly 13,850 cases of paralytic polio reported, I lined up in school to get my first shot of Salk polio vaccine so I could go swimming in the summer and my mother wouldn't be afraid that I would get paralyzed.

In 1965, the year I headed for college, there were 261,904 cases of measles and 6,799 cases of pertussis. By the time I graduated in 1969, there were 25,826 cases of measles, 3,285 cases of pertussis, 57,686 cases of rubella and 90,918 cases of mumps recorded. By the 1970's, American pediatricians were giving children 10 doses of 5 vaccines (diphtheria, pertussis, tetanus, polio, measles and rubella) starting at 2 months of age until six years.

By 2008, U.S. government health officials were directing pediatricians to give girl children 69 doses of 16 different vaccines; diphtheria, pertussis, tetanus, polio, measles, mumps, rubella, haemophilus influenzae B, rotavirus, pneumococcal, hepatitis B, hepatitis A, influenza, chicken pox, meningococcal, and HPV (66 doses of 15 vaccines for boys), starting at 12 hours of age and continuing until 18 years of age. American children are given and mandated by law to receive more vaccines during childhood than any child population in the world.

In 1970, 1 child in 1,750 was diabetic in America. Today, it is 1 in 450. In 1970, 1 child in 2,500 developed autism. Today, it is 1 in 150. In 1976, there were 796,000 learning disabled children. Today, 1 child in 6 is learning disabled in America. In 1978, there were 2 million asthmatic children in America. Today, 1 child in 9 has asthma. The child chronic disease and disability epidemic, which developed during the last quarter of the 20th century and continues today, has crippled and killed more children, most of them highly vaccinated, than any infectious disease epidemic in American history.

❧ ❧ ❧

I grew up in a medical family: my mother and grandmother were nurses, my grandfather was a dentist and I had aunts and uncles in the medical profession. After graduating from college with a degree in English in 1969, I worked as a writer at a teaching hospital before I married and became a mother in 1978.

I was knowledgeable about health and medicine and so, when I became pregnant, I did what well educated women in the 1970's did: I read everything I could get my hands on about pregnancy, childbirth and caring for my baby. I ate nutritious foods and took vitamins. I did not have an alcoholic drink or take so much as an aspirin. I attended Lamaze classes so I could give birth without anesthetic and I knew I would breast feed to give my baby the very best start in life.

But even though I was aware of health issues, I was no different from most new mothers in the 1970's in that I knew absolutely nothing about the vaccines that my pediatrician would inject into my baby. I had no idea that vaccines carried any risk whatsoever.

I'm not sure why I assumed vaccines were risk free, when I certainly knew that prescription drugs and surgery entailed risks. Perhaps it had to do with the fact that vaccines are supposed to guard against disease and keep well people well. The concept of risk associated with a prevention is quite different from the concept of risk associated with a cure. Anyway, I believed vaccines were 100 percent safe and effective until, that is, my son became a vaccine reaction statistic.

When I became a new Mom with the birth of my son, Chris, I never expected to feel the kind of love I did for my baby. I don't think any mother is fully prepared for so much joy, even with all the sleepless nights, and we dream so many beautiful dreams about the future.

Except for a milk allergy that gave him colic for the first few months of life, Chris was a lively, contented, adaptable baby who loved being around people and always seemed to be doing things ahead of schedule. He had begun saying words at seven months and was speaking in full sentences by two years of age. By two and a half, he could identify the upper and lower case alphabet and numbers up to 20. He could name every card in the deck and had created a card identification game to entertain himself and our family. He was starting to recognize words in the books we read together every day. One doctor told me he was cognitively gifted.

I remember that after his third DPT shot, when he was seven months old, there was a hard, red, hot lump that stayed at the site of the injection for several weeks. I called my pediatrician's office and was told by the nurse that it was 'a bad lot of DPT vaccine' and not to worry about it. My totally clueless response was to ask 'Should I bring him down for another one?' This because I thought she meant the shot might not have been strong enough and I wanted my baby protected.

The day of his fourth DPT and Oral Polio Vaccine (OPV) shots when he was two and a half, Chris was healthy except for slight diarrhea that was left over from a 48 hour bout with the stomach flu he had at the beach three weeks earlier. He had just come off of a round of antibiotics that a doctor had prescribed for the flu because back then antibiotics were prescribed for everything from pneumonia to the flu. The nurse who gave him his shots said he didn't have a fever and that a little diarrhea didn't matter.

What was different about that day was that Chris, who was usually happy to be at the doctor's office or any other place there were lots of people he could talk with, became upset when the nurse tried to get him to swallow oral polio vaccine. He spat it out. She asked me to hold him while she gave him another dose of OPV and also injected him with DPT. I had to hold my son down on the examining table as he fought with every ounce of strength he had in his body to get away from the nurse who was trying to inject him with the vaccine that would change his and my life forever.

Chris eventually calmed down and we went out for lunch. But when we got home, he seemed quieter than usual and didn't want to play. Several hours later I walked into his bedroom to find him sitting in a rocking chair staring straight ahead as if he couldn't see me standing in the doorway. His face was white and his lips were slightly blue.

I called out his name and watched his eyes roll back in his head and his head fall to his shoulder as if he had suddenly fallen asleep sitting up. I thought it was unusual because I had never seen him fall asleep sitting up before. I tried to wake him but it was like he had suddenly gone into a deep sleep. When I picked him up, he was like a dead weight. I carried him to his bed, where he stayed without moving for more than six hours, through dinnertime.

After dinner, I called my mother, who urged me to wake him. Sitting on the bed calling his name did no good and I had to get into the bed and put his back against my chest and roll back and forth calling his name to get him awake. He struggled for consciousness and when he was awake, he didn't know where he was, couldn't speak coherently and was unable to sit up or walk by himself. I had to carry him to the bathroom, where he had terrible diarrhea and then fell asleep in my arms. He slept for another 12 hours. This was 1980. I had been given no information by my doctor about how to recognize a vaccine reaction.

In the following days and weeks, Chris deteriorated. He no longer knew his alphabet or numbers and couldn't identify the cards he once knew so well. He would not look at the books we had once read together every day. He couldn't concentrate for more than a few seconds at a time. My once happy-go-lucky little boy never smiled any more but was now listless and emotionally fragile, crying or becoming angry at the slightest frustration.

Physically, the deterioration was just as profound. He had constant diarrhea that looked like attic foam insulation, he stopped eating, he stopped growing and was plagued with respiratory and ear infections for the first time in his life. All during this period of failure to thrive, the pediatrician told me it was just a stage he was going through and not to worry about it.

After eight months of deterioration, I took Chris to another pediatrician who tested him for cystic fibrosis and celiac disease but all the tests came back negative. None of the doctors knew what was wrong with my son, who had become an entirely different child physically, mentally and emotionally.

It would be another year before I saw the TV documentary 'DPT: Vaccine Roulette,' and called the television station in order to be put in contact with other parents as well as obtain copies of medical studies that had been used to factually support the documentary. It would mark the beginning of my research to find out the truth about pertussis and pertussis vaccine.

I came home from the television station with my briefcase full of copies of pertussis and DPT vaccine studies dating back to the 1930's. I will never forget sitting in my living room and reading clinical descriptions of pertussis vaccine reactions in the pages of *Pediatrics*, the *New England Journal of Medicine*, the *Lancet*, and the *British Medical Journal* which exactly matched the pertussis vaccine reaction symptoms I had seen my son suffer within four hours of his fourth DPT shot.

I read the 1948 descriptions by Harvard researchers R.K. Byers and F.C. Moll of pertussis vaccine reactions that ended with permanent brain damage. I learned that the British National Childhood Encephalopathy Study published in 1981 had found a statistically significant correlation between DPT vaccine and brain inflammation leading to chronic neurological deficits and that the UCLA-FDA study published in *Pediatrics* that same year had found that 1 in 875 DPT shots is followed within 48 hours by a convulsion or collapse/shock reaction just like my son had suffered.

As I leafed through more than five decades of medical literature documenting the fact that the encephalopathic complications of pertussis disease or whooping cough were identical to the encephalopathic complications of whole cell pertussis vaccine, I was stunned. I felt betrayed by a medical profession I had revered all my life.

The day my child suffered a vaccine reaction, he should have been in an emergency room, not unconscious in his bed. As his mother, I should have had the information I needed to recognize what was happening to him and take steps to deal with it, including calling my doctor and later making sure the reaction was recorded in his medical record and reported to the vaccine manufacturer and health officials.

At age six, when Chris could not learn to read or write, he was given an extensive battery of tests that confirmed minimal brain damage which took the form of multiple learning disabilities, including fine motor and short term memory delays; visual and auditory processing deficits; attention deficit disorder and other developmental delays. He was removed from the Montessori school he attended and placed in a self contained classroom for the learning disabled in public schools, where he stayed throughout elementary, junior and high school despite repeated efforts to mainstream him.

As a teenager, Chris struggled to deal with the big gaps between certain aspects of his intelligence – like his creativity and unusual ability to think on an abstract level – that was mixed with an inability to concentrate for long periods of time or organize and process certain kinds of information he saw or heard. He was angry and frustrated because he couldn't do what his peers could do in school and so he found ways to act out that were self destructive. There were times I thought I would lose him. Whenever I see a news report about some young kid with learning disabilities and ADHD who ends up on drugs or in prison or dead on the streets, I am haunted with the though it could have been Chris.

I find it devastating today watching the young mothers and fathers, who are searching for ways to help cure their vaccine injured children. I understand too well the price we have paid for the stubborn reluctance of those in government, industry and the medical profession, who make and promote vaccines, to listen to us, nearly three decades ago, when we begged them to investigate why our healthy children became sick and regressed into chronic illness and disability after vaccination.

My son, born in 1978, was part of the first bubble that turned into a tidal wave of learning disabled, hyperactive, autistic children that required the creation of special classrooms in the U.S. public school system to deal with this new phenomenon. It is becoming painfully apparent that he and his classmates were the canaries in the coal mine, ignored because, as German immunologist and DPT vaccine critic Dr. Wolfgang Ehrengut once suggested 'What must not be, cannot be.'

The right to know was the guiding principle that served as the foundation for those of us who launched the vaccine safety and informed consent movement in the U.S. We were all parents who had watched the Emmy award winning television documentary *DPT: Vaccine Roulette* produced by NBC-TV reporter Lea Thompson in the spring of 1982. Each one of us who saw that remarkable show knew, for the first time, as we watched it, what had happened to our once healthy, bright children and why they had changed before our eyes after vaccination.

We founded the non-profit, educational organization that today is known as the National Vaccine Information Center (NVIC) with the mission of preventing vaccine injuries and deaths through public education. Later we would expand that mission to include defense of the informed consent ethic. In 1982 our first goal was to persuade the government to license a less toxic DPT vaccine for America's babies. We knew that Japan had used technology developed in the U.S. that reduced endotoxin content and made pertussis toxin less bioactive to license an acellular pertussis vaccine (DtaP) for Japan's infants in 1981. However, it took more than 14 years of lobbying before the FDA licensed the purified DTaP vaccine for American infants in 1996.

To make parents more aware of the need to protect their babies from vaccine injury by making well informed vaccination decisions, I co-authored the book *DPT: A Shot in the Dark* with medical historian Harris Coulter, which was published by Harcourt Brace Jovanovich in 1985. The first major book to criticize the science, policy, law and politics of mass vaccination, it was met with hysterical, vitriolic reviews in the *New York Times* and *Wall Street Journal*. We knew then that we had hit our target with precision.

Shortly after we organized in 1982, initially calling our fledgling non-profit organization Dissatisfied Parents Together (DPT), we were asked by Congress to work on legislation that would provide federal compensation for children injured by government mandated vaccines. The drug companies making and selling vaccines and pediatricians giving vaccines had been trying unsuccessfully for years to persuade Congress to pass 'exclusive remedy' legislation that would give them total liability protection from lawsuits for vaccine injuries and deaths.

In the 1970's and 1980's, attorneys for the drug companies were settling most product liability and medical malpractice lawsuits out of court on the courthouse steps. Desperate parents and plaintiff's attorneys without deep pockets were willing to take several hundred thousand dollars rather than take their chances with a court trial and end up with nothing. The stipulation for most out-of-court settlements was that all medical and court records would be sealed from public view.

It was the rare vaccine injury lawsuit that generated a million dollar plus award. But in 1982, drug company lobbyists, stunned by national publicity revealing the fact that vaccines can injure and kill, told Congress that they would leave the country without any vaccine supply if they didn't get liability protection. The American Academy of Pediatrics suggested their pediatrician members might not want to give vaccines in the future without liability protection.

Politicians on both sides of Congress told our young group of parents with vaccine injured children: Come to the table and fight for what you think the families should get but we are going to pass a law with or without you to protect the vaccine supply and mass vaccination infrastructure in the United States.

So we went to the table and did the best we could at a time when few people had ever heard of a vaccine reaction, there were no personal computers, cell phones, or the internet, and we were facing pharmaceutical companies, government agencies and medical organizations with far more money and political clout than we could ever hope to possess.

We did what we could to even the playing field, including organizing the first public demonstration ever held in front of the Centers for Disease Control (CDC) in Atlanta in May 1986 as well as leading a candlelight vigil at the White House in November 1986. Over protests by government health and justice officials, who maintained until the end that vaccines do not cause injury and death, President Reagan signed the National Childhood Vaccine Injury Act into law that year.

The 1986 Vaccine Injury Act was historic because it was the first societal acknowledgement that vaccine injuries and deaths are real and that families, whose children have been injured or have died from the effects of government recommended and mandated vaccines, should be financially compensated. The law also instituted the first vaccine safety reforms in the mass vaccination system, for which parents were directly responsible:

• mandatory recording of vaccine-related health problems in the child's medical record by the vaccine provider;

- mandatory recording of the manufacturer name and lot number of each vaccine given in a permanent record by the vaccine provider;
- requirement for doctors to give written vaccine benefit and risk information to parents before a child is vaccinated; and
- requirement for vaccine providers to report hospitalizations, injuries and deaths that occur within 30 days of vaccination to a federal Vaccine Adverse Events Reporting System (VAERS).

Parents fought for and won the right to access the civil justice system if they were turned down for federal compensation or offered too little to take care of their vaccine injured child's lifetime care needs. We also protected the right to go to court and sue vaccine manufacturers for unlimited punitive damages if it could be proven that the company engaged in criminal fraud or gross negligence in the manufacture of the vaccine.

Between 1988, when the federal Vaccine Injury Compensation Program created under the Act became operational, and 2008 nearly $2 billion in compensation was awarded to vaccine injured children by the U.S. Claims Court in Washington, D.C. However, because U.S. Department of Justice and Health and Human Services officials fight every vaccine injury claim, two out of three vaccine victims are turned away empty handed. More than $2.5 billion sits unused in the Vaccine Injury Trust Fund, which is financed by a surcharge on vaccines that the people who get vaccinated pay as a kind of 'self-insurance.'

Drug companies, pediatricians and federal health officials are trying now to persuade Congress to let them raid the Trust Fund and use money that belongs to vaccine victims to conduct vaccine 'safety' studies to prove vaccines do not cause injury and death.

The 1986 law also contained provisions secured by parents that required the Institute of Medicine (IOM), National Academy of Sciences, to review the medical literature for evidence that vaccines can cause injury and death and report to Congress. In

1991 and 1994, the IOM published landmark reports confirming that childhood vaccines can cause brain and immune system dysfunction as well as death, including the following conditions:

- acute encephalopathy (DPT vaccine)
- chronic nervous system dysfunction after serious acute neurological illness within 7 days after receiving DPT
- shock and "unusual shock-like state" (DPT vaccine)
- protracted inconsolable crying (DPT)
- anaphylaxis (DPT, DT, Td, T, MMR, hepatitis B)
- acute and chronic arthritis (rubella vaccine)
- Guillain Barre Syndrome (OPV, DT, Td, T)
- Brachial neuritis (DT, Td, T)
- Thrombocytopenia (MMR)
- Death (from polio or measles vaccine strain viral infection);

However, the IOM physician committees reviewing the medical literature noted that there was a lack of sound scientific research into dozens of other reported serious health problems following vaccination. Therefore, they were forced to conclude that 'the evidence was inadequate to accept or reject a causal relation' for many of the adverse events reported after vaccination.

In 1991 IOM acknowledged there were 'many gaps and limitations in knowledge bearing directly or indirectly on the safety of vaccines':

These include inadequate understanding of the biologic mechanisms underlying adverse events following natural infection or immunization, insufficient or inconsistent information from case reports and case series, inadequate size or length of follow-up of many population-based epidemiologic studies, and limited capacity of existing surveillance systems of vaccine injury to provide persuasive evidence of causation. The committee found few experimental studies published in relation to epidemiologic studies published.

When I was interviewing parents of DPT vaccine injured children in the early 1980's while writing *DPT: A Shot in the Dark*, I was struck by how the mother's descriptions of vaccine reaction symptoms were identical to the symptoms physicians had described in the DPT vaccine medical literature. It soon became apparent that the 'reactions' to DPT which pediatricians told parents were 'normal' and of no consequence, were anything but normal and nothing to worry about.

In 1985, Dr. Coulter and I pointed out that mild to severe brain inflammation following vaccination could not only lead to severe and profound brain damage but could also result in milder forms of brain dysfunction that included learning disabilities and ADD/ADHD. We were also the first to publish an association between vaccination and autism, specifically DPT vaccine induced brain inflammation that left the child with a constellation of brain and immune system dysfunction symptoms which could result in a diagnosis of autism.

After nearly three decades of collective denial by government, industry and the medical community that use of more vaccines are harming more children, a third generation of young mothers contacts us at the National Vaccine Information Center reporting exactly what those of us, whose children reacted to DPT vaccine in the 1980's, reported. Mothers tell us how they took a happy, healthy, bright, normally developing son or daughter to the doctor to be vaccinated and then, within hours, days or weeks, their child regressed physically, mentally and emotionally and became a totally different child.

Mothers describe how within days of vaccination, their babies ran fevers, screamed for hours, fell into a deep sleep and woke up screaming again; started twitching, jerking or staring into space as if they couldn't hear or see; were covered with body rashes; became restless and irritable, or had a dramatic change in eating or sleeping habits.

These mothers and others, whose children do not have such obvious clinical symptoms within hours or days of vaccination, will describe a gradual deterioration in overall health, a picture that includes constant ear and respiratory infections; sudden onset of allergies, including milk allergy and gluten intolerance; asthma; unexplained rashes; persistent diarrhea; sleep disturbances that turn night into day and day into night; loss of developmental milestones like the ability to roll over or sit up; loss of speech, eye contact and communication skills; and development of strange or violent behavior that includes hyperactivity, biting, hitting, social withdrawal and repetitive movements such as flapping, rocking, and head banging.

Older children (and adults) who become chronically ill after vaccination complain of muscle pain and weakness, joint pain, crippling headaches, disabling fatigue, gastrointestinal disorders, heart and vision problems, and loss of memory or inability to concentrate and think clearly. Many are unable to engage in athletic activities or excel in school as they did before the vaccine reaction.

The once healthy, normally developing child becomes a totally different, sick child. And the mother, who carried that baby inside her for nine months and gave birth to that baby and spends much of her waking time caring for that baby, knows her child in a way no one else does. And she knows something has changed, even if she doesn't know why.

Depending on the child and therapy interventions, there is either gradual full recovery or the child is eventually diagnosed with various kinds of chronic health problems. My son regressed after his DPT shot but stopped just short of autism. Why? I don't know. It may have had something to do with the fact that he only received four vaccines that day – DPT and OPV. If Chris had been born in 1998 instead of 1978, he could have received 10 vaccines that day and he might have had a more severe brain inflammation that caused him to become autistic, mentally retarded or he could have died.

Although Chris suffered a mild brain inflammation and was left with minimal brain dysfunction that took the form of multiple learning disabilities and ADD, and had to stay in a self contained classroom for the learning disabled throughout public school, we both know he was one of the luckier ones. He has learned to compensate for his learning disabilities and has adopted a wellness lifestyle that helps him maximize his mental and physical health. After working in warehouses and mail rooms following public school, Chris attended a technical school that had a strong support program for the learning disabled and earned an associate degree in videography. He is currently filming, editing and producing educational videos for NVIC and takes great satisfaction in helping others learn how to prevent vaccine injury.

Vaccine induced brain injury appears to be on a continuum, spanning from the milder forms like ADD or ADHD to multiple learning disabilities; and from seizure disorders and autism to severe and profound mental retardation with the most severe consequence being death. On the vaccine injury continuum, often coinciding with brain dysfunction, is immune system dysfunction of varying degrees. Clearly this reflects the relationship between the immune and neurological systems and the immune mediated mechanism of neuroimmune dysfunction induced by vaccination in some children. It is also interesting to note that the most serious complications of vaccines are very similar to the most serious complications of the infectious diseases they are designed to prevent.

Leo Kanner observed in the 1940's that most autistic children had very intelligent, high functioning mothers and fathers. My experience interviewing parents of children, who became autistic in the late 1970's and early 1980's following DPT vaccination, was that many of these children had above average development before regressing into autism after vaccination. They were left with a mixed profile that included learning disabilities, ADHD, and autistic behaviors but they also frequently retained above average intelligence in key areas.

Many of the parents, who contact NVIC, report their child suffered previous vaccine reaction symptoms that were written off by their doctor as unrelated or unimportant. Some say their child was sick at the time of vaccination, often on antibiotics.

Others describe a strong family history of allergy and/or autoimmunity, such as thyroid disease, lupus, rheumatoid arthritis, diabetes, severe allergies to milk, pollen, medications and vaccines. (After I realized my son was a vaccine reaction statistic, I intuitively concluded that there must have been something that made him more vulnerable than other children to suffering a vaccine reaction and realized our family history of allergy and autoimmunity was a good possibility). Still other babies, especially those who die after vaccination, were born premature, were underweight or had a history of health problems prior to being injected with multiple vaccines over and over again.

In other words, these are children with potentially identifiable genetic or other biological high risk factors, which are being ignored in the one-size-fits-all national vaccine policies that allow few contraindications and say it is safe to inject a baby with as many as 10 vaccines on one day. The pre-licensure clinical studies vaccine manufacturers conduct to prove a new vaccine is safe do not include certain children routinely vaccinated in America, including premature, underweight and sick babies and those who have suffered previous vaccine reactions.

There is a familiar pattern to vaccine reactions and this pattern has been reinforced over and over again by almost every vaccine reaction description by parents in the U.S., Britain and other countries during the past three decades. This commonality of experience contributes in no small way to why the vaccine risk debate will not go away. It will not go away in part because industry, government and medical organizations have failed to convince the public that, when serious health problems follow vaccination, it is always just 'a coincidence.'

While it is illogical and unscientific to assume that *all* serious health problems following vaccination *are* causally related, it is more illogical and even less scientific to assume that *all* serious health problem following vaccination are *not* causally related.

If I had not walked into my child's room when I did after his DPT shot, I would not have witnessed the post-pertussis vaccine convulsion, collapse shock and six hour state of unconsciousness which, not counting the few minutes I was able to rouse my son to a state of semi-consciousness, was actually an 18 hour plus state of altered consciousness. If Chris had been a four month old baby and not a precocious two and a half year old, the regression he underwent following vaccination may not have been so clearly apparent.

How many mothers are not in a child's presence to witness a seizure after vaccination, which could easily occur in the middle of the night? And how many infants are regressing after unrecognized vaccine reactions, such as a mild brain inflammation whose signs can be subtle, but are never diagnosed until long after the damage has been done, which prevents even a time relationship between vaccination and the regression from being recognized?

During the several decades that I have been calling for the institution of vaccine safety and informed consent protections in the mass vaccination system, I was appointed to serve on government vaccine advisory committees and Institute of Medicine (IOM) forums including the National Vaccine Advisory Committee (1988-1991); Institute of Medicine Vaccine Safety Forum (1995-1998); the Vaccines and Related Biological Products Advisory Committee of the Food and Drug Administration (1999-2002) and the Vaccine Policy Analysis Collaborative sponsored by the Centers for Disease Control (2002-2005).

In 2001, I was invited to make a presentation to the IOM Immunization Safety Review Committee at the outset of their deliberations. I forwarded a hypothesis that biologically vulnerable children may suffer from repeated atypical manipulation of the immune system with multiple vaccines in early childhood:

> There is a compelling argument to be made that the dramatic increase in chronic brain and immune system dysfunction in children, especially the rising number of reports of regression in previously healthy children, is due to an early exposure that is being experienced by all children but which is harming an expanding minority of them ... many biological responses are at least partially under genetic control. If, for example, adverse responses to vaccination are tied to the genes responsible for predisposition to autoimmunity and immune mediated neurological dysfunction, then it is possible that the addition of more doses of vaccines to the routine schedule in the past two decades has affected more and more children with that genetic predisposition ... therefore, when all children only were exposed to DPT and polio vaccine in the early 1960's, a tiny fraction of those genetically susceptible responded adversely. But with the addition of measles, mumps, and rubella to the routine schedule in 1979 and then HIB, hepatitis B and chicken pox in the late 1980's and 1990's, far more of those genetically susceptible have been brought into the adverse responder group.

This hypothesis, which essentially acknowledged biodiversity, could not be examined by the IOM in their 2002 report on *Multiple Immunization and Immune Dysfunction*, which admitted that:

> The committee was unable to address the concern that repeated exposure of a susceptible child to multiple immunizations over the developmental period may also produce atypical or non-specific immune or nervous system injury that could lead to severe disability or death (Fisher, 2001). There are no epidemiological studies to address this. Thus, the committee recognizes with some discomfort that this report addresses only part of the overall set of concerns of some of those most wary about the safety of childhood immunization.

In the past quarter century as the numbers of doses of vaccines our children get has tripled from 23 doses of 7 vaccines by age six to 69 doses of 16 vaccines from birth to age 18, the numbers of children with asthma, attention deficit disorder, learning disabilities and diabetes has tripled and autism now affects one in 150 children. Our public school systems are unable to build or staff special education classrooms fast enough to serve the millions of highly vaccinated, chronically disabled and ill children. And the trillion dollar annual health care price tag to treat chronic disease in our society continues to climb.

The larger unanswered question is: has the repeated manipulation of the immune system with multiple vaccines in the first three years of life, when the brain and immune systems develop most rapidly, and throughout childhood been an unrecognized co-factor in the epidemics of chronic disease and disability plaguing so many highly vaccinated children today?

When you look at the possible biological mechanisms for vaccine-induced neuroimmune dysfunction, the scientific picture is complicated by the presence of heavy metals such as mercury and aluminum; foreign proteins; yeast; MSG; formaldehyde; phenoxyethanol; sodium borate and antibiotics that, together with residual DNA and possible adventitious agent contamination from animal and human cell substrates, have unknown biological effects.

Atypical introduction of viruses and bacteria into the human body via vaccination has yet to be evaluated for its potential negative effects on chromosomal integrity. The medical literature contains reports of chromosomal breakage after smallpox vaccination and yet there are no studies today evaluating this possible effect with other vaccines. It is worth scientific investigation as the past two generations of highly vaccinated children give birth to their children.

There is a surprising lack of scientific understanding about how microbes causing disease or live virus and inactivated bacterial vaccines act at the cellular and molecular level to disrupt immune and brain function. And there have never been any prospective, long term studies comparing the long term health of highly vaccinated individuals versus those who have never been vaccinated.

The 1991 Institute of Medicine committee agreed that there is a general lack of scientific knowledge about precisely how infectious diseases as well as live virus and inactivated bacterial vaccines may negatively affect immune and brain function:

Such shortcomings relate, for example to pathologic mechanisms of specific infectious agents, the molecular basis of vaccine injury, and the national history of conditions such as encephalopathy, mental retardation and chronic arthritis.

The 1994 IOM Committee admitted:

The lack of adequate data regarding many of the adverse events under study was of major concern to the committee. Presentations at public meetings indicated that many parents and physicians share this concern ... The committee was able to identify little information pertaining to the risk of serious adverse events following administration of multiple vaccines simultaneously. This is an issue of increasing concern as more vaccines and vaccine combinations are developed for routine use ... The committee was able to identify little information pertaining to why some individuals react adversely to vaccine while most do not. When it is clear that a vaccine can cause a specific adverse event, research should be encouraged to elucidate the factor that put certain people at risk for that adverse reaction."

Other potential co-factors in the rise in chronic illness and disability in American children is increased exposures to pesticides, chemicals and other environmental toxins; overuse of antibiotics and other pharmaceuticals; nutritionally compromised food sources and unhealthy lifestyles. But there is a compelling argument to be made that the rising number of reports of regression in previously healthy children is due to an early exposure that is being experienced by all children that is harming an expanding minority of them.

A healthy, mature immune system capable of responding well to the challenge of infectious microbes requires an equal balance of cellular (innate) and humoral (learned) immune system responses. A disruption in this balance can lead to development of allergy and autoimmune disorders, including neuroimmune dysfunction.

Vaccination attempts to fool the body into believing it has come in contact with the real microorganism that causes infection. But vaccination does not exactly mimic the natural infection process and often by-passes cellular immunity in favor of humoral immunity. When I was sitting on the FDA Committee, I learned that vaccine developers do not fully understand the biological mechanisms involved in the immune response to natural infection or vaccination and so the achievement of vaccine induced mucosal (cellular) immunity has been elusive.

Philip Incao, M.D., a holistic family care physician in Colorado explains:

> *Physically, health is about balancing acute inflammatory responses to infection, which stimulate one arm of the immune system, and chronic inflammatory responses to infection, which stimulate the other part of the immune system. Overuse of vaccines to suppress all acute, externalizing inflammation early in life can set up the immune system to respond to future stresses and infections by developing chronic, internalizing disease later in life.*

Could the suppression of most infectious disease in early childhood help disrupt the balance of cellular and humoral immune responses and cause susceptible children to suffer chronic inflammation that leads to chronic neuroimmune dysfunction, including autism? If so, those children genetically predisposed to mounting atypical inflammatory responses, such as those with a personal or family history of allergy or autoimmune disorders, may be at special risk.

In September of 1997, NVIC sponsored the First International Public Conference on Vaccination in Washington, D.C. It was the first conference on vaccination not sponsored by the pharmaceutical industry or the federal government. Among the physicians, immunologists, neurologists, microbiologists, ethicists, attorneys, and journalists I invited to speak about vaccine science, policy, ethics and law was a young gastroenterologist working at the Royal Free Hospital in London. He was studying the relationship between inflammatory bowel disease, persistent measles virus infection and measles vaccination.

Andrew Wakefield, M.D., was the first physician to speak publicly about a possible causal association between receipt of MMR vaccine and subsequent development of chronic inflammation of the bowel. Although parents, doctors and the U.S. media were aware of the debate about the ability of the whole cell pertussis vaccine in DPT to cause brain inflammation and brain damage, there hadn't been any public discussion about the ability of other vaccines to cause chronic health problems.

Dr. Wakefield and I had several telephone conversations before he left London for Washington, D.C. to make his first public appearance at a major U.S. conference. He was planning not only to speak about the association between MMR vaccine and Crohn's disease but also mention that many of the children with inflammatory bowel disease (IBD) he was treating had developed autism shortly after MMR vaccination.

Following protocol, he informed his superiors at the Royal Free College Hospital that he would be speaking at our conference. A few days before he was scheduled to fly to Dulles International Airport, he telephoned me to express concern that he might be barred by airport immigration officials from entering the U.S. He was being subjected to intense pressure from senior health officials in the UK to cancel his appearance at our conference.

The day after he arrived, he received a telephone call from his employer asking him to reconsider speaking at our conference and suggesting he may not have a job waiting for him when he returned to the UK if he did speak. At this point, I urged him to withdraw from the conference to protect his job and told him I would explain to the audience that he was unable to present at this time. But he refused to cancel and explained that if he did not speak he would live in fear for the rest of his life and he wasn't going to live like that.

I knew then that Andrew Wakefield, although perhaps he did not realize it, was going to play a key role in confirming the relationship between vaccination and brain damage and would likely suffer persecution at the hands of those in the medical community who would try to stop him from telling the truth. I also knew that he would change the course of the history of the vaccine safety and informed consent movement we had launched 15 years earlier.

Less than six months after he presented at our conference and talked about his concerns that most of the original studies in the 1960's and 1970's evaluating the safety of live measles and MMR vaccines only included a three week follow-up period, Dr. Wakefield and 13 colleagues published evidence in the Feb. 27, 1998 issue of the *Lancet* that measles infection and measles vaccine may be linked to the development of inflammatory bowel disease and autism in previously healthy, normally developing children. In reviewing the medical factors common to eight out of 12 previously normal children who simultaneously developed severe intestinal dysfunction as well as autism, they found that five of the eight children had developed these after MMR vaccination.

During the course of their investigation, Wakefield and his colleagues discovered that in 1961 Hans Asperger had observed a high rate of gastrointestinal (celiac) disease in those diagnosed with autism. They hypothesized that persistent viral infection, either from natural disease or live virus vaccines, can cause chronic inflammation of the bowel and damage to central nervous system development in some children. The authors emphasized that they had not proved a cause and effect relationship between MMR vaccine and a non-specific colitis which they described as 'autistic ileal-lymphoid-nodular hyperplasia.' They simply called for more studies to investigate the hypothesis.

Their case report in the *Lancet* was met with a firestorm of criticism in the U.S. and Europe. An editorial in the same issue of the *Lancet* by U.S. health officials charged that 'vaccine safety concerns such as that reported by Wakefield and colleagues may snowball' when the public and media 'confuse association with causality and shun immunization.' They discounted the study's importance and suggested the children's regression into autism after vaccination was 'coincidental' and not caused by the MMR vaccine.

A Reuters newswire story quoted Neal Halsey, M.D., of John Hopkins' and chair of the American Academy of Pediatrics Committee on Infectious Diseases, as saying it was 'highly inappropriate' for Wakefield and his colleagues to discuss a possible connection between the health problems of the children in his study and measles or MMR vaccines. Halsey cited 'good evidence for genetic predisposition and other factors, including intrauterine exposure to rubella, head injuries and encephalitis as "possible contributing factors" that explained the children's autism.' [i]

In response, NVIC joined with the Autism Research Institute (ARI) founded by Bernard Rimland, Ph.D. and Cure Autism Now (CAN) and issued a March 1, 1998 press release calling the attack on Wakefield and his colleagues 'a threat to independent scientific research and the public health.' We also called for independent studies to be conducted by non-governmental researchers into the possible link between vaccines and autism using a portion of the one billion dollars appropriated by Congress to the Department of Health and Human Services every year to create, buy and promote mandatory use of vaccines by all children.

NVIC separately challenged federal health agencies to publish an article in the medical literature detailing the prospective, case controlled clinical trials and other safety data used to license the live MMR vaccine and recommend a second dose of measles vaccine for all children in 1991. Dr. Rimland added: 'It is ludicrous to claim that the link between many cases of autism and vaccination in just coincidental.' CAN founder and president Portia Iverson said 'Approximately one-half of the hundreds of parents who call our office each month report that their children became autistic shortly after receiving a vaccination. Isn't it the responsibility of the government to take a proactive position on behalf of these children rather than a defensive one?'

I wrote to the *Lancet* defending the Wakefield study and quoted Herbert Spencer: 'There is a principle which is a bar against all information; which is proof against all argument; and which cannot fail to keep a man in everlasting ignorance. That principle is contempt prior to investigation.' My letter was published in abbreviated form by the *Lancet* in May.

Part of Dr. Wakefield's hypothesis was that the combining of three live viruses into one vaccine (MMR) was exposing children to an atypical simultaneous presentation of the three viruses, which in past generations were experienced by children at different times in childhood. In other words, children almost never naturally become infected with measles, mumps and rubella at the same time. His suggestion that children receive the three vaccines separately, rather than in the combination MMR vaccine, became the central focus of the anger of the vaccine establishment on both sides of the Atlantic. They saw the suggestion as a threat to future public acceptance of vaccinations that bundle many different antigens together into one shot.

Following the controversy that ensued from publication of his article about MMR vaccine and autism, Dr. Wakefield was invited at my request by the Institute of Medicine (IOM) to present his findings at an October 1998 workshop sponsored by the Vaccine Safety Forum, which I had been a member of for four years. At the public workshop, he presented evidence for identification of measles viral DNA in intestinal tissues of autistic children using In-cell Taq/Man PCR. He explained to government officials that immunological studies, including antigen-specific lympho-proliferative and cytokine responses and FACScan lymphocyte activation studies, were underway. However, the information he offered was met with resistance from those most anxious to discount the validity of it.

Less than a year later, in the summer of 1999, the Environmental Protection Agency (EPA) and FDA announced that they were directing the vaccine manufacturers to remove a mercury preservative (thimerosal) from childhood vaccines. Under a provision in the 1997 FDA Modernization Act, health agencies had been directed to calculate the level of mercury in all medical and over-the-counter products. Their calculations revealed that mercury in childhood vaccines exposed children to mercury levels that exceeded EPA threshold guidelines for safe exposures.

Within a year of that announcement, the IOM convened a new Immunization Review Committee at the request of the CDC and National Institutes of Health (NIH) to evaluate scientific data that would answer outstanding questions about vaccine safety. In April 2001, the first report of the newly created Committee stated that 'the evidence favors rejection of the causal relationship at the population level between MMR vaccine and autistic spectrum disorders.' However, the IOM added a caveat: 'The proposed biological models linking MMR vaccination to autism spectrum disorders, although far from established, are nevertheless not disproved.' IOM recommended that further scientific research on the occurrence of autism in children following MMR vaccination be done.

NVIC issued a press release in which I stated:

The Committee clearly acknowledged the biologic plausibility that MMR vaccine could be a co-factor in causing autism in some children. The conclusion by the IOM Committee that current scientific evidence favors rejection of a causal association between autism and MMR vaccine should not be taken out of context. There has been limited scientific research to date to investigate the relationship between vaccination and autism. Until a more rigorous examination is conducted, the case is open, not closed.

The same month that IOM published their report on MMR vaccine and autism, an article entitled 'Autism: a novel form of mercury poisoning' was published in *Medical Hypothesis* by Bernard et al. Since then, the idea that mercury poisoning is the primary cause of autism increases in the U.S. and has eclipsed recognition of the potential role that live MMR vaccine (or any other vaccine) may play in the development of autism in some children.

The hypothesis that mercury preservatives (thimerosal) in vaccines has exposed children to bolus and cumulative amounts of mercury and caused regressive autism was forwarded by parents whose children regressed into autism in the 1990's after being repeatedly injected with thimerosal containing DPT/DTaP, HIB and hepatitis B vaccines starting at birth. Maintaining that they are 'pro-vaccination' and simply want mercury removed from vaccines, some parents went on to found advocacy organizations, and lobby Congress and state legislatures for laws that would ban mercury preservatives.

Six months after the mercury hypothesis was published and three weeks after Sept. 11, 2001, the IOM Immunization Review Committee published a report on 'Thimerosal-containing vaccines and neurodevelopmental disorders.' IOM acknowledged that 'mercury is a known neurotoxin' and concluded that 'the evidence is inadequate to accept or reject a causal relationship between thimerosal exposures from childhood vaccines and the neurodevelopmental disorders of autism, ADHD and speech or language delay.' The IOM urged that 'full consideration be given to removing thimerosal from any biological or pharmaceutical product to which infants, children and pregnant women are exposed.'

Parent groups in the U.S. did not think the 2001 IOM reports went far enough to acknowledge the relationship between vaccines and autism, while government health officials and vaccine manufacturers were furious that IOM had publicly called for the removal of thimerosal from vaccines.

Between 2001 and 2004, the publicity surrounding the association between autism and vaccines greatly increased public awareness among Americans that vaccines can cause harm. By 2004, frustrated public health officials requested that the IOM Immunization Review Committee re-examine their 2001 reports on MMR vaccine, thimerosal containing vaccines and autism and issue a revised report.

Parent groups advocating the mercury hypothesis went to Congress in an unsuccessful attempt to block the IOM re-examination. There were unconfirmed reports that IOM Committee members received email threats from parents of children with autism before the public workshop was held to discuss new data.

In May 2004, the IOM issued a new report on autism and vaccines. Despite the mounting clinical evidence and studies by independent researchers that there is a causal relationship between vaccination and regressive autism, this time the IOM categorically rejected all clinical, biological mechanism and epidemiological evidence that vaccines may cause autism or other neuroimmune disorders in some children.

In an unprecedented fit of pique, the IOM Committee went one step further and declared that no more scientific research should be funded to investigate the relationship between vaccines and autism. The prestigious scientific body, which had a decade earlier confirmed vaccines can cause brain and immune system dysfunction, was slamming the door on any further scientific research into the growing number of reports that children were regressing after vaccination and being left with neuroimmune dysfunction that took the form of autism.

On May 18, 2004, NVIC issued a press release that characterized the report as 'a case of political immunology masquerading as real science.' I criticized the undue influence of funding government agencies on the Committee's conclusions and the dismissal of biological mechanism evidence in favor of relying on flawed epidemiological studies primarily using old medical records to draw conclusions. I added 'With this report, the Institute of Medicine takes a step toward weakening its reputation as an independent body capable of making an objective scientific analysis of complex medical risk issues which are influenced by government policy and industry profits. When the real science comes out demonstrating that vaccines can cause autism in genetically susceptible children, this Committee's conclusions will be meaningless.'

Although there is a general mistrust among young parents of IOM and other institutions defending vaccine safety, I continue to hope that one day the Institute of Medicine will reconsider their opposition to funding of scientific research into the biological mechanisms and high risk factors for vaccine induced autism. The 1991 and 1994 IOM reviews of the scientific literature for evidence vaccines can cause harm, which were requested by Congress under the 1986 law, are among the most comprehensive that have ever been published. Perhaps one day there will be another review by IOM of the link between autism and vaccines and the conclusions will be different.

It is clear that those promoting and profiting from mandated use of multiple vaccines to prevent all infectious disease are determined to hold the line, as they have done for more than a quarter of a century, and deny the extent and severity of vaccine risks. The stubborn refusal to fund studies to compare long term health outcomes of highly vaccinated and unvaccinated individuals is telling. The unwillingness to study the biological mechanisms of vaccine injury and death has prevented pathological profiles from being developed to separate out what is and is not vaccine induced. Without that knowledge, genetic and other biological high risk factors cannot be identified so the lives of susceptible individuals can be spared.

The question, which those responsible for protecting the public health in every country have not answered, is: why are so many highly vaccinated children so sick? The most vaccinated child populations in the history of mankind should be the healthiest and not the sickest if vaccination to prevent most infectious disease in childhood truly results in better health.

Could it be that the public health policy of removing all experience with acute infectious disease in early childhood, together with the atypical manipulation of the immune system from birth via vaccination, is directly responsible for new epidemics of chronic disease in the U.S., Britain and other developed countries?

We cannot wait any longer for those who do not want to address the question, to answer it. It is time for citizens in every country to stand up and defend the freedom to make informed, voluntary vaccination decisions. If we are not afraid, we can protect ourselves and our children from exploitation by profiteers and ideologues who justify throwing some of us under the bus in the name of the greater good. Only when we are free to exercise the human right to informed consent and vote with our feet, will we have the economic and political leverage to force policy change and protect our health and the biological integrity of future generations.

Endnotes

i. What the story did not disclose was that Halsey is a measles vaccine developer who helped direct studies in underdeveloped countries using an experimental high potency measles vaccine. The studies were eventually halted after the discovery of an excess number of deaths in girl children given the vaccine.

CHAPTER TWO

Suffering in Silence

*We should not make any judgement on the motivation
of parents who in seeking for a cause of their
children's illness seek also to further
the cause for treatment of their children.*

Josh's GP

It was lunchtime, Christmas Eve 1985, and we had just finished work. A load of us decided to go to our work's social club, as there was always a good Christmas atmosphere, the disco and drinks were cheap. I didn't want to have too many as we'd arranged to go night clubbing in the evening. It was my turn to buy the next round, that's when I met Nick at the bar accompanied by his brother and sister-in-law and two children.

Nick was very loud, the complete opposite of me, I was quiet, lacked confidence and hated to be the centre of attention. He asked me if I would like a drink and we got chatting. He worked for a double glazing company, I knew he was quite a few years older than me but wasn't sure about his age.

I said I had better get the drinks back to my friends; having asked what had kept me, they started teasing me, shouting 'Heather's pulled', 'Get in there'. I told them to be quiet, I could see Nick was looking. The DJ began to slow things down by putting on slow stuff, I could see Nick was coming towards me. Was he going to ask me to dance? I hoped so. As I nervously got up to dance I could feel myself having a hot flush. Was it the drink or embarrassment? My friends' jeering rang in my ears.

I hoped I wasn't sweating too much as he drew me closer to him. As the music stopped he kissed me. I responded. I blamed this on the drink, as it was really out of character for me. Nick always insisted it was because I fancied him, more like the other way round I say. Nick tells me he fancied me the first time he saw me but felt I was too young. This was something his mates ribbed him about, six years difference in our ages, I was 18, he was 24.

At the end of the dance, Nick asked me for my phone number and said he would ring me on Boxing Day. Would he remember, or even bother to keep my number? When he did ring, on Boxing Day I played it cool, casually I said 'I forgot that you said you would ring'. Still you can't play hard to get when you really fancy someone. We went out for a drink that evening.

We married in May 1990. We did not know when planning our big day that it would be on the football cup final day, much to the annoyance of many of Nick's mates and his dad, all big football fans. We had a wonderful wedding; everything went smoothly, after having had a migraine the day before. On the actual day I had no nerves at all and was so excited when the horse drawn carriage arrived to take dad and me to the church.

Aaron, our first child, was born on 23rd February 1991 weighing 8lb 11oz. I had already decided I wanted to bottle feed him; he was a very greedy baby, always draining his bottles dry. Aaron wasn't the easiest of babies, he continually woke during the night and was very demanding, which is one of the reasons why we did not want to leave it too long before trying for a brother or sister for him.

Again I felt I was so lucky to fall straight away, Aaron was 13 months so it meant there would only be 22 months between them.

Luckily I did not suffer as many migraines this time but did suffer the sickness and was prescribed Avomine. I also had three urinary infections and was prescribed antibiotics.

Josh was born on the day he was due, 13th December 1992, after a normal delivery. He weighed 8lb 11oz, exactly the same weight as Aaron. The midwives all called him a little bruiser, he was very chunky and looked muscular, he looked gorgeous in his little bodysuit. I decided to breast feed Josh; he took to this and fed very well on several occasions putting on 1lb a week. After six weeks when my milk did not seem to be satisfying him, I put Josh on the bottle to which he immediately took. Now Josh was sleeping right through the night; we couldn't believe it, at two Aaron was still waking up.

Josh was so different from Aaron, such a happy baby, always smiling and very content. He adored Aaron and would get so excited when Aaron played peek-a-boo with him and did pat a cake with Josh's little hands. Josh was the perfect baby; he had such a lovely affectionate nature everyone wanted to take him home with them.

Josh developed normally and reached all his milestones as expected, he sat unaided at just over six months, and although he was the slowest to walk at 11 months, I didn't consider that to be late. Aaron used to fetch things for Josh, with Josh being content to sit and let Aaron do that. Josh had a bit more weight to carry around at a year; he was 25lb compared to Aaron who was 23lb. By 11 months Josh was saying single words such as 'Mamma', 'Dada', 'Ta', 'Gone', 'Juice' and 'Bye'.

Josh had his MMR vaccine at 13 months; on the evening of the vaccination he had a high fever so we gave him Calpol. The following morning he woke with severe diarrhoea, it had leaked all through his baby grow and onto his cot bedding. This was bright yellow and then changed to what I can only describe as being like Oxtail soup. This continued for five days, he then became constipated. Prior to the MMR he had opened his bowel every day, sometimes twice a day.

I contacted the health visitor regarding his constipation when Josh was only opening his bowels once a week, she told me to buy a tin of prunes and let him drink the juice. I did this but it had no effect. We began to notice changes in him, my happy contented little boy now seem to always be miserable and upset and would scream and cry for no apparent reason; he no longer liked to be picked up and cuddled. He seemed not to like being touched, and changing his nappy was a nightmare, anyone would have thought I was hurting him. He became withdrawn and stopped playing with Aaron, preferring to be on his own. This was devastating for us all and extremely upsetting for Aaron who kept asking 'mummy, why won't Josh play with me anymore, doesn't he like me? He won't even look at me'.

How could our little boy have changed so quickly within four weeks of having had the MMR vaccine? Josh's behaviour was what I can only describe as 'odd'. I put this down to his constipation, but soon began to realise that there was more to it. He became obsessed with light switches and would climb on chairs and tables to get to them, turning the light on and off. It was the same with door handles and opening and closing doors. He was getting a lot of enjoyment from this repetitive behaviour and clearly had to do it. It was now a real struggle to get any eye contact with him; before he loved posing for the camera, he now ignored any camera that was pointed at him.

Taking Aaron to playschool was very stressful, as Josh seemed to be frightened of going outdoors; every time he saw me put my coat on he would scream and throw himself on the floor. I became a prisoner in my own home as he continued to have these tantrums every time we tried to leave the house.

Other mums would comment and ask 'isn't he happy again?'; he never seemed to be happy. I found myself trying to avoid the other parents and would leave a little later so they would have already dropped off their children. Josh would scream even louder if there were too many people around his pushchair. I always made sure I had a pocket full of little lollipops and when his behaviour got too embarrassing I would give him a lollipop to keep him quiet. However, he began to get through them too quickly and I knew this would not be doing his teeth any good so I stopped it.

It was now six weeks since his MMR vaccine and we had heard no language from him for at least two weeks. The single words he had gained had vanished and he made no attempt to say anymore. Having got him used to sitting on the potty at an early age he no longer knew what the potty was for.

Josh had always been a good sleeper, sleeping through the night from six weeks old. He now became hard to settle down to sleep and woke up every couple of hours kicking and banging in his cot. He spent long periods awake babbling to himself, and when going in to him he was unaware of my presence except to take his bottle from me; he had developed an increased thirst.

At his 18-month assessment concerns with his behaviour, poor interaction, little eye contact and a total loss of speech were noticed. He was still only opening his bowel once a week, I was being told not to worry as all children are different with their toilet habits. Anything I said about MMR was completely ignored; it was as if I hadn't spoken.

Josh's behaviour got worse, he would stand spinning and spinning around and flapping his hands whilst doing this. Meal times became a real challenge, his appetite was now very poor and he refused to eat certain foods. Josh used to love yoghurt but now he became more interested in the packaging than the contents, he would tip all the yoghurt on to his high chair tray, just so he could have a good old chew of the plastic container. He would throw a big tantrum if we tried to remove it from him.

It had always been a joy and pleasure to watch the boys both splashing and playing together at bath time but not any longer. Now, Josh would scream as I lowered him into the bath and after a few weeks he no longer wanted his brother or anything else with him in the bath. Any bath toys would be thrown straight back out, and he didn't even like a sponge or a flannel left in with him.

At this time, I was working in the evenings 6pm until 10pm five nights a week in a factory and consequently going to bed physically and mentally exhausted. I remember begging Nick on several occasions not to go to work as I was so tired and I didn't know what sort of day I had in front of me.

Josh seemed now to also suffer from feverish episodes and persistent unexplained vomiting. It was during the Christmas just after his second birthday that he seemed to suffer seriously from this. This time it was much worse: Josh was very lethargic and vomiting, he wanted to be cuddled then he didn't, he wanted to sleep all the time but would only sleep for 10 minutes at a time. He was clearly agitated and in pain. When the doctor came out on Christmas day, he said it was a virus.

Josh seemed to deteriorate further during the night and he seemed not to be able to tolerate the light being turned on and screamed and covered his eyes with his hands. Even daylight seemed to cause him a problem. Calpol did not keep his temperature down. We called the doctor out again, the same doctor arrived and prescribed antibiotics. We seemed to spend the next 48 hours rocking Josh off to sleep and letting him sleep on our laps while he whined in his sleep. He slowly began to recover with the antibiotics and took fluids only for the next week.

Having nursed him through this 'virus' we noticed Josh seemed to be more distant and isolated from us, if that was at all possible. After a few months went by, we became convinced Josh was not hearing us. As many parents of autistic children do, we suspected deafness. After a long haul of appointments and tests under anaesthetic Josh was found to have a hearing loss in both ears. They felt his right ear required a hearing aid. Due, however, to his autistic tendencies the doctors felt Josh would not be able to tolerate this.

A doctor from the child development centre told us Josh had the right to hear like anyone else, whether or not he had autistic tendencies he should be given the opportunity to try a hearing aid. How wrong could the audiologist have been, Josh took to the hearing aid from the first day, he would come and give it to us if it was not turned on. It seemed to calm Josh down and help his concentration, and he continues to wear it. We do not know for sure whether the virus contributed to Josh's hearing loss, but years later we found it written up in Josh's medical notes as Unspecified Meningitis.

Josh was nearly two and a half before he was seen again by a health visitor, who apologized saying that he should have been reviewed sooner but the previous health visitor had moved on. I could tell by the look on her face that she had real concerns about Josh as she watched him. As a consequence of this visit we were advised to take Josh to our GP who very quickly got him an appointment at a child development centre. The centre confirmed what I was now already thinking myself, Josh was showing signs of autism. But this did not necessarily mean he was autistic.

At this time, Josh was tested for fragile X chromosome but the results were negative, as they have been with other children damaged by vaccination. Within weeks an educational physiologist visited to observe Josh. She told him what a handsome little boy he was, not that this meant anything to him, all he wanted her to do was read a Thomas The Tank Engine book to him, over and over again.

At almost three years of age it was suggested that Josh started at an assessment unit, a little like a special needs nursery. I agreed to this thinking it would help him to socialise with other children and be with teachers more able to help Josh than I was. At home he continued to spend long periods occupied with the light switches and his latest diversion was running up and down the landing screeching with delight as he banged each bedroom door shut.

Josh attended the Unit two whole days a week; I missed him terribly but did make the most of those two days. It meant I could even put my feet up if I wanted to as I was now four months pregnant; we needed to get Josh settled before the new baby arrived. Josh cried every morning when I left him and liked to stand on a chair and watch me through the window until he could no longer see me, I felt encouraged by what seemed to be a normal child reaction.

In February 1996 our beautiful baby girl was born, I was so desperate for a girl that, not quite believing I had one, I kept taking her nappy off to check. She was darker than the boys, had a bit more hair, lovely olive skin and little rose bud lips. Having been told throughout my pregnancy that I was carrying a smaller baby I was surprised, as she was the biggest of our three children weighing 8lb 12oz. We stuck to the original girl's name we had picked when we had the boys, Jodie.

She was just like Josh at that early age, very content, only crying when hungry, she slept well and just fitted in with our daily routines; sometimes I did not have time in the mornings to bath her so I kept her in her baby grow and bathed her after I had got the boys to school, this was also less work for me, as Josh always wanted to jump in her baby bath when I got her out.

Josh showed very little interest in Jodie when she was first born, but now and again when she cried he tried to put her dummy in her mouth. Aaron was all over her, which was nice, as he no longer had any brotherly bond with Josh. I did not return to work after having Jodie as I took redundancy. Josh was attending the Unit four whole days a week and I was trying hard to potty train him. It was very much hit and miss, he didn't really understand, but he did prefer to sit on the toilet rather than use the potty. With the continued persevering of his teachers we were only having a couple of accidents a week, probably three pairs of wet pants.

I suppose like many other parents, I had more or less accepted the assurances of the doctors that the onset of Josh's problems were not related to the MMR vaccine, and that the timing was just a coincidence. So when the time came for his MMR booster at the age of three years and nine months, I took him. Josh immediately developed diarrhoea, just as he did after the first MMR vaccination. The diarrhoea only lasted three days but then his constipation became much worse, he was soon only opening his bowel twice a month; surely this could not be a coincidence. For Josh to develop diarrhoea and regression once may be, but twice surely not. There was now NO WAY Jodie was going to have the MMR.

Josh's behaviour regressed even further with constant screaming, and his refusal to walk to nursery. Having only one car at the time, which Nick needed for work, I usually had to sit Josh on the end of Jodie's pram. This was very heavy to push and made by back ache. I also needed to get Josh to school as quickly as possible so that he could use the toilet.

Although he had previously been doing well with his toileting he now regressed with it. Two months after Josh received the MMR booster and having been in pants for four months, with much regret I had to put him back into nappies not only for his wetting but now for his continual soiling. No sooner had he been cleaned and changed, he had soiled himself again; he was getting through 7-8 pairs of pants a day and making his little bottom very sore.

Although it didn't seem possible, Josh became more obsessive. One day I changed the ornaments around whilst polishing; when he came in from nursery he noticed and put each and everyone back in their original place. He developed an amazing memory, he memorised every last word on every page of his growing number of Thomas the Tank Engine books, and because of this he knew exactly when to turn the page. This was even more odd as Josh couldn't read. Taking Josh out in the car was traumatic for him; he would kick and scream if we did not go the way he expected us to go. He found it hard to accept that sometimes we needed to go right and not left. It became harder to do anything as a family.

Now, when I look back I realise that Jodie had to grow up too quickly. She was walking at nine months after only a short while in a pushchair, mainly because on trips such as the ones to school, I couldn't push her and hold on to Josh at the same time and as well because Josh wanted to sit in the pushchair on top of her. I knew I could no longer use the pushchair and have Josh walk alongside after he had one of his regular tantrums on the way to school. He suddenly let go of my hand and ran straight in front of an oncoming school taxi, luckily the taxi was about to stop so he did an emergency stop and Josh continued through the school gate oblivious to what he had just done.

With tears streaming down my face I tried to apologize to the driver, who said he understood, but I knew I couldn't let it happen again. Josh was a danger to himself as well as others. If it had been on a busy road the driver could have hit him.

Josh seemed to enjoy the structured environment at school and he appreciated the daily routine with a schedule; knowing what was coming next. During the end of March and early April 1997 several professionals went into school to observe Josh and try to interact with him. They followed these observations up with reports of their findings, which were then sent to Southampton General Hospital where a Consultant Paediatrician and child Psychiatrist along with a clinical Psychologist studied them. This process ended with an appointment to which we brought Josh so that other professionals could assess him again, whilst we watched in another room with an expert from an autistic school.

While Nick observed the various tasks they were trying to get Josh to do, I spent an hour trying to convince the sympathetic autism expert who sat next to me, that my son was not autistic. I explained how he could do this and that, how loving he was, how his eye contact was improving and how he was slowly beginning to cope with change. In my heart, though, I knew he was autistic and would have been shocked if he hadn't been diagnosed as such. Our next appointment in two weeks was only for Nick and myself.

It was my thirtieth birthday, on the day that Josh was diagnosed as being autistic. I couldn't hold back the tears, I cried uncontrollably, the pain I felt was indescribable. In the car on the way home I could hear the words of the psychologist as she told us, 'I'm very sorry but Josh is autistic, it is a life long disability and he is still very young, we don't know what the future holds for him, or whether he will be able to live an independent life, all we do know is the right school and education is crucial for all autistic children'.

Josh's teachers could not understand why I was so upset as we had all expected it, but unless you have been through it yourself you can't begin to understand. You live in hope and then suddenly that hope is taken away. Perhaps this will sound silly to you, but its like a death, you can't really begin to grieve until after the funeral, I was feeling this after the diagnosis. I was grieving for my little boy whose life had been taken away by vaccines. The diagnosis was so final and the problem was left with us. I cried for days until my friend Sue said to me 'Heather, he's still the same little boy he was last week'. Of course she was right and I still loved him deeply; I had to pull myself together, I had other children and they didn't need to see me so upset.

Josh was now back in pants and doing well – no wetting and less soiling but still only opening his bowel twice a month. Josh's GP refused to listen to what I was saying and indicated his toilet habits were due to his autism and it was neurological, rather than a bowel problem. Josh would get there in the end, it would just take him longer to learn he had to sit on the toilet and do a poo. Josh spent long periods sat on the toilet crying and hitting me in pain, it wasn't that he was afraid to go, he clearly couldn't.

I began to think perhaps all autistic children have these gastrointestinal problems, especially as Josh would regularly vomit. The same GP again told me he would expect Josh to be sick sometimes as autistic children eat things they shouldn't, like paint, crayons and so on. This was not Josh, although he liked to chew things like pen tops, shampoo lids, yoghurt pots and also the sleeves of his school sweatshirts, he would not eat or swallow anything. I felt Josh's GP was being very ignorant and putting all autistic children in the same category when in fact autism is a very broad spectrum, and like any other child, an autistic child is an individual. Of course, what the GP was really afraid of was admitting that Josh had regressive autism triggered by his MMR vaccinations.

Josh started at a special needs school and settled well. He had a medical during October 1998. At the medical the doctor informed me that Josh's opening his bowels every sixteen days was not normal; by then he was nearly six years of age. A letter was faxed to our local hospital and we were given an appointment for the following day. At last, we thought, someone was going to listen to us.

I began taking Josh to the hospital twice a week for the next six months. After failing to respond to large doses of laxatives, suppositories and regular full phosphate enemas he underwent manual evacuation for impaction under general anaesthetic. Having had three of these procedures it was then recommended he had an anal stretch and rectal wash out at Southampton General Hospital. This hopefully would improve his bowel, and prescribing laxatives again would stop him becoming impacted. However, despite these procedures, after three weeks Josh had to have a manual evacuation under anaesthetic again. I was taught to administer enemas, and continued to take Josh to our local hospital weekly for the next six months.

In the meantime Josh was referred to Professor Milla at Great Ormond Street Hospital (GOSH) and our local paediatric unit was shut in early 2000. During our visits to GOSH, we saw Dr

O'Connell at a private clinic for secretin injections after seeing on a television documentary how this treatment had helped another autistic boy. Josh had three injections, which altogether cost £2,500. After urine tests it was suggested that Josh start on a gluten and wheat free diet. We did not see the response we had hoped for with secretin so we discontinued it. Although the diet made little difference to Josh's bowel movements, it did seem to help his autism; his behaviour was much improved and he became calmer and more sociable.

Josh was admitted to GOSH in April 2000 for an endoscopy[i] and a anorectal manometry.[ii] The results of these procedures were explained and reported to me and I will explain them as the doctors related them to me. There was inflammation of the laminar propria in the duodenum, terminal ileum and colon; there were also focal collections of eosinophils[iii] within the laminar propria. It was recommended we removed dairy from Josh's diet as the consultants suspected Josh had Gilbert Syndrome: abnormal functioning of the liver involving missing enzymes. He was prescribed Sodium Cromylgate for allergies; this did reduce his vomiting and instead of occurring weekly it only happened once every few weeks.

By this time Josh was scrawny, pale and underweight. Where had our chunky little boy gone with the dimples in his bottom and ripples on his legs; the boy that we had used to call 'our little sumo wrestler'? Professor Milla at GOSH had exactly the same negative response when we mentioned MMR, as had previous doctors and psychologists; there was no discussion. We requested a referral to the Royal Free Hospital, which Professor Milla was more than happy to give us. No doubt he saw it as an easy way to get rid of us both and the awkward questions that Josh raised.

We finally received an appointment for 5th December 2001 to see Dr Murch and his clinical team at the Royal Free. This appointment was sent 18 months in advance. I rang up the Hospital to see if they had made a mistake; should it have been

December 2000? While we waited we continued to be seen by Southampton Hospital. Although I have never met such a rude and arrogant man as *Dr Difficult* whom we saw there, it was still better to have him than no consultant at all.

The arguments we had with *Dr Difficult* all centered on his blind, dogmatic and unevidenced assumptions that Josh had nothing more than constipation and was probably autistic before the MMR vaccine but we just hadn't noticed. His anger towards Dr Wakefield appeared pathological; he clearly hated him with a vengeance.

By the time Josh was seen by Dr Heusckel at the Royal Free his weight had fallen to only four stone. The doctor could not believe I had been administering enemas for almost three years, and that Josh had only opened his bowel three times in two years without the use of the enemas. He listened with interest as we went over Josh's history and how he was fine up until he had his MMR. He did not seem surprised when we told him that he regressed further after the booster. At last, I thought, we had found a doctor who was listening to what we were saying. He sent Josh for an X-ray, which showed severe impaction throughout his lower intestines. This was why he was vomiting so frequently. He told us that he wanted to admit Josh very soon and he would phone me the following day with a date. My faith in the medical profession had fallen so much that I was surprise when he did call; he explained that Josh would spend three days in hospital having investigations; this was booked for the following week.[iv]

Josh had a number of gastrointestinal procedures. I found myself continually confused by the technical terms and felt as if Josh's life was being taken out of my hands. However, the doctors at the Royal Free were very attentive and explained everything to Nick and myself. Josh had an OGD[v] and a Colonoscopy.[vi] This procedure showed reddening at the gastro-oesophageal junction as well as erythema in the gastric antrum.[vii] There was also a loss of vascular pattern in the rectum and sigmoid, known as

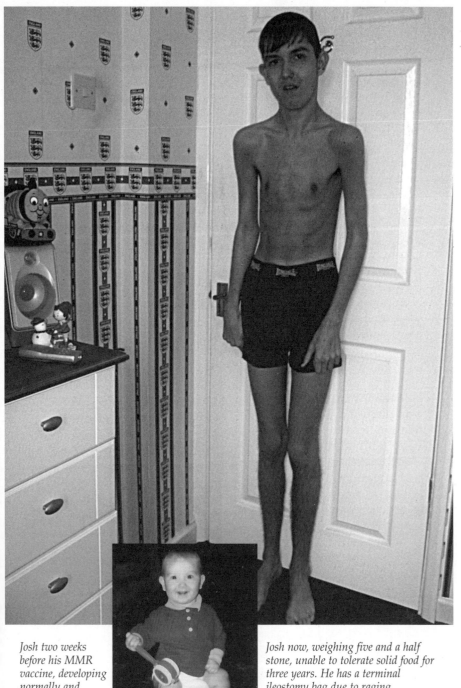

Josh two weeks
before his MMR
vaccine, developing
normally and
happy to use his
potty from the age
of ten months.

Josh now, weighing five and a half
stone, unable to tolerate solid food for
three years. He has a terminal
ileostomy bag due to raging
inflammatory bowel disease that led to
his colon being removed.

lymphonodular hyperplasia.[viii] Histology revealed severe eosinophilic oesophagitis[ix] with chronic inflammation, ulceration and multiple allergies. Although they said it was hard to get a clear picture on Josh as his severe impaction blocked the scope, all together this amounted to a bad case of Inflammatory Bowel Disease with severe impaction. This diagnosis fitted with many other cases of vaccine damaged children seen at the Royal Free Hospital. Josh was prescribed Sulphasalazine, Probiotics, Ranitidine and Domperidone.

Josh continued to need regular enemas and had persistent vomiting. In February 2002[x] we returned to the Royal Free Hospital, as we were unhappy that not enough explanation had been given when we had visited three weeks earlier. I asked the consultant outright if the results we had been given were what they would expect to find in vaccine damaged children. He explained that Josh's bowel was exactly as they had expected it to be, even though it was hard to get a clear picture. But while he said that he understood what we meant he could not confirm vaccine damage. It was at this appointment that, for the first time, surgery was discussed for Josh, and we were told that he should be referred to the Chelsea and Westminster Hospital to a top Paediatric Surgeon. Doctors at the Royal Free described Josh as the worst case they had seen out of the hundreds of children now being treated at the hospital. At this time Josh had only been under the Royal Free's care ten weeks. At this point too we joined the legal action underway against Merck and GlaxoSmithKline (GSK) for MMR vaccine damage.[xi]

Life was extremely stressful having to respond to solicitors' letters and fill in forms. I was also fighting the local education authority as I felt Josh's school was not meeting his needs. Although meetings were held and the principal special needs officer from Hampshire attended, they still argued with me that they could meet Josh's needs; yes, written down on paper they could, but they were failing to meet them in practice. The battle over Josh's education dragged on until eventually a referral was made to another school which was out of our county. Josh was given the placement and transport. I think this was the best thing we did, to move Josh, as the new school did wonders with him, they never looked at what he could not do, but worked on what he was capable of doing. The Head Teacher in this school said she had seen so many autistic children come through her school since the MMR vaccine had been introduced in 1988, she felt that she would not risk giving it to her own son. She gave us the number of a private clinic where she had taken her own son. Nick and I both felt single vaccines were what we wanted for Jodie, rather than leave her unvaccinated. Nick, Jodie, Josh and I attended the clinic in March 2002. Jodie was given her first single measles vaccination. On arrival at reception, we were asked to complete a registration form for Jodie. There was a question on the form asking why we had decided on single vaccines. I gave details about Josh and his reaction to the MMR.

When I gave the completed form back to the receptionist she read our comments about Josh, she asked us whether we had heard of secretin. I told her that we had used it before, but did not see the response we had hoped for. Having only given Josh three injections of secretin, she went on to say we needed to give it at least six before we would start to observe a positive response.

We arranged an appointment to see Dr David Pugh, the doctor who organised the clinic, in the middle of April to discuss secretin and Josh's bowel problems. After explaining we had not seen the response to justify continuing the treatment, again we were told we had not given enough injections and also left the gap between each injection too long. Although Dr Pugh felt the hospital investigations should take priority, he wanted us to let him have one last shot at using secretin that in his opinion had helped children with bowel problems.

He went on to tell us about a little boy he had treated who had similar problems and no speech. After giving him the sixth injection, he said to the boy 'see you next time', and the boy turned round and asked him 'what time?'. I remember the story very clearly because it gave me hope that Josh may regain his speech.

Nick was unhappy about trying secretin treatment again but I talked him round. I became obsessed with the timescale for the injections and was adamant that the injections should be given exactly every four weeks and refused to be flexible with appointments. I remember getting very excited as we approached the sixth injection.

However, Josh still showed no improvement after eight injections. It was suggested Josh convert to secretin nasal spray where he would get the same monthly dosage but on a daily basis, one squirt up each nostril. I spoke to the consultant at the Royal Free Hospital regarding using secretin again, he told us if we were using it to try and help Josh's bowel we should stop as we were only wasting our money. He went on to explain that Josh had been on very potent drugs which seemed to have no effect, and out of the many children they had seen Josh was clearly the worst.

In January 2003, just before Josh's first surgery procedure, I telephoned Dr Pugh's clinic to order another secretin nasal spray. I tried for several days but nobody answered the phone. I did not understand why until I saw a Tonight Programme that had carried out an investigation on Dr Pugh, his vaccine clinic and his medical centre, both of which had been closed down by the National Care Standards Commission. According to the investigation and charges later brought against Dr Pugh he had been administering out of date vaccines, storing them insufficiently and falsifying blood tests.

Jodie had to have two separate blood tests and both showed no antibodies for measles, so to this day remains unprotected and unvaccinated against measles, mumps and rubella. I was consequently the only parent called to give evidence for the GMC in Dr Pugh's case.

Josh was seen by Mr Haddad, the Paediatric Surgeon at Chelsea in May 2002 and was admitted in August that year to have yet another manual evacuation under general anaesthetic and biopsies taken from his rectum and anus to rule out Hirschsprungs disease; [xii] the results came back negative. This meant they could proceed with what they call an ACE,[xiii] a surgical procedure which involved inserting a tube directly into Josh's colon through his stomach into the abdominal wall, so I could administer bottles of enema and sodium chloride through the tube to try and keep his colon empty and stop his impaction. This procedure was performed in January 2003.

For the first couple of weeks we did see a slight response, then one evening I went to administer the drugs through the tube but it had completely disappeared into Josh's stomach. It had been dragged down the abdominal wall by hard stools; the specialist stoma nurse from Chelsea had to talk me through how to get it back out over the phone. I put him in a warm bath and gradually massage around the area and gently pull it back out; I was frightened I was going to hurt him, when it came out it was all slimy and bloody. Laxatives were prescribed to try and prevent this from happening but it still continued, Josh's GP even had to come out one night to force the tube out again.

Five months later the tube was replaced with a button similar to a washing up bottle top. Eventually Josh stopped responding altogether, the bottles of daily enemas were making him violently sick as I was told to administer enemas into his bottom again. Josh could not go on like this, he kept holding his head, I could only assume it gave him bad headaches. His poor little bottom was regularly bleeding; we were told it was because little blood vessels kept bursting from years of enema use. I now had to syringe local anaesthetic into his bottom to relieve the pain he was in.

The X-rays showed no improvement, the Royal Free Hospital Consultant said he had never seen such impaction. Josh went on to be admitted several more times to be emptied out before both hospitals decided the next step would be a colostomy. Whilst the consultant at the Royal Free wanted the whole of Josh's large bowel to be removed the surgeon did not. As he explained to us his job is to save as much of the bowel as he possibly could.

A year after his ACE was inserted, in January 2004, he went back into theatre to have the button removed and a colostomy was performed. Josh had his sigmoid colon removed. He now had a bowel bag, he spent three days in a high dependency unit and then ten days on the ward, he had his own room, as I needed to be with him all the time. After being shown by the specialist stoma nurse how to change and care for Josh's bag, I was concerned how we were all going to cope with this as a family. Josh seemed to accept this was now going to be part of him and did not seem at all worried or confused by it.

One evening, two weeks after coming out of hospital, Josh seemed to be in some pain and was holding his tummy. As I got nearer to him to lift up his top I could smell an awful smell and found his t-shirt was covered in blood, I shouted to Nick to come quickly. Josh's bag was full of blood and falling off but having removed the bag there seem to be no blood oozing from his stoma (opening in his stomach). Although the bleeding had stopped Josh was clearly troubled by it and we rang for the doctor to come out. On arrival, the doctor said he had thought Josh was an old man in his seventies with a bag. I don't know why he expected that! The doctor panicked and said Josh needed to be admitted to hospital immediately.

Josh had scans and X-rays and was kept in for observation for three days; the most likely cause was put down to a kink in the scarring tissue inside his abdomen. When Josh was well enough to return to school the specialist nurse travelled down to train his teachers how to change and empty his bag. Although she was happy to do this she felt I was more than capable of it, but obviously I did not want the teachers to be frightened by the process, and I also needed the support from her.

One advantage of the surgery and the very serious developments with Josh's medical condition was that at least he was relieved not to have the constant enemas. At this time, Josh was having days were there would be no output in his bag so we were still told to give laxatives daily. Not surprisingly knowing Josh's past history, this did not help.

One Saturday morning in May 2004 I went running up the stairs as Josh was screaming in the bathroom. I found him trying to remove his bowel bag; as I removed it for him, he was sick all over me: Josh had a huge hard stool he could not pass through his opening. I tried to stretch the skin around to make the opening wider, then broke the stool off with a tissue, as this happened he vomited again.

This incident and others combined with the fact that Josh was frequently having no output, led us to another X-ray at the Royal Free Hospital that again showed severe impaction. The consultant said that the first operation had made no difference and that Josh needed his whole colon removed, which should have been performed previously, as Josh's colon was dysfunctional. He said he was concerned about Josh and his impaction and that he was going to liaise with the surgeon at Chelsea.

In July 2004 we discussed Josh's next operation with the surgeon; this was booked in for 29th September 2004. He was unsure as to what procedure would be carried out on Josh and would decide once he had 'opened him up' and had a thorough look. In the mean time he would make arrangements to admit Josh for a manual evacuation. This meant they needed to go through the stoma as he no longer functioned from his bottom end.

This admission got overlooked. I tried several times during the summer to arrange it but each time were told that, due to surgeons and doctors annual leave, I would have to get back in touch in early September. Towards the end of August 2004 Josh had not had any output in his bag for five days, his stomach was very distended and he was vomiting. I rang the Royal Free Hospital; they said they would get a consultant to ring me within the hour.

We were then told to bring Josh in straight away. Having spent five days in hospital trying to empty Josh out with laxatives, and even antibiotics in the hope that these would produce diarrhoea, Josh still did not pass any stools and his bag remained empty. One last attempt was made to put a nasal gastric tube up Josh's nose and down into his tummy so drugs to 'wash him out' could be administer. After agreeing to let them use light sedation on Josh, he was still unable to tolerate it and each time the tube hit the back of his throat he pulled it out.

It was 10 days since Josh had passed any stools and we were transferred over to Chelsea and Westminster Hospital where Josh would be evacuated in theatre under general anaesthetic. The only thing was we had to make our own way there, as the hospital could not supply transport until the following morning. We were told if we waited until then the hospital could not guarantee a bed, so we were urged to take the opportunity offered to us. Knowing it would take Nick probably three hours to get to us, I had no choice but to gather up all our belongings and get a taxi. I could not manage all my bags and Josh's videos, which he always insisted on having in hospital, as well as hold on to him. The ward sister asked a nurse to help me, and said the quickest way to get a cab was to walk to the end of the road and flag one down. Josh seemed to be excited; he obviously thought we were going home. His mood soon changed as he noticed we were going in the wrong direction as it was an unfamiliar route. Josh has always been good with directions. He was getting very distressed and smacked me several times.

I was relieved as we approached the entrance to Chelsea Hospital, but this only confused Josh and he started to scream. This time I had to struggle with all the bags myself as I tried to stop Josh escaping, the driver said that the fare was £25.00. I thought the least he could have done was help remove the bags from his cab. Needless to say I didn't tip him. I was near to tears as I struggled up the escalator and on to the ward. Josh soon calmed down as the nurse brought a television so he could watch his videos.

Josh went down to theatre and was emptied out the next day, but was not getting discharged until two days later, due to the sickness that always occurs after anaesthetic. I had been in contact several times with Kirsten Limb, who was working on my legal case against the pharmaceutical company. Since Josh was likely to need a part of his intestine removed, the solicitors were keen for me to ask if a sample of the colon tissue that was to be taken from Josh during his next surgery could be frozen for viral analysis. I wrote down the exact procedure which needed to be followed in order to preserve this sample, as I knew how important this was to get it right.

As Nick, Josh and I made the journey for the planned operation the atmosphere was tense between me and Nick. We were unsure what was going to happen and how long I would be in hospital with Josh. Nick always found it hard having to leave us. As Josh was wheeled down to theatre I could feel the tears whelming up. I tried to be strong as I had done this on numerous occasions, but this time was the hardest, I did not know what was going to happen nor did the doctors. Just as he was drifting off to sleep I bent down and gave him a big kiss and told him how much we all loved him. I looked at the time: it was 10.35am. I was glad to have some company as my friend Lyn had arrived with her mum Val in time to see Josh before he went into theatre.

I only met Lyn in 2003; when Josh had his first operation her son was in hospital at the same time. We have kept in touch ever since, I feel I have known her for a very long time. Josh took to her straight away, she understood him as she has fostered many special-needs children. Josh adores her and always shows her lots of affection. She has been a great support to me whenever Josh is in hospital, visiting and phoning me, as she only lives half an hour away from Chelsea hospital. We went for a coffee and a bite to eat; they then left at 12.30 pm. I sat in Josh's room and looked through a magazine.

It was 1.30pm when a registrar came from theatre and said 'I'm afraid we have had to remove the whole of Josh's colon'. It was so badly diseased, he would now have a terminal ileostomy bag; the output would never be formed, it would remain as a liquid. Arrangements were then made to keep the entire colon for research. It was sent to the lab and frozen as the hospital could not get hold of any dry ice to have it transported to Coventry Microbiology. It was 4.10pm and Josh was now in recovery, vomiting as he usually did after anaesthetic, no matter how many anti-sickness drugs he had beforehand.

At 5.30pm Josh was taken to the new High Dependency Unit, and I was then told I would not be able to sleep in the room with him. They no longer allowed parents to sleep due to lack of space; if there was an emergency, they said, they would not be able to get the crash trolley through. I understood but did not like the thought of Josh waking up and finding me not there for him. I was given keys to a room a few floors up; Nick, Aaron and Jodie were able to stay there when they visited for the weekend. Josh was still very sleepy so I decided at around midnight to go to bed. It must have been an hour later when there was knocking at my door; a security guard shouted that I was needed on the ward.

Josh was crying. They weren't sure what was the matter with him, I tried to comfort him but he did not want to be touched and was clearly agitated. Eventually he seemed to calm down and drift back to sleep. I went back to my room at 4am. I was worried about Josh so returned to him at 6am to find him asleep. The nurse said he did seem distressed about half an hour before, she thought it was because he had woken up to find me not there.

When the day shift nurse came to see him he was crying and was very upset, she asked me if I felt he was in pain. Although he was unable to have any pain relief for another hour, he was trying to bring his knees up. This was strange as he should have had no feeling since he had an epidural tube in his spine. All his pain relief drugs were being administered through this. The nurse went and got a cold metal spoon and touched Josh's tummy with it, he let out an almighty scream and again when his legs were touched with the spoon.

Pulling back the bed covers to take a look at Josh's epidural, we noticed his covers were soaking wet. While we had all assumed his behaviour was down to waking up and finding me not there, in fact his epidural tube had snapped and he was in pain. I felt sick, upset and guilty, the pain he must have been in and not being able to tell me. Who knows for how long he had not been receiving the pain relief drugs. I slept in the Unit that night on a chair; I was not prepared to leave him again. I could not wait to see Nick and the children, who were coming the next day for the weekend.

Nick could not hide his shock; he remarked that Josh looked like death. To me he looked better than he had two days before. On the whole doctors were pleased with Josh's progress and he was allowed to go home after two weeks. Before we left the hospital I checked that Josh's colon had been stored; I was told it was safe in the freezer of the immunology laboratory.

Apart from Josh's high output in his bag, which we were told would gradually reduce over the next few weeks, he recovered well. I then began arranging a courier to collect the sample from the hospital. I told the hospital that a courier would be able to collect the sample the next day bringing dry ice and a suitable container. To save the courier waiting around, could they make sure the colon was within easy access of the freezer?

As I worked this out with the hospital I felt confident and reassured. You can imagine my shock when a few hours later I received a phone call to inform me that though the box had been found in the freezer it was empty. The box was also clearly labelled, ready for the courier with Dr Wakefield's name, although who wrote this it was a mystery.

The immunologist was distraught and could not explain what had happened. The colon sample was later found at the other end of the lab on a workbench; it had by then deteriorated so badly that it was useless for research. The colon had not been logged in on the system and therefore did not need to be logged out. Whoever did this knew how important it was. We had lost an irreplaceable piece of evidence.

Hammersmith Primary Care Trust offered their apologies. After a private internal investigation, the hospital claimed that there had most likely been a breakdown in communication. The hospital then changed their story saying they did not think that the colon had ever been put in the freezer; they evidently forgot they had already told us that the box had been found in the freezer empty. Josh had stayed in hospital for almost two weeks following his operation and there was clearly no possibility that the colon could have remained on the lab benches unnoticed during this time, deteriorating like a piece of rotting meat. Having been invited to look around the labs we could not believe how little security there was in place.

Two further investigations were carried out by the Healthcare Commission and the Health Service Ombudsman. Tighter security is now in place, with CCTV installed and all samples, routine and non routine, are now logged in on the system. This story of Josh's missing and abused body part, was later covered by Peter Hitchens in the *Mail on Sunday*, under the heading 'This boy's illness may be linked to the MMR so who destroyed the crucial evidence'.[xiv]

Josh's operation was having a huge impact on the whole family; it was like having a baby, as he needed to keep being changed and having his bag emptied during the night. It was disturbing Aaron's sleep. Josh needed his own bedroom and so we had to put our house on the market. We bought a four-bedroom house; Josh settled well and liked having his own room. I continued then, and still do, to get up twice during the night to see to Josh's bag.

Having to begin a twenty-year mortgage again, doubling the amount we borrowed put immense pressure on Nick and me, but I am pleased to say we are still together. Josh seemed to be coping well with his ileostomy bag, but did not understand why he could not go swimming with his class. On the first occasion he went in the pool, his bag had leaked putting the pool out of action; they could not risk that happening again.

In July 2005 Josh was awarded a Diana princess of Wales's memorial award for young people. He was nominated by his school for all he had gone through and the adversity he had overcome. He was presented with a special certificate signed by the then chancellor Gordon Brown, he also got a gold lapel pin, and an invite for the family to visit Althorp House, childhood home of Diana.

We were all so proud when Josh received this award at a special assembly, our whole family had tears rolling down our cheeks, and even Aaron who keeps his feelings well hidden had tears. He has been so proud of his brother and how he copes with everything.

Josh's output in his bag increased all the time, we were now being told to measure the daily output. This was around two litres a day; the average adult is 800mls, just under a half. Josh was regularly fainting and had several admissions for severe dehydration. Josh craved salt at every opportunity in an effort to keep up with his losses. On one occasion I found him pouring salt out of the canister onto the kitchen work top and licking it. He had a severe sodium leak in his blood and urine, which still continues today.

At this time, Josh was still under three hospitals: Southampton, the Royal Free, and Chelsea and Westminster. Doctors at all three had concerns about Josh. Each blamed the other for failing to provide the responsibility, ongoing care and treatment that Josh so desperately needed. After begging Dr Heusckel at the Royal Free Hospital for his help in April 2006, the best he could offer us was his sympathy. He even told us he would not let his own children suffer in the way Josh was, yet he concluded that nothing could be done for Josh now at the Royal Free.

We could not understand why he would not investigate Josh's symptoms as tests kept indicated that bowel disease could still be present. We even said that we would forget the issue of MMR and what initially caused Josh's condition. We felt that in relation to Josh's health at that time it was irrelevant. The only real question was how we were to move him forward and get him the right treatment and investigations.

Dr Heusckel was a consultant who four years previously could not do enough for Josh. We would have followed him across the country had he moved to another hospital. Why had he changed? He agreed with everything we were saying to him and even showed him photographs of the mess Josh was in most mornings, covered in faeces up to his chest where his bag had leaked. His only reply was that he had never once disbelieved us, so we did not need to show him the evidence.

We did not return to the Royal Free Hospital again, although Josh has never been discharged from there. A caring journalist helped arrange for Josh to be seen by Dr Fell, a gastroenterologist at Chelsea. He could not believe how Josh had to live, nor could he understand why had he not been brought in earlier to be helped as Josh was already a patient under the surgical team. Dr Fell said Josh needed further investigation; after several surgery procedures things were clearly not as they should be.

Josh was admitted to Chelsea Hospital in June 2006 and several tests were carried out. Because his upper body had lots of inflammation it was recommended that the way forward was to remove all food. Josh's sole source of nutrition became Modulen, a powder that had to be mixed with cool boiled water. This is used in patients with Crohn's Disease and Inflammatory Bowel Disease during active episodes; it gives support during remission and helps malnourished patients. Josh continued to vomit daily, but gained two stone in weight. This was very misleading for the doctors, as this nutrition had helped him gain weight the previous year when prescribed by the Royal Free. It gives the bowel a complete rest. Josh continued to have persistent vomiting, fainting and severe dehydration.

After several hospital admissions for dehydration, during which Josh was put on drips for a few days, at the end of August 2006 he had a white blood cell scan that showed an abnormal increased uptake in his small intestine and around the ileum; this indicated further bowel disease. Steroids were introduced, but after two months of Josh having been on them with no improvement, we decided to take him to the United States. It was only there that amongst other diagnostic aids, Josh could have the endoscopy capsule, the only procedure that can fully examine the whole of the small intestine.

We got full support from Josh's GP for this trip to the States. He put together a letter discussing all Josh's history, his treatment and medications. Although we have not always seen eye to eye over the years with him, we now have a good parent-practitioner partnership and if he can help he will. He actually admitted to us that if there ever was a vaccine damage payout regarding MMR damage, Josh is clearly one of the children who should receive it. Here is what our GP said to us generally about compensation, it is worth quoting:

> As soon as you suggest that a medical intervention (such as Vaccine) might have been contributory or even causal, it is automatically assumed that you are only after compensation. It is iniquitous that anyone should even suggest that parents of a handicapped child are motivated in any way by greed, but this is all too often the 'elephant in

the consulting room' when a parent wants to discuss the possibility of vaccine damage. Even if you are seeking compensation, people need to see that for what it is ... *compensation, not ever a reward.*

However, doctors can sometimes be a bit like lawyers, hedging their bets, and our GP is keen to make it clear that it does not mean he is admitting the MMR causes autism and bowel disease. A bit strange that, I thought!

With much support from both Dr Fell and our GP, Nick, Josh and I made the long and expensive journey to Thoughtful House in Texas where Dr Wakefield has been practicing since 2002. Josh had never been on an aeroplane so we were not sure how he would cope. Apart from the fact that his bag kept filling up with air from the pressure, he loved flying!

Josh had no trouble swallowing the Endoscopy Capsule with water, we were very proud of him as it was quite big; he was intrigued by the light in it. We all expected this capsule to travel extremely quickly through Josh's body as his transit is so fast. To everyone's surprise the capsule had not been excreted into Josh's ileostomy bag before the battery ran out of its eight-hour life span; it appeared about an hour later.

The capsule did seem to travel quickly to begin with but then sat in his stomach for six hours. Josh had another endoscopy and ileoscopy carried out in Dr Wakefield's presence by Dr Krigsman, who flew in from New York. These results showed that Josh was suffering extensive ulceration, lesions, stomach abscesses and papillomas (inflammatory related growths). In his oesophagus one of these growths was so big that it had to be surgically removed. Josh continued into the next day being violently sick. Dr Krigsman told us that Josh's body may never be able to tolerate food again.

Having had the bowel disease confirmed by biopsies and images taken throughout Josh's body, we were then contacted by Dr Heusckel from the Royal Free Hospital. He was interested in any results found. We felt that it was a shame he had not been as interested six months earlier. He said he was pleased that now Josh would get the right treatment. Josh was prescribed a different steroid, more powerful, higher dose, along with anti-inflammatory drugs and many supplements, including a change of nutritional source formula.

Josh began rapidly losing weight. Within three weeks he had lost a stone. Having been treated for a year a white cell scan confirmed no improvement, steroids do not seem to have any impact on Josh's condition. Being on immune suppressants, which kill off the white cells in the blood, he has to be monitored closely by fortnightly blood tests. This drug worried us terribly. Josh's hair began to get very thin and we all hoped that it didn't fall out.

Josh's output remains high. He is still unable to tolerate any food without immediately vomiting it back up. We recently tried a small jar of baby food; it looked promising as he kept it down for half an hour before being sick. We have since tried baby rice but the same happened, it is now three years since Josh has eaten ordinary food.

After Josh's weight dropped to just over five stone he was admitted into Chelsea and Westminster Hospital, reassured that Josh would not be discharged until we had some answers. The plan was to hospitalise Josh for a whole month to carry out further investigations, and monitor and measure his fluid intake and output both in urine and stoma.

After two weeks I had to ask for Josh to be discharged, as he could not cope with being on the ward. He had coped extremely well but it was clearly too much for him. He became increasingly violent towards me and was like a wild animal. I had never seen Josh so aggressive, he was grabbing and pinching my face so hard my face was swollen and aching like I had been to the dentist. Josh was shaking me like a rag doll with frustration; I could not calm him down.

Even though he was screaming nobody came to see what was up with him. I decided to take him for a bath in the hope this would calm him down. As I gathered up my toiletries he was throwing them at me. I quickly pulled back the curtains from around his bed, there were no nurses at their desk, I ran to the bathroom and he ran behind me. I then locked the door, sat on the bathroom floor and cried uncontrollably.

I stayed there for an hour, Josh broke the toilet seat by slamming it down to sit on it, this then upset him as it had broken into five pieces. I managed to run back to his bed and pull the curtains around. With tears rolling down my face, I rang my friend Lyn and asked her to come and get us. With that the nurse came in to do Josh's temperature and pulse, which should have been done first thing in the morning, along with his medications, which still had not been given. The nurse asked me what was up and I said we needed to go home, as Josh could not cope any longer. I said 'could you please get Dr Fell for me?' They bleeped him and eventually his registrar came.

Also the teacher from the hospital school came to work with Josh and said it was unacceptable that Josh had been made to cope on the ward and that he should have his own room. She was told off and it was said that she was getting too personally involved. Although a room was empty Josh could not have it as it had to remain empty for emergencies.

It was agreed we could go home after Josh had had blood, stool and urine tests and been weighed, as long as we came again in a couple of days for review and a further bone scan. I never ever want to put Josh through that again. He needed to be weaned off the steroids as the impact they had on his bones is frightening, we now had to have Josh seen by a bone specialist to discuss what is going to happen regarding treatment for his bones.

Back home I had never felt so drained and exhausted. Had we gained anything? We were no further forward with his weight; in fact, due to only having half of his feeds one weekend, as the hospital did not order them in time, he now weighed less than when he went in.

Returning to the hospital on the Wednesday, we were shown the images of Josh's endoscopy capsule. These indicated there were no improvements in Josh's bowel disease from the previous images taken three years ago in the States. In fact, the consultant said the recent images looked even more prominent, and went on to describe Josh's insides as raggy. **Forgive me, Is raggy a medical term?**

When we questioned the cause of Josh's condition, we were told that the hospital didn't have the answers. It was suggested that Josh's bowel reacted to something when he was younger. Well we could have told them that and what it was!

To add to Josh's terrible iatrogenic injuries, we now have the damage done to his bones by steroids; we have a boy of sixteen with the bones of an old man. The consultant is hopeful that, providing Josh can stay off steroids, and with added medication to build and strengthen his bones, the damage caused will be able to right itself as Josh is still growing. He will be monitored and scanned regularly regarding this.

Although we are no further forward in treating Josh's bowel disease, nor do we have answers to why Josh cannot hold any food down, he is now putting on weight and is six and a half stone due to a fat solution liquid originally designed to help build up premature babies.

None of us can be sure what the future holds for Josh and we try not to dwell on it. Having recently paid for private blood tests to be carried out, Josh was found to have a mitochondrial dysfunction,[XV] mitochondrial blockages and abnormalities in many of his antioxidant pathways. We need to figure out why his chemistry is so disrupted. We had been hoping to get some answers from GOSH, as Josh's consultant at Chelsea said they will go into depth and be able to tell us if Josh's mitochondrial disorder is primary or secondary. It also seems to me to be the case that the NHS use 'private' test results as an excuse not to do anything. They suggest we are paying for the results we want and the tests are inferior.

Recently, I found out we will probably not receive another appointment at GOSH; Josh is clearly being denied treatment and help. Doctors are not even prepared to see him. Most doctors feel they have nothing to offer and are even questioning the lab results that we have obtained privately. It seems once again doctors are afraid to cross the line as they have seen what will happen to them – in the form of Dr Wakefield – if they do.

Now we tend to take each day at a time. Will Josh ever eat again? Will he ever talk and call me mum? Will he still be watching Thomas The Tank Engine when he's 30? Although caring for Josh is extremely hard and tiring, having to still get up twice during the night to change or empty his ileostomy bag, sometimes not getting to it in time, I don't think I could ever let him go into residential care.

Inevitably, my mind is filled with the same questions that affect all parents, although in our case the questions and answers are more extreme: am I being selfish and holding Josh back? Would he gain independent life skills if I were not around to do them for him? I just cannot bring myself to trust anyone else to look after Josh the way I can. I admit I am often exhausted and have dark moments while Nick thinks I do not help myself enough. I have never been offered respite care nor have I pursued it. I can see this matter becoming a major problem for Nick and me. Especially as at present Josh has gone from being generally calm, placid and affectionate to very aggressive, and now does not like even to be spoken to. We have noticed he does not like to be told he is a good boy and cannot cope with being praised, although he seems to accept the words 'Well done'.

The only explanation I can imagine for Josh's changed behaviour is hormones. Having said that perhaps his new behaviour is understandable in light of all the pain from GI issues, chronic refluxing, his inability to eat and being disturbed every night. Whatever the cause, how do I communicate to Josh that hitting out and slapping my face is unacceptable behaviour?

When I read about parents who have killed themselves and their disabled child, I have no trouble at all imagining how someone got into that state of mind. I could not do that, however. Perhaps because I feel that the rest of my family needs me. But there is so little help and support offered to families like ours that I understand how people arrive at the point where they can no longer carry on.

I no longer grieve for the 'perfect' child I should have had because without his disability Josh would not be Josh. We all love him for who he is now and we know he loves us. I would not give Josh up for anything, but I wish I could spare him all the pain and suffering that he has to go through every day of his life. At those times when he is not frustrated or in pain, I hope he is happy but I don't really know what it is like in his world because he cannot tell me. I know he is often scared, frightened and confused, and that makes my heart heavy.

Our children were toddlers when we started this fight; they are now young adults, and we still come up against the same brick walls. It's difficult to believe that no doctor in Britain would work with Josh with the understanding that his damage might have been a consequence of MMR. Meanwhile three wonderful doctors, the only doctors willing to properly investigate and treat Josh and other vaccine damaged children and treat their parents with respect, have been brought before the General Medical Council.

The only reason these doctors are on trial is because the *Lancet* report published in 1998 referred to MMR vaccine having been given to the children cited in the case review study. Eight of the twelve children's parents blamed the vaccine for their child's condition. If MMR vaccine had not been mentioned, or had another cause been suspected for the Inflammatory Bowel Disease suffered by the children, there would have been no criticism of the *Lancet* paper and no GMC hearing, and consequently our children would have been able to get the treatment they needed in the UK.

We feel honoured to have met Dr Wakefield and communicated with him, he is a wonderful, caring man and a brilliant doctor. He had the courage to stand his ground when others bailed out. His research has a valid foundation; the fact that not all children are affected by the vaccine surely means that some children may have pre-conditions that cause disastrous effects when they have the vaccination. These pre-conditions should be investigated without researchers fearing government or pharmaceutical company intervention. Why should 'questioning' be considered a disciplinary offence? Surely this is the basis of any scientific research, or have the rules been changed by the government and pharmaceutical companies?

If Dr Wakefield were to be struck off at the end of the present hearing, the investigation on the role of MMR in bowel disease and autism would come to a complete end in the UK. Autistic children exhibiting symptoms of the serious bowel disease that Dr Wakefield researched would receive even less treatment than they do now. Doctors and scientists in the UK would be effectively gagged and put off doing further research that questions the safety of the MMR or other vaccines. For the sake of children like Josh and others this cannot be allowed to happen.

As parents, we are not anti-vaccine, although obviously now I wish in Josh's case that I had been. As responsible parents we wanted to do what we thought best for our children. In doing so we lost our little boy to autism. A boy who now should be off out with his mates and like his brother dating girls. It takes only a short time to do the damage, but a lifetime, if ever, to put it right again.

Many parents tell us that they don't know how *we* cope but it is surprising where you get the strength to cope. We have met some wonderful parents and others along our journey, people who we never could have hoped to meet in usual circumstances. I do shed a tear when people speak with great sympathy for us and what we have coped with, and I am always very touched by the words of strangers. But I feel I am only doing what any mother would do, its not about whose child has been affected the worst. As parents of vaccine damaged children we are all in this together. Let's hope we will one day get justice for our beautiful but terribly damaged children.

Recently, we have been given strength by our GP, the best GP we could ask for. We now have tremendous respect for him and after a long journey we seem to have won him over. We now have a good parent-practitioner partnership. I would like to end this chapter with another quote from him, a quote that might give strength to other doctors, having to deal with patients with similar conditions:

Parents whose children have autism need all the help we can offer. I do not think you want anybody's pity in this matter. What needs to be made clear is that parents of sick children need the admiration and affirmation of those of us who are fortunate to have healthy children. If we feel uncomfortable it is because we often have a sense of guilt that we, the 'lucky' ones, do not do enough.

Endnotes

i. **Endoscopy** – Procedure carried out to look at the inside of the body using a device called an endoscope – a thin long flexible tube containing a light and camera so images of the body can be relayed.

ii. **Anorectal Manometry** – A test to measure how well the muscles and nerves in the rectum and anus work. A catheter (flexible plastic tube) is inserted into the bottom from where it goes into the rectum. A small balloon on the end of the catheter is then inflated gradually causing the nerves and muscles in rectum and anus to squeeze. Signals are then picked up by sensors in the catheter and recorded by a machine.

iii. **Eosinophils** — White blood cells that actively promote inflammation. They accumulate in tissue such as the oesophagus, stomach, small intestine and sometimes in the blood. They can cause allergies and severe reflux.

iv. This was the procedure that the children cited in the *Lancet* paper were put through, although according to the prosecution they were not ill. The prosecution also claimed, completely against the evidence, that Dr Wakefield had manipulated and arranged the procedures so that he, Professor Murch and Professor Walker-Smith could experiment on the children. Josh was admitted for these procedures four or five years after Dr Wakefield allegedly committed the offences for which he is presently on trial at the General Medical Council.

v. **OGD, oesophago-gastro-duodenoscopy** — A procedure that enables the doctor, usually a gastroenterologist, to examine the oesophagus, stomach, and duodenum using a thin flexible tube or scope that can be looked through or seen on a TV monitor. Also called upper endoscopy.

vi. **Colonoscopy** — Looks into the colon (sometimes known as large intestine / large bowel.) The colon is the part of the gut that comes after the small intestine. The last part of the colon leads into the rectum where stools are stored before being passed out through the anus.

vii. **Erythema in the gastric antrum** — Erythema is redness of the skin caused by capillary congestion, in this case in the last third of the stomach.

viii. **Lymphonodular hyperplasia** — A condition in which there is an increase in the number of normal cells in the lymph nodes.

ix. **Eosinophilic oesophagitis** — Eosinophilic esophagitis is an inflammatory condition in the wall of the esophagus in which it fills with eosinophils. Most cases are seen in people with allergies such as hay fever and asthma.

x. In 2002, Dr Wakefield left the Royal Free to live and work in the United States, his research grants having been withdrawn and attacks in the press continuing.

xi. This case had been in preparation from around 1993. It had around 1,500 claimants listed. However, in 2003 legal aid was withdrawn from all claimants and despite an appeal, which was turned down, the case collapsed.

xii. **Hirschsprungs Disease** — Nerves that control muscles in the bowel are missing. Faeces cannot be pushed through the bowel in the usual way. Often babies born with this do not pass meconium — dark faeces — in the first two days of life.

xiii. This operation can be performed for patients who have difficulty evacuating waste matter or for those who experience faecal incontinence. The aim of the procedure is to give an enema through an opening on the tummy instead of through the back passage. The enema will flush out the waste matter downwards through your bowel while you are sitting on the toilet.

xiv. Hitchens, Peter. 'This Boy's Illness May Be Linked to the MMR, So Who Destroyed the Crucial Evidence?'. *Mail on Sunday*, March 25 2007.

xv. **Mitochondrial disorders** — Mitochondria take oxygen and glucose and, through a complex chain of chemical reactions, turn them into carbon dioxide and water with the release of energy that can be used by the cell. Failure to generate sufficient energy, a feature of mitochondrial disorders, means that cells and tissues do not function properly and are at risk of premature death. These disorders may be congenital or acquired. More important are acquired mitochondrial disorders. Mitochondria are very sensitive to environmental insults such as heavy metal poisoning and infection. Toxic injury or sustained stress due to infections, for example, can damage and deplete mitochondria. Mitochondrial disorders are associated with childhood encephalopathies and tests for such disorders are merited in children undergoing developmental regression.

CHAPTER THREE

Our Children's Children

Due, no doubt, to a continuing post-war shortage of building materials, we waited a long time for the completion of this house where we still live in Wilmington, Kent. When in 1959 we finally moved in our son, Graham, was already two and Iris was expecting our second child.

With unmade roads and gardens, it was a hot, dusty and, for Iris, an uncomfortable summer at the end of which, after a long and arduous labour, Deborah Jane weighed in at eleven and a half pounds! Those were the days when family doctors made home visits and ours, called by the midwife, arrived at 4.15 am with his suit over his pyjamas just after Iris had been safely delivered. Although I'd not yet seen the baby or Iris since the birth, I was thrilled to have a daughter and it obviously showed as I opened the door to the doctor, who came again before 'surgery' that morning and later returned accompanied by a paediatrician. The paediatrician's main concern was that breast milk would need to be supplemented so that the baby would not suffer a sudden weight loss.

My parents had moved to Nottingham to live next door to my eldest sister who moved there when she married; consequently we saw very little of them. Iris' sister Elsie, being single, lived in Bromley with their parents who were as thrilled with their grandchildren as we were. Iris tells how, when she and Elsie were small, her mother would tie cushions to their feet with dusters and let them 'skate' along the lino in the hall, thus making chores fun. Iris has also been that sort of mother, always with time for the children and me.

We had no car or outbuildings at first and my bike was kept in the back bedroom! Every week, Iris took the children by bus and train to Bromley where I would join her after work in the City of London, where Elsie was also employed, so that I could help with the journey home. On each occasion Iris' mother would give us something to take home, if only something like a couple of bananas. Iris' mother was the eldest of eleven children and was the nucleus of her large family, so that when we visited at weekends, there were usually some uncles and aunts to indulge these, the only grandchildren in the family.

Iris' family would often come for the weekend when her father would help me with the garden, laying a terrace as well as a lawn for Graham and Deborah to play on. Nanny enjoyed reading to the children and in the morning before the household was up and around, the children would climb into bed with her and Granddad to be read to.

Until now, Iris' family's Christmas was celebrated at her parents' house but from our first Christmas in this house, when we had 24 to sit down to lunch and supper, the celebration moved here. There were then only two cars in Iris' wider family so a number of our guests had to stay over and slept, as was usual on such occasions, on the floor. My own experience of extended families having been rather different, these occasions taught me the value of family and we believe they had a significant and beneficial influence on our children's development as they learnt through love and example, often from older people. As for discipline, quietly spoken Iris had only to raise her voice 'half a decibel' to bring the offender or offenders into line!

Most of our neighbours at that time were in a similar position to us with small pre-school children who all played happily together in the various gardens or in the cul-de-sac where cars and motorbikes were a rarity. There was therefore ample opportunity for the children to pass around those common childhood infections such as measles, mumps and chicken pox. The only inoculation administered then in infancy, as in our own early years, was that for diphtheria which was indeed a potentially fatal childhood illness. Later, of course, Deborah and Graham received the oral vaccine against polio. If one traveled abroad, there would be smallpox and tetanus vaccinations, the latter was also usually given to child accident victims as when Deborah fell and cut her head open trying to ride a bigger child's scooter! In the event, our children did not succumb to measles, mumps or chicken pox until Graham started school, which was also the way of things in our day. It had long been considered best that children gain life-long immunity from these common ailments whilst young and so no attempt was made to isolate the sick child and naturally Deborah soon followed Graham into the sickbed!

As the children grew up, we kept a fairly open house here for their friends; one of Graham's school friends who had two similarly 'hungry' brothers at home was well known for coming at dinner time when Iris would invite him to sit down and have some pudding: 'Oh, no thank you', he would say and then without much urging: 'Oh, alright then.' Even on Christmas mornings some of the children's friends would often come around. Iris and I felt quite flattered by such visits.

Deborah was always a home-loving girl and as she reached adolescence it seemed her main ambition in life was to marry and have a family of her own. On leaving school after 'A' levels she joined Unilever. In April 1987 she married a local boy, Jeremy, whom she had known as a friend of Graham's. Her American Godmother came over bringing some warm Florida sunshine and the friendly neighbours in our little cul-de-sac community all contributed something to make her day a real success. That she and Jeremy bought a small house not far from us was later to prove a great blessing.

Iris and I were naturally pleased to learn a couple of years later that we were to become grandparents and were excited at the prospect of a new baby in the family. Deborah was not well when she left work some six weeks before her baby was due, but her indisposition was attributed by the family to her condition. In the event, however, she went into premature labour two days later and Jennifer was born in the early hours of the following day. Whilst Jennifer remained in the special care baby unit, the nurse visiting Deborah after her return home insisted that she should have the doctor in but, in contrast with our Doctor of thirty years before, he persistently refused to come and invited her, despite her being unwell, to visit the surgery. We later took our complaint about the doctor to the Family Practitioner Committee but to no avail.

In desperation, Jeremy finally asked his family doctor to call and Deborah was soon in the local hospital where she remained, having antibiotics intravenously for a heart infection until, invoking our medical insurance, she was transferred to the London Bridge hospital for open-heart surgery at the beginning of January. It was a traumatic time for all concerned but for Deborah, being separated from her new baby on top of everything else, was all but unbearable. Nevertheless, as we left the Hospital the night before her surgery, it was Deborah who told us not to worry: 'I'll be alright', she assured us.

Iris and I and her paternal grandparents shared the care of Jennifer when she was finally discharged from the special care baby unit and, as Deborah recuperated, even whilst still being treated for the infection, being now retired, I would commute with Jenny in her carrycot almost daily to the 'London Bridge' to see her. Iris and Jeremy would usually join me after work and other members of both families visited when able to do so.

After this experience, when expecting again, Deborah looked forward to being able to breastfeed and bond with her new baby and, after a carefully monitored pregnancy, her son arrived on his Dad's birthday in May, 1993. Since Jennifer's birth, in the meantime, Iris had been giving whatever practical support she could to Deborah, helping with her household chores and the like and, as Deborah doesn't drive, taking her for the 'weekly shop', appointments and so on which, of course, she continues to do to this day.

Like Jennifer, David was a bright, responsive and smiley baby and a great joy to us all. Jeremy worked long hours at that time, so Deborah and the children would often spend much of the day with us even eating with us in the evening. As a result, Iris and I would doubtless have been the envy of many grandparents as we were able, almost daily, to watch David and Jenny's progress. As grandparents we may be biased but we honestly believe that David's progress was exceptional and his development in advance of the norm for his age. He was the perfect child; he interacted with people, quickly developed some vocabulary, slept and ate well, later even sitting at the table with us to eat our food suitably prepared, of course, and, once he got the hang of it, preferring to feed himself!

We celebrated Iris' 60th birthday in July '94 with a garden party here attended by a large group of family and friends. It was on this occasion that we noticed things going wrong. Quite uncharacteristically, David went virtually berserk in his effort to free himself from his pram and when released, it was found he was suffering severe (bright yellow) diarrhoea to which his behaviour was attributed but which, in the event, persisted for some years.[1]

From this time on, David's earlier promising development seriously regressed and it was Iris' sister, Elsie, without a family of her own but by now the favourite aunt to *two* generations, who some time later first mentioned the dreaded word 'autistic' in relation to David's condition. Until then I guess we had been in denial over the obvious change in David despite our loss to explain it. At that time, to us, as to most people including, we believe, medical professionals 'autism' was just a word. Now, of course, we know better even though most professionals still seem not to!

David's loss of skills and altered behaviour were alarming. I used once to wonder how parents could allow their small screaming children to thrash about on the floor of supermarkets. Now I think I know because I have seen David do it. In such a situation, screaming and lashing out, he was almost impossible to pick up. He lost the ability to cry and was unable to articulate in any way what he was feeling so he just screamed. If he were hurt, he would hit the offending part of himself. Today, we believe his distress when picked up, put into or taken out of his car seat, for instance, was a reflection of the stomach pain he was suffering. Indoors he would roll his tummy over the arm of the sofa. Unable to keep still, he would race up and down the living room, spinning as he went, dive headfirst onto a settee and throw his legs over his head and remain in this position for minutes at a time. He would no longer look at us, respond to his name or communicate in any way with those around him, doing his best, with screaming protest, to avoid contact with visitors, even family, altogether.

Being unable to give voice to his feelings, we believe it was his frustration that made him aggressive, when he would launch himself at the nearest person. Deborah would try to hold him to her until he calmed down. For a long time now, if their Mum is absent, Jenny will try to calm him in the same way. Sometimes, however, as soon as his Mum eased her hold, his tantrum would resume. He also suffered acute distress, screaming and struggling, if his Mum tried to trim his hair. Iris would endeavour to soothe him as she held him in a bear hug on her lap. As for myself, I could not bear to witness his anguish. Often the attempt had to be aborted as the stress caused David to perspire heavily resulting in him needing to remove his clothes. Deborah was then obliged to resort to chopping his hair while he slept. Nowadays

David is more amenable to having his hair cut, at home of course, but he still has what he refers to as his '70s' style and it suits him very well.

He also began to develop obsessions the most persistent of which is still, at the age of 15, his two toys 'horse and rider'. If these are mislaid, either one or the other or both, everything stops whilst a search is mounted to reunite them with their owner in order to minimise his despair at their loss. He has gone through a number of horses and riders over the years as they have been worn away by constant use, his current horse being now almost without legs and the rider without arms but nonetheless they continue to be vitally important to him.

For a very long time he could not settle to sleep at night and, at home, Deborah would go short of sleep herself as she lay with him until he finally went off at 2.00 or 3.00 in the morning. Both children were happy to be here with us, seemingly regarding this as their second home, and on rare occasions when Deborah and Jeremy were out to dine or entertaining at home the children stayed, Iris providing the company for David that Deborah did at home. Very often when Elsie knew the children were to be with us, she would make a point of coming too and she would then provide the reassurance for David. In recent times, however, David has been settling much earlier, whilst always obsessively insisting on being woken at seven.

Being constantly on the move, David had ceased to eat with us and his diet became very limited in the sense that he would now only eat home-cooked fish fingers, spaghetti, pizza or chips. His taste for these things tended to be relatively short-lived, each in turn becoming quite unpalatable to him, making him gag, which of course created another problem. One can never be sure how David's exaggerated sensitivities to taste, touch and sound will manifest themselves. When he was six, and not long after a hernia operation, David broke his leg in an accident indoors and, during the time he was wheelchair bound and in plaster, he acquired the taste for McDonalds, after seeing fast food advertisements on television, thereby illustrating the power of advertising! Since that time he has taken 'permanently' to a 'plain cheeseburger' diet. If anyone even suggests that he eat something different he protests violently. This has involved Iris in almost daily, sometimes twice daily trips to get his meals, while Jeremy naturally does this duty at weekends.

Between such meals, at home and with us he will only eat dry breakfast cereal or porridge for which he might ask at any time of day, he also enjoys a cup of tea with a biscuit or two or Nana's chocolate cakes! Sometimes he displays curiosity about what we are eating and might smell the food on someone's plate, but when invited to have a taste, he invariably declines to have any himself.

Even now David cannot tolerate noise, including the hubbub of conversation and has the TV volume so low that it is almost inaudible to the rest of us. As a result, he has inevitably missed out on a normal childhood with no friends other than Graham's children, his cousins, Gregg and Abbie who, happily for us, also live nearby. When Jennifer celebrated her eighteenth birthday last year, David, who was being looked after at home by Auntie Elsie, came along with her to the nearby hall, where the disco and everyone went quiet for him, while he did what he had come to do which was to sing 'Happy Birthday' which he usually likes to lead! He then withdrew and the party continued.

Like birthdays, Christmas is normally an exciting occasion for young children – and for us adults as we watch their wide-eyed wonder at all its colourful detail. It was extremely sad, therefore, that David's regression meant that the 'best of times' became the 'worst of times' with him unable to cope with all the changes that these occasions demanded. Early on in his regression he was unable to understand the concept of presents, he disliked 'new things' and even now we have problems finding presents for David. More recently he will sometimes ask for specific things liking any present that comes in a series, such as 'The Guinness

Book of Records'. It is always a relief, especially for Iris, who does all the Christmas shopping, when we strike on an acceptable present for David.

David has to be prompted to share and unsuspectingly one can easily 'get into trouble' helping oneself to one of his chips! On the other hand he will not take or accept anything unless specifically told it is his or for him. As he misses so much as a result of his condition, we are all constantly on the lookout for things he might enjoy and, since he developed an intense interest in all things equestrian, Elsie and Deborah took him to the Horse of the Year show at Olympia. This was whilst he was still in a wheelchair with his broken leg, which obliged them to watch proceedings from the wings, as it were, at arena level. Later we all took him again but now, in the tiered seats surrounding the arena, the bright lights and loud music severely distressed him and he screamed to be taken out, before the event had begun. Having spent approximately £150 on tickets and more for the Programme, which he regards as an essential addition to his collection of such literature, we spent the evening in the cafeteria drinking tea, while David enjoyed studying his Programme. The Olympia staff were kind and helpful offering us earplugs for David but, having been driven out, nothing was going to entice him back in.

Jeremy takes David to Point-to-Point meetings and to Hickstead where much of the noise is, of course, carried away on the breeze and he also enjoys watching the show jumping and other equestrian events at the County Show. He always knows when important Race and Three Day Event meetings are being televised and his insistence on watching them, here or at home, can decide the day for the rest of us. We are not sure how or when he learnt to read so competently but he has done so for a long time now and a necessary accompaniment when viewing racing is the appropriate part of the Sports Supplement.

David insists every day on having *The Times* newspaper, which he then monopolises to the extent that everyone else is denied access. This is another facet of his obsessive behaviour, which includes collecting Leaflets, Programmes, Guides and such, many of which have to accompany him everywhere, other than to school fortunately. If something is forgotten, as in the case of his horse and rider, the item has to be retrieved as soon as possible, which could, of course, mean an extra car journey for the purpose. Recently, he has been carrying a large framed early photograph of himself (the only one he likes), together with a number of books including a heavy world atlas, videos and DVDs which he never watches or listens to, as well as the inevitable bundle of leaflets and his horse and rider.

David followed Jenny into the small, first rate mainstream Wilmington Primary School, the motto of which was: 'Big Enough to Cope, Small enough to Care', where eventually he was receiving one-to-one tuition pretty well full time from the school's new Special Needs teacher, Mrs. Smith; she like most who come to know David and understand him, is very fond of him to this day. Mrs. Smith became like a second mother to David and it gave her great pleasure when he mistakenly called her 'Mum'. David presented the school with its first experience of autism and so for all the staff it was a learning curve. The Head teacher, Mr. Finlayson, the teachers, and the children showed him considerable understanding. He was spared the customary discipline of lining up to enter school by class because of the noise of the assembled children. Then there was Mrs. Haughton who had to have her hand held in the playground and insisted it should be David's hand that held it! The school caretaker, Mr. Marden, organised individual games for David at playtime.

However, in view of present day fear of the consequences of being 'familiar' with another person's child, Deborah and Iris were obliged on one occasion early on to go and clean up David's diarrhoea, although the teacher would have been quite willing to do so had she been allowed. Of course, there were times when other problems arose but neither Deborah nor David were ever blamed, in fact the Headmaster frequently reassured Deborah that

David was not a naughty child. Nevertheless, with his acute memory for dates and events, when problems, however minor, did arise David would assume that such problems would repeat themselves the following week and the week after and so on, creating in him an unwillingness to attend school on those days. We are happy to say that Jenny coped well with having the only 'autistic' sibling in the school and occasionally came home with tales of David's antics, like the time when he stood up in Assembly and invited, 'Everybody dance!'

After some hesitation, fearing to offend Iris over her age, she was finally invited to address a class at school on her own early schooldays during the Second World War. Later, as part of a history project at the school, she gave a demonstration of the limitations of WWII cuisine. This happened to coincide with an Ofsted inspection. As a visiting inspector left the room he made the mistake of pointing out that powdered egg would have been used in those days. As Iris waved her packet of dried egg, she was able to assure him: 'At Wilmington we do things properly!'

In 1996 Iris and I visited family in Australia and brought back with us a tape of Australian folk songs. These caught David's attention and he would play them over and over again here, listening through earphones or 'dancing' to them with his sister on cushions spread out upon the floor. Some years later, we were amazed to be told that David was to enter the school talent contest; we thought: 'He'll chicken out at the last minute' but he didn't and with his unaccompanied rendition of one of the Aussie songs, 'Blinky Bill', complete with the 'musical' interludes between verses – he won. Even though we knew that David could carry a tune and that he was well known and liked throughout the school we still could not believe it: 'it must be the sympathy vote', we thought but no, everyone, not least his fellow pupils, one of whom said he was 'real cool', were bowled over by his performance. Another when asked about it said he didn't pay that much attention to David, as he had been mesmerised by the sight of some teachers being moved to tears by the whole affair! The following year David entered the competition again but we might say, fortunately, he was unwell and sent home before the event began. We feel that otherwise he would have expected to win again!

Despite his perfect spelling and his easy familiarity with the computer, and his phenomenal memory for factual information, David is behind his peers academically. He only very rarely has the simplest of homework and he is obviously not destined to take examinations at the Special Needs Secondary School, which he now attends after a considerable fight for an all too scarce place. Government policy is closing these schools in face of ever increasing demand whilst the displaced victims of Autistic Spectrum Disorders (ASD) are forced into Main Stream schools where they are liable to be 'excluded' for behaviour over which they have no control.

David now has transport provided to carry him to and from school. With Jennifer's schooldays coming to a close very soon, it is worth reflecting that Iris has been doing the 'school run' for Deborah for thirteen years, which has involved many early mornings for both of us. Not that we mind; we feel we are fortunate to have a reason to 'get up and go'! 'But what next to motivate us in the mornings?' we wonder.

Deborah and Jeremy had long been hoping to take both children to Walt Disney World in Florida. They had last gone with us in 1993 when Jenny was three and Deborah was expecting David. In 2004, it was finally decided that David was sufficiently improved to enable him to face the long trans-Atlantic flight. Jennifer was now 14 coming up 15 and would be keen to experience all that the theme parks have to offer, much of which we all realised David would be unable to contend with so Iris and I agreed to go with them and help out.

Waiting to depart from Gatwick, David consumed two litres of water, taking literally the advice to drink plenty on such journeys, with the result that, by the time we boarded, and having endured an hour delay, he was complaining of tummy ache, which turned out to be no more than an urgent need to 'spend a penny'! Once that problem was dealt with, and with the TV screen to watch in front of him as well as his prearranged special meal, he coped with the long period of inactivity very well.

We preferred the independence of rented accommodation and obviously knew this would be better for David in any case so we took two bungalows one in Orlando the other on Marco Island on the south west coast of the peninsular where we spent our third week. Undoubtedly the most universally popular amenity at each house was the pool. This was particularly so for David, safely equipped with a life jacket, and Jenny who both had great fun with inflatable toys, lilo and such. David liked some parts of Disney World, particularly the Animal Kingdom with its drive in a 'Safari-style' truck through the cleverly confined animal enclosures.

On our last day in Orlando, Hurricane Charley was on its way and, by lunchtime, virtually everything, fast food outlets and the theme parks had shut down and we were advised to shelter, if possible, in an inside room the only one of which was Iris' and my bathroom. David was unperturbed; we took cushions in to sit on and David had a bed made up in the bath where, with his game-boy, he was quite content. In the event, by the time the storm reached Central Florida, traveling northeastwards from the Gulf coast, it had moderated considerably and we suffered no damage.

Once we discovered, by reference to his Medical Health Record Book, that David's decline began just four days after his MMR vaccination, at the age of 14 months, we have been left in no doubt as to what caused the sudden onset of his regression. It may well be that the toxic thiomersal in the earlier DPT triple jab had a part to play but it was undoubtedly the MMR that pushed him over the edge.

Having read 'Silenced Witnesses',[ii] we know we are most fortunate that an eminent immunologist told Deborah and Jeremy at a private consultation: 'On no account should David have the "booster MMR"' although he omitted to say this in the letter he later sent out.

As can be seen, David has progressed to the point where some would doubt he was ever as badly afflicted as he was. His recovery began almost as soon as Deborah adjusted his diet and added dietary supplements on the advice of a nutritionist friend. Thereafter, as nothing was or is available from the NHS for victims of Autistic Spectrum Disorders, except, perhaps, Ritalin[iii] we were all on the watch for anything that might help David, whatever the cost. The first avenue pursued was Homeopathy. Iris remembers that she and Deborah were never told beforehand what each remedy was supposed to achieve but each proved beneficial, although the benefits were sometimes preceded by a brief worsening of his overall condition. We were assured by the homeopath that this was to be expected and was not a cause for concern.

We read of the beneficial effect of secretin, which had been stumbled upon in America, and when in December 1998, Iris and I visited Deborah's Godmother and family in the United States we brought home information on the hormone from the Internet, via the Autism Research Institute. Even on holiday, our days can be affected by consideration of David's condition. Eventually, Elsie discovered that the story of Billy Tommey, the 'first' child in the UK to be given secretin, was going to be shown on television and that Doctor O'Connell was offering injections of the hormone at a clinic in London. Iris and Deborah duly took David along for a consultation in 1999 and eventually, over a period of time that spanned both his hernia operation and broken leg, David had four injections at a total cost of some £3,500 to which various members of both families contributed but Elsie most of all. Deborah later had David put on 'Homeopathic Secretin'. As a direct result of these secretin treatments David had bouts of German Measles and Mumps thereby appearing to remove some of the harmful effects of MMR from his system.

One of the most remarkably effective 'treatments' David was given was 'Developmental Brushing'. While we were initially sceptical, even his teachers were so impressed with its effect on David's communication skills and improved attention that some arranged to see the homeopath themselves to learn more about it. This therapy involved the repetitive application of small artists' brushes, to various parts of the face, hands and body, stimulating nerve endings by producing a very light massage. One session might be devoted to his upper lip, another to his hands and yet another to his back. When any of us tried being the subject of this, it just tickled, sometimes unbearably but David displayed no outward reaction at the time. Later, its benefits showed with his more settled behaviour at school and improved speech.

In all, Deborah tried the following therapies all of which had some benefit, albeit not always long-lasting: Secretin Injections, Homeopathic Secretin, Homeopathic 'Anti-MMR', Developmental Brushing, Auditory Integration Training, Cranial Osteopathy and Dietary Supplements.

David has indeed come a long way but he remains autistic. He has obsessions, he still runs up and down the living room and his conversation is very repetitive; he obviously thinks hard how to phrase what he wants to say but having said it, perhaps with some hesitation, he'll say: 'Wait, I'll say that again' and this might go on for half a dozen attempts before he has said it to his satisfaction. Iris' roast dinners are universally popular amongst the family, bringing us all together quite often. Sadly, of course, David is on the perimeter of such family gatherings as the rest of us sit and talk at the table but he will often want to monopolise the conversation. As he screws up his fists by his ears, he almost screams: 'Why do you all talk?' His Mum brings him up short: 'David! Excuse me?' 'Sorry, excuse me' David will say and then proceeds into one of his long-winded and repetitive statements. Sometimes he is hilarious and we have seen his cousins reduced to tears of laughter: 'No, I'll start again' for the umpteenth time! Nowadays he enjoys his cousins who are, without exception, very understanding and patient with him.

The opening sequence of the Television Drama 'Hear the Silence' with Juliet Stephenson, in December 2003, served as a poignant reminder of an experience we ourselves had had. It was in the early days, when we were unaware just how his behaviour was being affected, and on the day in question Deborah and I were taking him for a walk in the local wood where there are plenty of paths and broad rides. I don't recall how he managed to slip our hands but suddenly he was off. Deborah called him but he failed to respond, he didn't even hesitate and by the time we decided that he wasn't going to come back to us and we'd have to go after him, he had a good head start, charging heedlessly through the undergrowth. As we followed him downhill, we had trouble keeping him in sight let alone catching up with him and we became increasingly anxious, wondering where it would end. I think he must have run the best part of a mile before we finally caught up with him, as he grew tired!

The whole story of 'Hear the Silence' was a mirror image of our experiences with David and we have to admit that we were on the verge of tears the whole way through it as it brought back our memories and gave us a new understanding of David's experience. It stands out in my mind that we have received no help from the NHS or the orthodox medical profession. Not all the doctors we have consulted have been as arrogant as the one in 'Hear the Silence;' most of them, seemingly answerable to the pharmaceutical companies, are utterly blind to the idea of vaccine damage.

David taught himself to ride a bicycle here in the garden, the layout of which provides him with various permutations of circuit. Jenny would watch him proudly through the window and I cannot believe, even now, how happy I was to see my lawn ruined! Away from home, of course, he requires constant supervision and so, with company on foot, he will now sometimes ride in the nearby woodland, going at his own pace but, happily, no longer wishing to lose his 'minders'. He most enjoys his cycle rides with his Dad at weekends when they go together variously down to the river, onto the heath where there are lots of 'humps and bumps' or into the woods. He also has here in summer, a miniature set of 'show jumps,' which he now sets up himself on the lawn and pretends he is any number of well-known show jumpers and their mounts whilst someone is required to time him as he races round jumping each one in turn.

In the days when we were young parents, the pursuit of a career in Medicine was still regarded as a vocation and the family doctor displayed a strong sense of responsibility towards his patients. Doctor Andrew Wakefield is now one of a rare breed of such practitioners as his unselfish concern for vaccine damaged children and their parents show.

Today it seems to us too many GPs regard their profession as a nine-to-five, five-day-week occupation where the general aim in life – as is all too common these days – is to do as little as possible for the maximum reward. In some ways their attitude is understandable, controlled as their practices and performance are by Central Government via the Department of Health with bonuses for meeting particular targets such as childhood vaccination schedules. We have read of families being turned away from their GP's surgery for refusing to have a child vaccinated.

We find it difficult to believe that there are not more doctors about like Dr Wakefield, doctors with the nerve to step up and be counted. For many establishment figures, of course, and researchers such as Doctor Wakefield himself, their jobs or funding would no doubt be at risk. But what about your average GP; why can't more of them open up a little and pay more attention to their patients and less to their received views from government and Big Pharma? Or perhaps, though 'heaven forbid', the average GP himself accepts the official line on MMR without question and really knows no more about the potential for vaccine damage than the 'man in the street'.

It is a sad fact that even some of those close to David have found it difficult to understand the nature of autism. Autism has no guile or deceit; what is sometimes seen as manipulative behaviour is purely the victim's obsession with routine and aversion to change. In our experience this manifests itself in the various traits I have described and by being governed by the clock, in David's case this is typified by an insistence on being home by a certain time, having his pyjamas on by a certain time and so on. If any of us fail to accommodate the idiosyncrasies in David's make-up, he is likely to respond aggressively, usually accompanied by a muted scream of protest. Although David invariably apologises immediately for the outburst, with 'Sorry', it is just as likely to resume. David seems unable to grasp the meaning of 'sorry'. Because David fails to understand certain things, we all have to consider carefully not only how we phrase things but the very subjects we address.

David cannot handle more than one question at a time, however innocent: 'Did you have a nice ride with Dad? Where did you go?' Fists screwed up by his ears in a subdued scream: 'I'm not telling you'. He regularly interprets a question as a statement resulting in more anguish and confusion. Although now fifteen and well over five feet in height, in his relationship with his Mum and, to a lesser extent Iris, much of David's behaviour and conversation are those typical of a much younger child. Especially, in his obsession with animal noises which he expects his Mum to imitate on demand. We have never seen Deborah turn either of her children away with a "Not now, I'm busy" or similar and we don't believe she ever has. For years she has sat with Jenny to provide moral support and guidance as Jenny contends with her homework but if David comes to sit on her lap (even now) and gain her attention, she will happily welcome him. It is the sight of this closeness and dependence that affects Iris and me most when we consider David's future.

Iris and I have long come to the realisation that it is better not to try to persuade David into situations that we think he 'should' enjoy, but which he would find stressful, so we are always available for 'child minding'. Whilst it is great to keep things on offer, forcing the situation does not work. Obviously we would all dearly love him to participate more in family events and everyday outings but if it causes David distress then it is upsetting for everyone and can increase his general level of anxiety. We are all keen to ensure that Jenny doesn't feel that she has missed out because of David's condition. David of course most certainly does miss out but thankfully he is probably unaware of the fact. Obviously, his parents are saddened as we are by the knowledge that David has been unable to participate in things that his peers enjoy such as team sports, the cinema, and outings with friends, which situation, barring a miracle, is likely to continue.

We have been writing letters to various individuals and organisations on the matter of MMR, vaccine damage and autism since 1997. However, following letter after letter, we have arrived at the inescapable conclusion that there is a deep and widespread conspiracy embedded in the MMR controversy and that a part of this involves a muzzled Press, which, with the occasional erstwhile exception of the *Daily Mail* and *Mail on Sunday*, seems to have been all but silenced. All the papers now appear effectively to publish only articles, denigrating Dr. Wakefield and his work, often working this in to an article on another subject entirely, such as the article by quackbuster Damian Thompson, *Daily Telegraph* Saturday 26th April 2008 on the matter of alternative medicine.

It be of course that the media has been got at in this way 'in the National Interest.' Recently there was an 8,000 strong vaccine protest march in Washington D.C. which, as far as we can determine, was not reported here either in the press or on TV. The interconnection, for instance, between the Legal Services Commission (LSC), an organisation supposedly 'independent' of government and the Department for Constitutional Affairs (DCA), an arm of government, leads one to believe that there is no such thing as an 'independent' organisation set up by government.

We have submitted countless letters to the *Daily* and *Sunday Telegraph* protesting at their editorial bias towards MMR. Most of these are not favoured with so much as an acknowledgement, but in February 2004, we actually had one printed in the *Sunday Telegraph* letters page, which was however considerably edited. Below is our full letter including the passages in italics that were cut.

In *all* your items on the MMR and Doctor Wakefield, *including that by Dr. Darymple*, you fail to acknowledge that the Legal Aid to parents of the afflicted children has been withdrawn *on the basis that medical research is an inappropriate use of such funding even though without the research, affected parents will be unable to seek redress through the courts. The matter is now subject to judicial review* and *in the meantime* Dr. Wakefield and co. must rely upon *charitable* donations to continue this vital *medical* search for the truth.

My generation began to acquire natural immunity to childhood ailments such as measles as soon as we started school and I do not believe that they pose anything like the danger to our society that Dr. Darymple and his like claim. Autism, on the other hand is a lifelong disability and only those who have watched the regression of a thriving child can begin to appreciate what it can do not only to the victim but also to the *wider* family.

I would suggest that the solution to the government's difficulties over the take up of the triple jab is to reinstate immediately parental choice in the matter of SINGLE vaccinations whilst at the same time releasing funds for thorough and open clinical (ie not epidemiological) research into the whole question. Sadly, we know this will not happen; too many vested interests at play!

Need we wonder why the last paragraph of our letter was edited?

Over the years, we have written to Dr. Brent Taylor at The Royal Free Hospital – no reply, Sir Liam Donaldson – no immediate reply – however, after a further exchanges of letters with the Department of Health Customer Service Team, *almost two years* later we were 'rewarded' with a comprehensive reply from Dr. D.M. Salisbury, Principal Medical Officer at the DoH. There are no prizes for guessing the gist of that missive which came accompanied by the complete 'MMR Information Pack', which incidentally, declares that MMR 'initial trials lasted up to nine weeks'!

We have written to the former Prime Minister as well as MPs of all three major Parties, all of whom have endorsed the 'official line', except Julie Kirkbride who alone attempted to introduce a Bill in Parliament to restore parental choice in the matter of single vaccines. At one stage, we were assured by the then 'Shadow Health Secretary', Dr Liam Fox, that the Conservative party intended, if they were elected, to allow single vaccines. Of course, they have long since reneged on this.

Our correspondence with the Legal Services Commission (LSC) is ongoing and, in the meantime, Clare Dodgson, former Chief Executive, has moved on. If, as they claim, they were not *instructed* to pull the plug on funding, we have been trying to pin them down on the who, how and why, after eleven long years, it was suddenly found to be 'inappropriate' for the LSC to fund medical research in legal cases. At the time that the LSC was denying us a further £10 million, it should not be forgotten that there were reports in the Press[iv] that Asylum and Illegal Immigrant appeals were absorbing £200 million a *year* of the LSC's budget which incidentally, the LSC was being told to reduce.

Evan Harris MP's tirade during the interview on Channel Four News on 16th July 2007 was particularly offensive and misleading and we wrote to him and others accordingly. We have also suggested to Brian Deer that his investigative talents might be better deployed looking into the MMR conspiracy itself, rather than pursuing his personal vendetta against Doctor Wakefield! As you would expect, neither of these were answered.

As observed in the MMR Information Pack, autism is a lifelong disability and we have an uncomfortable feeling that there will be many more victims of autism than, to quote the Pack, 'cases of congenital rubella syndrome' requiring life-time support 'both in human and financial terms'. Autism may not be as extreme as Thalidomide or as obvious but the evidence, much of which we glean with our own eyes and ears, points to the numbers of children who have an autism spectrum disorder being far greater and, as things are, the cost of their education and lifelong care will fall on the taxpayer.

We have no doubt that the incidence of vaccine-induced autism continues to grow and because it is apparent that the 'Yellow Card' system doesn't work, we have urged the creation of a National Register of victims in order to keep track of the size of the problem. The Department of Health disclaim responsibility and refer us to our local Primary Care Trust (PCT) who they tell us will know what demands are being made upon Educational and Social Services in our area! We have yet to pursue this. However, if they deny vaccine-induced autism it is difficult to know how they will write up this account.

One of the problems, as we see, it is the general lack of aware-ness of therapies that might help other victims as they have David. For some parents, of course, it may be a simple matter of afford-ability. Homeopathy is getting a bad press at present but when it was announced in October, 2004 that 'Greater use of complimenta-ry and alternative therapies on the NHS is to be encouraged by Government', we were prompted to write to the then Secretary of State to suggest that the 'availability and potential benefits of these treatments to victims of autism should be widely publicised by the NHS in the same way, for instance, as are the benefits of immunization'. Once again the DoH referred us to our local PCT who, when Deborah sought funding for a session of Auditory Integration Training (AIT) for David, refused it on the grounds that its benefits were not proven. Elsie had previously funded a course of AIT, which Deborah found to be helpful with David's noise tolerance following which, for about a year, we noticed he no longer covered his ears with his hands.

And so that 'lack of awareness' of the potential benefits of complementary therapies will continue to deny many victims the chance to alleviate their condition and the stress it creates within the family. Deborah's own therapy of choice is gardening. Her own garden being small and largely occupied by the clothesline and the children's trampoline, our garden benefits greatly from her attention. We installed a small greenhouse in which she nurtures young plants for summer colour in what would otherwise be a very green outlook for us.

Iris and I are unashamedly proud of our strong, united and mutually supportive family, the linchpin of which is and always has been Iris, herself. Fortunately, Deborah's experiences have made her strong yet she remains, as ever, very generous and considerate of others as her earlier participation in a local autism Forum, as well as a parent support group and her efforts in the MMR/autism struggle show.

Knowing that little can be done to redeem David's future, she nonetheless pursues these issues in the hope that other parents might be spared the agony which she and Jeremy and so many others have endured and for those parents she encounters in a similar position to herself, trying to draw their attention to potential treatments and therapies that might help to ameliorate the victim's condition.

Doctor Peter Fletcher, a former Chief Scientific Officer at the Department of Health, was quoted by Sue Corrigan in the *Mail on Sunday* of February 5th 2006. 'The refusal by governments to evaluate the risks properly will make this one of the greatest scandals in medical history' and again, 'There are very powerful people in positions of great authority in Britain and elsewhere who have staked their reputations and careers on the safety of MMR and they are willing to do almost anything to protect themselves.' The only word we would question in this is 'almost' but these remarks sum up perfectly our own views of the present scandalous situation!

There is no plausible explanation for the refusal of Government to acknowledge the fact of vaccine damage in some children other than its fear of the financial and personal career consequences, which, as the incidence of such damage increases, is bound to become ever greater. The existing arrangements for compensation and the compensation itself, even if a case can be proved, are totally inadequate, especially when set against the long-term care that the victims will require.

Unlike in North America where the vaccine manufacturers are obliged to contribute to a fund specifically created for the purpose of meeting vaccine damage claims, it would appear that our own Government has agreed with these companies that this is unnecessary and furthermore that it has indemnified the companies against claims. If this is so, how could the Government allow the legal aid-funded litigation to come to court when it was going to be the taxpayer who was going to pick up the bill for damages?

When Dr Wakefield warned throughout the second half of the 1990s about the possible dangers of MMR, and in 1998 recommended the use of single vaccines pending further research, his persecution began immediately, leading us to the inescapable conclusion that there already existed an understanding between Government, Health Authorities and Pharmaceutical Companies over MMR. Dr. Wakefield's persecution continues unremittingly today, every opportunity being taken by the media to denigrate him and his work, no matter how tenuous the link with the primary subject of any published article. The further research that

Dr. Wakefield and his colleagues suggested is that which the Government and its agencies have steadfastly refused to commission.

We have seen endless reports of dubiously based epidemiological studies by this and that organisation purporting to 'prove' that the vaccine is safe and an impressive tome from the Medical Research Council (MRC) supposedly examining autism and its causes pointing to anything and everything, apart from clinical studies of the vaccine-damaged children. Indeed, it would appear that some Doctors here are even refusing to treat sick vaccine-damaged children for fear of what they might find in the process.

What of the MMR, itself? Where is the health benefit in combining three vaccines? Is it effective, giving lasting protection? The evidence seems to indicate otherwise. Why the need for another round of MMR immunisation every time an outbreak of mumps or measles is reported? Surely these cases alone illustrate the need for single vaccines. So why has the Government set its face against single vaccines for all this time when the 'herd immunity' that they claim is necessary could so easily have been achieved with single vaccines from the outset? Although in our experience, parents are not anti-vaccine, the Government's continuing failure to face up to the evidence and resolve the matter openly and honestly, is likely to make people distrust not only MMR but the medical profession and immunisation in general.

Finally, we would like to emphasise that living with autism is not a passing inconvenience. Rather, it is for all concerned a life-changing, ongoing condition with which the victim and those around him or her have to contend day in day out, year in year out. Like others faced with the same situation our greatest worry is who is to care for David when the people who *really* care for him are no longer there. We have found that it doesn't do to dwell too much on this as it can give rise to considerable emotional upset and sleepless nights. And so we live one day at a time and give thanks for the David we know.

Endnotes

i. Deborah's account of her son's birth and following vaccine damage was included in the first volume of *Silenced Witnesses*.

ii. The first volume in this series. Now distributed by Sensinet. See contact details on page ii.

iii. Ritalin, an amphetamine often prescribed, particularly in the United States, to control hyperactive behaviour.

iv. *Daily Telegraph,* Saturday, May 1st 2004.

CHAPTER FOUR

Adam

In my dreams Adam can speak. In my dreams we have intelligent witty conversations and Adam is a charming companion. He is not the stroppy 'Kevin' that would be the inevitable fifteen year old reality if all that has happened had not happened. In my dreams Adam is going to conquer the world, he is dazzling and amazing and is going to give me loads of grandchildren.

Neither is my reality, my reality is a life wherein I am driven, striving to achieve for Adam the most that he can be, for a future that is the most that it can be, to protect him from dependence upon a system that is in itself responsible for the destruction of all that his life could and should have been. To tell this story I have to go back seventeen years, to when I met Adam's father and we were sharing his dreams.

We had met in Australia while I was on a business trip, his parents were friends with my parents, and we shared some respite time away from the busy demands of my trip. He had dreams of running an outward bound centre, teaching bush skills and survival to stressed executives, coupled with the easy going lifestyle and wonderful climate this was very alluring. Our plans, however, were not in line with his parents' aspirations for him and, to put it frankly, they bought him off.

By the time he went for the money, I was carrying Adam. Wounded, I returned home to England determined that I would instil somewhat better values in my own son or daughter. Since then I have had no contact with Adam's father although, sadly, Adam often expresses the wish to travel to Australia to seek him out. A prospect which terrifies me for the awful risk that it carries for Adam of acceptance versus rejection.

Back in England, I lived in Hampstead, so by some peculiar stroke of fate, I found myself having a far from easy birth in the Royal Free Hospital. After a relatively happy pregnancy, Adam was born fourteen weeks prematurely by emergency caesarean surgery, a hefty 1,162 grams.

By the time I got out of the hospital I had spent four weeks as an in-patient, due to post natal complications, then a further thirteen and a half weeks with Adam. First it was just sitting with him holding his hand and talking to him. Trying to hold back the tears. Eventually, I was allowed to hold him and this tiny amazing scrap fitted into the palm of my hand. Kangaroo care they called it, holding him bare to my chest, skin to skin. It was wonderful this time of bonding, even with the grey haired old consultant leering at me. I have some treasured photos of this time and the happiness and pride shines out from me.

Some of the other photos however are harrowing, they stay firmly in the box; they bring back the other memories, those I choose to, or have tried to, forget. I think going through an extremely premature birth must be one of the worst things that can happen to any woman, and going it alone was the hardest thing I have ever had to do.

Despite the emotionally difficult times Adam and I bonded closely; indeed nurses commented from the beginning how they saw him respond when he heard my voice. On one occasion when I was cuddling him and whiling away the time chatting to another parent I became upset, with silent tears creeping down my cheeks, unable to push them back. My friend co-preemie-parent Nina, said 'Celia, stop it you're upsetting Adam, look' pointing to the heart monitor attached to him. His heart rate had shot up to double the rate it should have been, and amazingly, as my emotions ebbed and flowed, his heart rate ebbed and flowed. The invisible umbilical cord is not a myth but a reality. I have found over the years since that this continues to be true, and I have a tendency to experience the same symptoms as Adam when he has some medical issue or a pain of some kind. I see it as a kind of check to remind me how he feels, when the tendency is for people, especially doctors, to dismiss or overlook completely the non verbal feelings of those who cannot describe how they feel. I have only ever mentioned this once before and now everybody will know. It feels very strange. Before you judge me as mad, think about identical twins and the accepted invisible bond between them.

Adam's discharge from hospital was carefully planned, he still needed nursing but it was felt to be better for him to be at home rather than in long-term hospital care. And I could not wait to get him home, to get away from the confines of the baby unit, the machines with their beeping and constant reminder of the fear, and the unfolding tragedies around me. In preparation, Adam's medical regimens were taught to me and I even had to practice resuscitation techniques on a plastic baby dummy, you can imagine how that felt!

I had no choice over the first set of vaccinations, Adam was jabbed in my presence by Omar, a tall commanding African registrar, a kindly man; I have a photo of him holding Adam and smiling beneficently. There was no discussion on the merits of it or of the timing, it was routine – for their convenience. I did not know then what I know now about mercury and other things.

On the 22nd November 1993, the day Adam came home, it was snowing. It seems hard to believe now with current climate patterns but on this day the sky was thick with a dirty grey blanket and fine snow was falling fast and covering everything white. It was crisp and cold as I climbed into the taxi holding my precious bundle, a far cry from the hot house that was the Special Care Baby

Unit, home for the past seventeen weeks, a place where tropical clothing was essential, and to which we were both acclimatised. This must have been amazing to Adam.

Entering the flat I was acutely aware of its emptiness, this large vacant space, silent but comfortingly familiar and that contrast from the bustle and traffic of a big hospital, the utter peace and quiet was wonderful. We were home, back to normality, or so I thought.

My return from the hospital, however, turned my home into a surrogate hospital and really things have never been normal since, whatever normal is, I no longer remember.

Due to Adam's prematurity, he needed continual oxygen, which was provided via a machine called a concentrator, and a very long length of plastic tubing connected to a mask over his nose. The Oxygen flow needed constant adjustment, by me 'Nurse Forrest', to maintain optimum blood oxygen levels, checked by means of a hospital monitor, which also had to be attached to Adam by means of an electronic probe taped to his foot. This delightful piece of equipment became an instrument of torture at night with its continual alarm, sounding each time Adam's oxygen levels dropped a whisker, or he twitched his foot. I was supported by three weekly visits from community paediatric nursing sisters, monitoring Adam and recording in medical notes. These medical notes became critical evidence in the later High Court case against Merck, vaccines purveyors.

The special bond which had developed between us in SCBU meant that Adam always knew how I was feeling and this was expressed in various ways. On one occasion when we were visited by the community paediatric sisters they were accompanied by the Specialist Clinical Nurse, Violeta who said she was delighted to see Adam doing so well and attempted to pick him up for a cuddle. Each time she approached him he screamed and screamed, much to her consternation, and the amusement of her two colleagues.

She suggested that perhaps Adam did not like black people, which was nearly my undoing, since I was doing a great job of being the gracious hostess, but it had nothing to do with colour. The truth was that I loathed her, and this fact was apparent to Adam it seemed, since I have never known him react that way to anyone else! The little star...

Adam also had weekly home visits from a physiotherapist and an occupational therapist, they picked up on some physical difficulties quite early. Transient dystonia[1] was suggested, as it is common in premature babies according to a paper I was given to read by the occupational therapist. If he has cerebral palsy I will eat my hat she said. Transient dystonia causes physical twitching in limbs amongst other things, and usually only persists for the first twelve months of infant life. I, of course, didn't know then about the constituents of his DPT vaccination, or the fact that mercury can cause cerebral palsy or worsen existing cerebral palsy. It appears that the doctors didn't know either that published research showed that premature babies are at greater risk than the general baby population due to their not having a fully formed blood brain barrier for several months; they were in effect administering a mercury cocktail straight to Adam's brain.

Almost inevitably, a diagnosis of cerebral palsy was made in May 2004. It was still a huge shock, and my world came crashing down. I was devastated, I had no experience of disability at all and had no idea what to expect and what it would mean to our lives. I remember crying a lot. In clinic, Doctor Andrew Lloyd-Evans, the neurodevelopmental consultant, told me that Adam would probably not walk until he was five and that he hoped he would not grow particularly tall since tall people have more mobility problems. This was not good news since Adam's father is nearly six foot six and it was likely that Adam would indeed be tall, in fact he is now nearly six foot and just turned fifteen.

Despite everything my beautiful son was a miracle and doing great developmentally: his first word at 9 months when he said hello to me early one morning, his first sentences around 12 months, his delight in playing games, in particular sharing the solving of puzzles and number games. At 13 months corrected age, counted from his birth due date, he could tell you that 17 came after 16! Occupational therapy assessments at the Royal Free at fifteen months were amazing, I have video footage of him scoring as a 4 yr old on some tasks, and you can see how motivated he was and how proud of his achievements. He was very happy and very sociable; a cute, clever little boy. Through Betty Hutcheon, Head of Paediatric Occupational Therapy, he was used by The Royal Free in the hospital brochure on paediatric services. I also have video footage of him just before the MMR, playing with his physiotherapist, seriously determined to engage her in his tea party game, repeatedly filling her cup from his teapot and forcing the cup into her mouth chuckling joyfully at her pretend noises of drinking and enjoyment. This child had autism? I don't think so!

He was scheduled for his MMR vaccination in late December 2004, but it was postponed because he had developed flu the day before – despite being given a flu vaccine on 16th November, effective eh – just another shot of mercury! It was rearranged for the beginning of February 1995, but was again postponed because he appeared to have a touch of a cold and the nurse decided to wait in case he had a cold coming on.

During this period, I heard a television interview which worried me. A Canadian parent was talking about children in Canada being adversely affected by the vaccine, she claimed that her child was brain damaged due to the MMR and that in Canada concern about the vaccine was widespread. A debate raged, with the TV programme doctor pooh-poohing the possibility. The Canadian parent sounded very sincere to me, not hysterical, very rational, she quoted facts and numbers. There clearly was an issue with the safety of the MMR. I raised concerns with my GP, with our community paediatric sister, and our health visitor. I was told by all three that there was no risk to Adam and that the only side effects that some children experience were a slight temperature, a slight rash and being a bit 'out of sorts'. I was told about the risks of not having him vaccinated, that 'measles can cause brain damage'. It was very difficult, I knew these people and they had always cared about Adam in a very sincere way, yet without exception they opposed any idea that there was any risk from having the MMR. I had no experience of this area, just experience of putting trust in doctors.

However, the passionate words used by the Canadian mother affected me very much and I remained uneasy about it, so I decided I didn't want to have him vaccinated. I then came under very strong pressure from my GP and from the Community Paediatric Sister, they told me that a common complication of measles is pneumonia, a very serious form of it, they said. I was told that it would be life threatening for Adam with his respiratory history and that I would be very irresponsible if I did not have him vaccinated. Again they stressed that there was absolutely nothing to fear from the vaccination and that my fears were groundless; I therefore felt that I had no choice but to have him vaccinated.

I was not given any published information or leaflets regarding the possible side effects and in those days I did not have access to a computer or the internet so I could not research that information for myself. Poor Adam, if I'd had the tools and the information was out there I could have saved him from what happened. I wonder now that any parent allows the MMR, given the results from the range of work in this area by reputable institutions and the access available to that information – unlike the misinformation the government has pumped out.

But that is what might have been. I remained concerned but the pressure was relentless and having no hard information to the contrary, I allowed him to be vaccinated. This turned out to be the worst decision I made in my life.

From the very first day following the vaccination Adam changed dramatically. His first reaction was recorded by visiting nurses on the 6th day following the vaccination as being miserable and out of sorts. On the 8th day following the MMR, Adam had loose stools, was vomiting, had a rash and was feverish. He continued to have pronounced measles symptoms for over six weeks and he also developed an ear infection. The visiting Community Paediatric Sister, Vicky Blackburn, identified the symptoms as a reaction to the MMR vaccination. Her notes recorded on 15th April 1994 include 'mother and respite nurse appear to have measles from Adam's MMR'. On 29th April 1994 she recorded 'Rash still evident on face from measles, appetite not improved'. The following day, Vicky Blackburn's notes state, 'ear infection diagnosed at Nuffield Hospital (Adam never had one before), a common complication of measles'. As I mentioned earlier, these medical notes provide a critically important historical record of events in great detail, and provided a concrete chain of evidence to underpin the case I later attempted to bring against Merck in the High Court. Sadly, these facts have never been open to public scrutiny thanks to the government shutting down legal aid funding for what can only be described as *political* reasons.

This period marked the beginning of a long-term change in Adam. The measles symptoms were followed by general malaise, intermittent fevers and rashes, temperature control problems and profuse cold sweats, which continued for over 15 months. Even today, Adam has cold sweats – some nights drenched – and I know that he is heading for a viral episode, it's as though his body cannot fight it off, it just lies below the surface like a malignant viral breath, not something tangible and obvious that I can fight, nothing that the doctors take seriously. But a damaged gut – a damaged immune system, they appear to me to be intertwined and I understand they are, that the front line of the immune system is the gut. So, poor Adam, but I didn't learn all this until later.

Frighteningly, Adam also became very withdrawn, losing interest in everything. Within days he became a different child, losing many skills he had previously acquired. The behavioural changes were very apparent during the summer although I thought he was lethargic and withdrawn because of his illness. I therefore paid more attention to his physical symptoms at that time and concentrated on trying to restore him to full physical health. However, my attentions turned to his personality changes when his physiotherapist, Susan Slater, returned to her job in August following a three-month leave. She found the change in Adam to be significant and serious. She described him as being like a *totally different* child. She could not engage with him and he had no motivation; it was as if she were not there. She had been a fixture in his life since he was born, she called him her little Rangers fan, due to a green and white stripy outfit, and he loved her. Now, she no longer existed for him.

By September 1995, the behavioural changes were more pronounced, Adam seemed to be regressing, he had no interest in communication, and he spent hours every day gazing at his hand, holding it up in front of his face and moving his fingers. He was in a world of his own. He lacked the motivation to play with his toys and he seemed to be regressing physically in that he was less co-ordinated and more floppy. His choice of foods became restricted. He craved gluten and casein foods such as pasta, bread, soft cheese, milk and fromage frais, and by the summer of 1996 these were actually the only foods he would eat. Before the MMR vaccination, Adam had been eating a range of foods including fish, meat, chicken, vegetables and fruit.

Back to the autumn of 1995, Susan Slater urged me to have Adam checked out and he was referred to the neo-natal paediatrician at the Royal Free. By this time he was sicker, his nighttimes were a nightmare, heavy cold sweats and hypothermic temperatures, indeed this sweating had rotted two mattresses by January. We had a couple of clinic reviews that autumn. Finally, reluctantly, the Consultant Paediatrician, Dr. Vivienne Van Someren agreed to investigate, and in my presence suggested to the Ward Sister that she wanted him admitted for observation 'because his mother is worried about him' – an intimation that I was the problem and not Adam's medical condition.

Unsurprisingly, there was a marked lack of interest in Adam on the ward. It was as though he was there merely to appease his worried mother. On one occasion I dragged the charge nurse off an evening ward round with doctors to 'come and see' for herself that he was hypothermic (less than 34° C) and drenched in cold sweat. Now that I have spoken to other parents, that I have had years to assimilate the first steps in this nightmare journey into illness for my son, I can recognise each early failure to see that Adam was suffering from an adverse reaction to a vaccine.

Adam failed to improve and I requested a referral to Great Ormond Street Children's Hospital. This was ignored and, encouraged by Adam's physiotherapist, I resorted to threatening the Consultant with a formal complaint to get her to do it. Adam was finally admitted to GOSH in December 1995 for a series of investigations over ten days. The only concrete thing they found was they discovered his reflux (which dated back to his prematurity days in SCBU) was not being controlled by the medications. The most significant thing was an opinion given to me by a consultant specialist in the autonomic nervous system, Professor Dillon, who said he thought it was viral in origin and that he would recommend CT scans be carried out. This was not followed through, and the specialist in infectious diseases, Dr. Novelli who was co-ordinating the case said there were no signs of viral or infectious origin. Though I suppose it rather depends on what you are looking for, doesn't it?

During this period in the hospital they requested that I attend an appointment with a Clinical Psychologist, the purpose of which was at first unclear. It later appeared that they were checking out *my* mental health; certainly I was the one being interviewed! I took the opportunity to express my concerns about Adam's behavioural changes, in particular one strange feature that had developed very early on in this 'illness'. The hours spent staring at his hand, held mostly in front of his face, often turning and waving his fingers. The psychologist said I should not worry about it; it was not a problem, she said, unless he was still doing it when he was five.

She counselled me about the importance of having a personal support network, and said that parents of children with special needs were very vulnerable to isolation and stress, and that others typically distance themselves from the situation, even previously close friends will drop out of the picture. You have to make an effort, she said, and plan to develop a social network of support – hospital wards are full of children whose parents cannot cope. Yes, very sensible advice no doubt, however, it completely fails to take into account that as a single parent of a special needs child you have few social opportunities; even if you have the time. It is true, sadly, that old friends drop away and you become isolated, you get a Christmas card saying sorry it has been so long, see you in the new year, and then they disappear.

New friends are found, friends who can identify because they are going through the same journey, friends who can share the pain and the joy that can come from such special children and the enormous pleasure that you have in each and every tiny step of recovery and progress. And best of all, you can depend on these people – they are not fair-weather friends – they are the bravest and strongest bunch around because they have had to be.

We left the hospital just before Christmas; the wards were full of colourful decorations, menus all cakes and ice cream and Mr. Blobby prowled around. For such a sad place – we were resident on the cancer ward – it was full of good cheer and optimism and smiling faces. Once home, we awaited the New Year, which would bring Adam back to the hospital for gastric investigations and then surgery for his reflux. Christmas was not a particularly happy time for us; it was quite lonely, with friends busy with family. It didn't appear to mean much to Adam, he was disinterested entirely in his

Christmas presents, not even opening them; not showing much interest in anything really. Just looking very pale, sick and sad.

We continued to have occupational therapy reviews at the Royal Free with Betty Hutcheon. This took place in a large treatment room, filled with toys and activities, very colourful. Adam had always loved it there as a baby. He was renown for being a cheeky boy and, still relatively tiny, would take off along the corridor once attention was distracted from him, crawling as fast as he could, dragging his oxygen cylinder, which was attached to him via a long nasal tube, behind him, laughing and giggling and enjoying making us run after him! Betty now commented on the changes in Adam, his lack of engagement and motivation and his lack of eye contact with her. On one occasion, without any warning of what she planned to do she dropped something very loud right behind him; he showed no reaction at all and this was very worrying. I asked her for an opinion on his strange hand behaviour and she said the 'autism' word; the first time I had heard that word. She used the word in the context of 'too early to say, autism does not usually manifest until 3 or 4 yrs old.'

Adam was reviewed regularly by the Royal Free community Child Development Team clinics, under the co-ordination of Dr. Andrew Lloyd-Evans. Adam's ongoing problem with temperatures and abdominal pain was of great concern to me, since we had no answers from any of the investigations. However, far from being of the view that it was in any way significant, Dr. Lloyd-Evans just kept telling me to give him paracetamol. In the autumn of 1995, Adam had begun to have severe stomach cramps that would make him cry out in pain. I thought initially that this was due to gastric reflux, and I think that was assumed by his hospital doctors. However, the problem intensified even after Adam had reflux surgery in March 1996.

Adam's abdominal pain became worse, both during the day and the night, they were accompanied by screaming for two hours or more each time. This necessitated daily paracetamol, sometimes two or three times per day; this for a year or more continued to be the only treatment considered for Adam. I did not know how much the paracetamol was a feature in the escalating problems – after all the community neurodevelopmental paediatrician kept advising it. I now think of this as laziness as well as ignorance, since the abdominal pain should obviously have been investigated – instead of which the incidents were put down to behavioural rather than medical problems.

Early in 1997 Adam went through the statementing assessment process, and a young progressive Educational Psychologist for Camden Local Education Authority, Charles Barnard, suggested autism and gave me information. My earlier concerns about changes in behaviour and the strange hand staring had been dismissed by professionals at GOSH as not a problem unless he was still doing it at five, however, Charles took this seriously. By mid-summer, Adam spend much of his day just lying on the floor staring into space or wailing; his eye contact had disappeared, even with me, and he was in a total world of his own. A world of pain, I later learned. The statement medical assessment was carried out by Dr. Lloyd-Evans who said Adam had autism and cerebral palsy (CP); in regard to the autism and the aetiology he said it was unknown, sometimes he said it was due to a viral insult, for example meningitis, sometimes it was due to organic global brain damage. He advised educational placement focused on autism not the CP.

I spent that summer depressingly researching schools, then discovered ABA through a home programme being run by a local parent that I had met at the Royal Free in 1995, whilst on that early admission for 'investigation'. Around this time Vivienne, a worker from Kids (a charity for children with Special Needs) sent me a conference flyer saying 'this may interest you'; Allergy Induced Autism (AIA) conference: does your child have any of the listed symptoms, in particular, unexplained abdominal pain?

I telephoned the conference organiser Meryl Nee and had a long chat. She talked about 'leaky gut syndrome' and told me about Dr.

Waring's work on sulphation issues in autistic children, about the Solihull study, parent funded, and about dietary intolerances and about the common factor in all the kids – massive unexplained abdominal pain. I asked her if she could provide me with any more information and she kindly posted me an information pack, produced by Dawbarns. The information was a revelation to me, and it was highly significant, proving to be the start of a long journey of discovery.

The Dawbarns pack contained lists of symptoms that coincided with Adam's condition. It seemed vital to look for the underlying cause of his abdominal pain; it was looking likely that Adam had really serious medical problems and that his behaviour was a consequence of those problems. When I rang the Royal Free, I found myself talking to Dr. Wakefield. He seemed like a doctor who really listened and after a long conversation with him about Adam he advised me to get my GP to refer him to Professor John Walker-Smith.

It was in the two days before and during Adam's first appointment at the Royal Free that I saw what a considerable difference there was between the doctors in the Royal Free department of gastroenterology and those outside it. The day before Adam's first appointment at the Royal Free, I took him to be examined by a leading paediatrician at a large hospital in South London and discussed Adam's symptoms including his pain episodes, which were very traumatic by this time. She immediately suggested that she should carry out a physical examination – 'Let's make sure he's not constipated'. 'No', she said, 'he feels fine, no sign of constipation, completely clear'.

The very next morning at the Royal Free Hospital, Adam was seen by Dr. Simon Murch. He said he appeared loaded, 'let's just send him down for an X ray'. Then Dr. Murch ascertained that Adam was completely packed, right up the descending colon, with a major impaction of faecal matter the size of a new-born baby's head that, he said, had probably been accumulating over 18 months or more. I was totally stunned; only a few hours earlier the paediatrician in South London had said with confidence that Adam was completely clear.

How long would it have been, I wonder, before this impaction had killed Adam? Thankfully we will never know the answer to that one. When I hear about parents being refused X rays to diagnose impaction, it terrifies me and upsets me at the same time while making me very angry. When the symptoms clearly mirror those that Adam suffered a proper examination is imperative and not just the assumption that the child's behaviour is due to autism. I am aware that gastro paediatricians have significant experience of feeling constipated colons, and that in a child, particularly a very young child, this requires a very sensitive touch and continual practice, so it would likely be difficult to identify by a general practitioner or even a general paediatrician, who are not doing this day in, day out. Dr. Wakefield gave me this generous explanation when I phoned him in outrage about the failure of the South London consultant; he sought to explain and defend that doctor.

Another feature, however, intermittent diarrhoea, is a major indicator of constipation and impaction. Parents cannot be expected to know this, until it is explained to them. However, I would expect any competent medical practitioner to know it, and to treat it seriously when accompanied by ongoing abdominal pain. It is scandalous that so many of our parents have to fight for the investigations which are so clearly needed on a clinical basis – why should any child be denied the same clinical investigations as their non-autistic counterpart? Some of these doctors should hang their heads in shame. Unfortunately, many of these attitudes persist due to Mad Ostrich Syndrome (MOS), a disease affecting doctors, the onset of which appears to be triggered by the terrifying prospect that vaccines may play a part in that escalating tragedy which is autism.

The Royal Free plan for Adam involved clearing the bowel, thereby alleviating his pain, then further clinical investigations and inclusion in a study. In relation to the clinical protocol I was asked some key questions: How had I heard of Andrew Wakefield? Had I formed an opinion of or made any connection between Adam's symptoms and the MMR? They obviously wanted to diagnose and treat children whose parents did not have preconceived ideas and who were not there because of the MMR or concerns about it. We met the criteria. Although, in hindsight, the medical records show a clear connection, it did not enter my mind at that time that there was anything wrong with vaccines and I had not made that association.

It took four months to clear Adam out with laxatives. Regular follow-up clinics meant contact with other parents and it was amazing to hear their stories, and in particular hear from them how their children had responded to the anti-inflammatory medication Pentasa,[ii] for the intestinal problems. As their children's gastro-intestinal problems improved, so they saw remarkable changes in behaviour, including, in some cases, speech where before there had been none. This was very exciting to hear and gave me great hope for Adam.

Clinical investigations were planned for January 1998. Adam was admitted onto the children's gastro ward and I got to meet Andy Wakefield's research nurse. I will never forget her kind words to me: 'Adam is lucky to have you for a mother'. After all the terrible guilt I had stored up, for having a premature birth, for failing to protect Adam and for all the feelings of powerlessness and all the doctors who had treated me like *I* was the problem, these words were very healing for me.

The investigations included many tests to look for any underlying gastro-intestinal pathology, infections, inflammation and so on. These included a colonoscopy of the small intestine and the colon. I was present during the procedure and saw for myself the internal filming by camera deep in Adam's intestine. It was very reassuring to be allowed to be present, and to have the privilege of seeing for myself the amazing sights on the big screen next to Adam. He was sedated and was sleeping so experienced no discomfort at all. The procedure was carried out by Dr. Mike Thompson and attended by Professor Walker-Smith, Dr. Murch and Dr. Wakefield. The doctors explained to me what was happening at each stage and what I was looking at. Swollen Lymph nodes were very evident, and could be seen clearly on the screen. The subsequent biopsy analysis revealed ILNH[iii] and non-specific colitis. Adam was started on Mesalazine (Pentasa) to treat the inflammation.

Adam was kept under careful review, although his abdominal pain continued. During that time we had consultations with Prof J. Walker-Smith and Dr. Simon Murch; although Andy Wakefield only ever pursued a research role, never suggesting any clinical treatments or procedures, he regularly attended clinics. I found Dr. Murch approachable at these consultations. Professor Walker-Smith appeared to me to be a very shy man and conversations were more stilted, I don't think he found meetings with parents easy.

It was hugely reassuring to have Adam secure under the wing of doctors who were specialists in their field, who understood what was going on, were willing to investigate and to listen to my concerns without dismissing them. I felt we were part of a team and that inspired confidence; it was obvious that they had only Adam's best interests at heart.

It appeared to me at this time that the number of children similarly affected was escalating, the children of parents I spoke with had study case numbers in the hundreds, as compared to Adam's number 41. It seemed everybody knew somebody with a child with autism and suspected gastric problems; it was quite frightening. Parents I met in the clinic had travelled from all over the country, desperate to find answers as to their children's mysterious and devastating illness.

In June 1998 Dr. Murch recommended we start Adam on a casein and soya free diet. This seemed quite daunting since we were going on holiday to Spain a few days later. I worried about finding casein and soya free foods in a different language. In the event, I took a suitcase full of rice milk with me and managed to talk my way out of the excess at the airport; as we had booked a villa I planned to cook much of the time. I took a Spanish dictionary along, but this was not terribly useful in supermarkets, reading the labels of ingredients in English is difficult enough! My efforts at speaking Spanish caused great mirth amongst Spaniards. We were in a very quiet area outside Conil de la Frontera, a small fishing town with very few tourists, in fact I don't recall seeing any others. I cannot say that I recommend starting a casein and soya free diet in such a place, where you don't speak the language, albeit very beautiful and hospitable. We managed though, I took extra pairs of hands, and the restaurants were wonderful and very tolerant of Adam.

The results of the diet were quite astounding, Adam first of all became so vocal – not verbal, but constant loud noise and vocal stimming[iv] – that I am sure he is remembered in Spain to this day! The locals adored him and found him hilarious. At the same time his dietary preferences changed almost immediately. He became determined to eat as much meat as possible – this has never changed – and he ate a wide range of vegetables. In restaurants it was easy to feed him as he would eat anything he was given. This from a previously self-limiting regimen of wheat and dairy and nothing else was astounding. His speech increased, he was very sociable and interactive. Best of all, his awful gut pain decreased dramatically from 2-3 times per day (of several hours duration) to three times per week of much shorter duration and with less severity.

Following the success of this dietary change, Dr. Murch considered gluten free, and asked me to contact Paul Shattock, Head of the Autism Research Unit at the University of Sunderland to arrange for urine testing of Adam. The purpose was to look for chemical markers called IAG to identify problems with metabolising gluten. Paul sent me the results which showed Adam had a marked problem with gluten, we had a long chat and he also advised me to consider avoiding certain foods associated with abdominal pain in similar cases, e.g. beef, tomatoes, corn, which I eliminated for a while, before introducing back slowly. Adam's diet was regularly reviewed with the Royal Free nutritionist who worked with Adam's team of doctors, and with her help I implemented a full GFCFSF diet. Unlike the effects of starting CFSF Adam displayed a physical reaction; marked physical self-stimulatory behaviour. His abdominal pain levels reduced further and it was now less frequent: 1-2 times per fortnight. Later, I found implementing Sarah's Diet (Lutein free)[V] for 10 months or so, on top of the GFCFSF, eliminated all abdominal pain episodes.

We settled to a pattern of review by Dr Murch at the Royal Free; a daily programme of laxatives to keep everything moving, dietary reviews, dietary supplements, and probiotics to help re-colonise Adam's gut. Unfortunately these were not available on prescription, the establishment does not apparently recognise the medical need for such things! I was told there was no apparent cure for Adam's condition – years away – said Dr. Murch.

It became clear to me very quickly as the treatment and the consultations at the Royal Free were on-going, that a considerable gulf was forming between the doctors who had become specialists at the Royal Free and the run of the mill NHS doctors. Even the senior doctors at GOSH where Adam was still going for regular check ups, seemed to be unwilling to entertain any ideas of vaccine adverse reaction.

I became increasingly concerned about a cramp problem in Adam's legs, muscles and ham strings. In searching for answers, through my own investigations I discovered the heavy metals toxicity connection to autism – discovered Adam probably had a huge load of mercury and possibly viral loads too. I learned that one of the things mercury does is disable the immune system, which likely set Adam up for the crash when he was given three live viruses in one MMR shot. I made huge attempts to engage a range of NHS Doctors in support of chelation treatment, all refused, despite test results showing high level of lead, and indicators for mercury.

Adam's cramp problem worsened and the only management implemented through his orthopaedic consultant was Diazepam.[vi] By this time Adam was taking 2-3 doses per day of Diazepam, spending days as a zombie in between bouts of pain. I spent a lot of time researching the connection between heavy metals and cramp and autism. For two years I spent my nights on the internet – Pubmed sites and others, studying published papers, and in collaboration with Ros Devrell, a SRN who was working for me as an ABA therapist, drawing up lists of full papers I wanted; using Ros's nursing student card to gain access to the medical libraries, we pulled all the key papers and put together an A4 arch lever file full of published peer reviewed studies relevant to the connections between heavy metals and cramp and autism, as well as another on the connections between viruses and bacteria with autism. I sent a copy to each of the Consultants at GOSH that Adam was under. I pressured the Orthopaedic consultant, Mr. Monsell, to get Adam investigated on these issues. In fact, I also sent him video footage of Adam screaming in agony being held down and restrained from desperate self-injury, and the stretching of his tortured legs, taking three people to manage it. I chose Mr. Monsell as somebody who was very sympathetic and kindly toward Adam and he seemed the most approachable. He agreed to pull together a team and admit Adam for investigations.

Around this time I was contacted by Andy Wakefield and asked to provide a blood sample via his research nurse who would visit at home. I was happy to agree to this as I very much supported Dr. Wakefield's work. After all, the government or the medical establishment showed no signs of looking into what was an obvious epidemic of children with severe IBD and autism; MOS again.

Subsequent results of this blood test, which had been sent to Dr. John O'Leary's laboratory in Dublin, showed Adam had very high levels of vaccine strain measles virus in his blood, which indicated the infection was multiplying – i.e. not dead fragments of protein. I called Andy Wakefield and he told me that Adam's level was nearly the highest in the group. Which explained a lot about his overall health and almost continual viral type illness.

I provided the laboratory report to a consultant at the large hospital where Adam was at that time having tests; he was adamant that he did not consider Adam to have any such problem and that Dr. O'Leary's PCR analysis,[vii] Pacman, had been discredited and was of no value. I had, however, done my homework, with a nurse to help with the research, and had information to hand to prove my points, and argued my case; at this point the consultant lost his temper and resorted to raising his voice.

The review meeting finished on a reasonably amicable basis, but the consultant realised that I was not satisfied with the conclusions. Dr. O'Leary has international respect for his work, and there are many testimonials to his integrity and the efficacy of his Pacman analysis. I suppose it is hardly surprising that the British establishment sought to discredit such work that was 'outside their control' and which supported Dr Wakefield's hypotheses.

Some of the GOSH test results had not been available for that review meeting, and were promised to me for a few days time. I was very disappointed therefore that I had to repeatedly request and chase those results, which included CSF Myelin Basic Protein Antibodies, samples of which had been sent to the National Hospital for Neurology & Neuro Surgery for analysis, and the heavy metals analysis via hair samples, again analysis by an outside specialist laboratory. Eventually, after writing to the consultant overseeing those particular tests, I was told that Adam's test results had been sent to Professor Dame Barbara Clayton for an opinion. She was a retired expert, I was told, a leader in the field. Two questions in my mind: one, why if the test results were negative or even neutral would they bother to send them to a leading expert? And two, who was she? On checking through the internet I found that she was Chair of the committee of public enquiry setup to investigate the Camelford incident, an episode of mass poisoning caused when aluminium, with other chemicals, was dumped into the local drinking water. The committee found that, although the local population had accumulated high levels of aluminium and had a range of severe symptoms, the chemicals had not caused people any harm. The outcome of the enquiry was later totally discredited and there were allegations of cover-up – hmmmm, and this was the person deciding if Adam's heavy metal levels should cause medical concern?

I never did get to see those test results, they were never made available to me. It did not seem a good idea for future relations to stir up a hornets' nest by doing a Subject Access Request, so I let it drop, and got on with the business of detoxifying Adam, and reducing his heavy metal burden. I had a group of 2,000 people holding my hand, through that wonderful medium of the internet, united in grief for our children and determination that they would not be consigned to the dustbin of no medical hope. During this period I kept detailed data, and was later able to graph Diazepam frequency and cramp episodes against the strategies I employed. Results showed dramatic decline in cramp and need of Diazepam, until, after a further year that included chelation therapy, the awful life-destroying cramp that had ruled Adam's life – life that had reduced him to living in harrowing torture from the most appalling pain you could not even imagine unless you have experience of it – just disappeared forever.

This was the driving motivation and I succeeded; however, the other remarkable benefit from this therapy was the recovery of Adam's intellectual abilities. But this is another story and maybe it is for later.

Adam's gut problems were also ongoing, however, something had to be done about the probable overwhelming measles virus and the debilitating effect that had. I discovered the work of Dr. Mary Megson, involving vitamin A therapy, and later, I found that this was backed up by the work of Dr. Jaqueline McCandless, an American Board Certified Neurologist, who had been researching and treating children with autism for their underlying illnesses, from a range of causes. I followed the discovery of the Vitamin A protocol by looking closely at published peer reviewed studies on Vitamin A and measles, benefits and risks. The work of these doctors in the US suggested that Vitamin A played a role in mopping up measles virus, indeed it is used as treatment of choice in third world epidemics.

I decided to implement the Vitamin A protocol as therapy for Adam in an attempt to reduce his measles virus burden. I am sure the establishment will say no proof of efficacy, but I can say definitively that although I have no double blind control study to put on the table, Adam got better. His health improved dramatically.

My view is that there is multiple causation of autism or ASD, and therefore multiple treatments are needed. My son, my beautiful son Adam, tragically through a sequence of events, but almost entirely due to vaccines, suffered multiple causal events. It has taken multiple strategies and treatments on the road to recovery to help him, each has played a part.

I believe in biomedical approaches to treating autism, and there is a big community out there now to help, for example in the UK, Treating Autism[viii] is a charity set up to help parents find their way through the maze of information on this very complex and devastating disorder and to understand the biomedical approaches to recovering. from it. This community of parents and professionals is dedicated and very knowledgeable, and they are recovering their children.

Adam has some way to go, we are not there yet, but my hope is that I can help him to be all that he can be. Will he ever speak? I don't know. Will he ever be the Adam in my dreams? I don't know, he cries because he thinks the whole world will not like him because he can not speak. But he is doing so well, he has his brilliant mind back, he is very clever, and he has the prospect of a future once more.

I was set on this road to discovery by Dr. Wakefield and his colleagues, it has been a long road in Adam's case, and very difficult. But we would not have got where he is now without Dr. Wakefield. I was therefore very upset by the treatment of him by the Royal Free when they decided to oust him, shocked by his abrupt departure and the political reasoning behind it.

I was very happy to continue to support Dr Wakefield in his work with Visceral,[ix] and for Adam to remain as part of his research project, after all nobody else was in the slightest bit interested in Adam's illness, or in treating him for anything but the most mundane, mainstream and 'acceptable' conditions. I think it is shocking and scandalous that other hospitals, including the main tertiary referral children's hospital in this country have maintained such a determined stand against parents of autistic children and the medical needs of those children.

I was deeply shocked to hear about the witch-hunt and proposed 'Trial' by the GMC of the doctors involved in the case review of children with IBD and ASD. To me, all three doctors before the Fitness to Practice Panel have the utmost integrity and are still highly respected in their field. Events show that they were very brave indeed to court the controversy and the vilification that this area of research was bound to bring them. As the parent of such a damaged child, to me they are true heroes and I will be eternally grateful to them for risking their careers and worse. If it were not for them, setting me on the road to understanding the basis of Adam's illness, for their caring, their clinical excellence, and their respect of me as his parent and advocate – where would Adam be now?

The damage that has been done, cannot be undone, and it is heartbreaking to think of the loss of a happy childhood and prospects of a normal fulfilling life, in the terms of what might have been – but thank God for the prospects that we do have due to the pioneering work of Andy Wakefield; from an understanding of what is needed, from experimental treatments, from a brave band of people who have not been personally touched by this tragedy yet have nevertheless dedicated themselves to help our children.

Endnotes

i. **Transient dystonia** describes an abnormality of muscle tone often demonstrated in infants under one year of age who were born preterm. Pedersen and Marestad (1996) also associate the condition with infants who have low Apgar scores, bacterial infection, and those infants not given breast milk during the neonatal period.

ii. **Pentasa** is an anti-inflammatory drug containing mesalamine, which helps to reduce inflammation in the intestine. Specifically, Pentasa is approved for the treatment of mildly to moderately active ulcerative colitis.

iii. **ILNH** is the acronym for Ileal Lymphoid Nodular Hyperplasia. The terminal ileum is the end of the small intestine, just before it goes to the large intestine. Ileal Lymphoid Nodular Hyperplasia is when the lymph glands are swollen, like during an infection, in this case, in the ileum of the bowel.

iv. **Vocal stimming** is sounds, not words, that are repetitive in nature.

v. **Lutein free:** Lutein is a yellow carotenoid pigment produced by plants. These pigments give yellow, green or orange coloration to vegetables. Lutein is naturally found in egg yolk and several plants including some flowers, red peppers, collard greens, kale, leeks, peas, roman lettuce, mustard and spinach. In the eye, lutein is the primary carotenoid present in the central area of the retina, called macula.

vi. **Diazepam,** first marketed as Valium by Hoffmann-La-Roche is a benzodiazepine derivative drug. It possesses anxiolytic, anticonvulsant, hypnotic, sedative, skeletal muscle relaxant, and amnestic properties. It is commonly used for treating anxiety, insomnia, seizures, muscle spasms, restless legs syndrome, alcohol withdrawal, benzodiazepine withdrawal, and Ménière's disease. It may also be used before certain medical procedures (such as endoscopies) to reduce tension and anxiety.

vii. **PCR analysis:** In molecular biology, the polymerase chain reaction (PCR) is a technique to amplify a single or few copies of a piece of DNA across several orders of magnitude, generating thousands to millions of copies of a particular DNA sequence. The method relies on thermal cycling, consisting of cycles of repeated heating and cooling of the reaction for DNA melting and enzymatic replication of the DNA.

viii. **Treating Autism,** a charity that gives advice on biomedical issues.

ix. **Visceral,** a charity dealing with vaccine/autism research.

CHAPTER FIVE

Being the Voice of my Child

Hello, my name is Deborah Heather. I was born in Limehouse in London's East End where I was brought up with my parents and my younger brother, Richard. I left school at the age of sixteen and was lucky enough to get a job straight after in a tea factory. I was very proud to have the job as it meant that I could pay back my parents Lawrence and Patricia for the hard work of bringing me up and instilling good values in me. I recall that with my first week's wages, I bought them an ornament, a black and white clown, which they were thrilled with.

I didn't last long at the tea factory and moved on to the Argos store in New Oxford street. I adored that job; I met people and made many friends. Dealing with the public put me in good stead for future positions. I had been bullied in my last two years of school life and had become a little withdrawn. I had to bring myself out, learn to communicate with people, and working with the public helped me achieve this. I worked in a delicatessen in Baker St and then went to work in an office for a lighting company that was also in Baker St.

In my late teens I ended up working with my mum at William Hill, the Turf accountants. The trouble was, someone would only have to look at me the wrong way and my mum would pounce like a lion. I was eighteen and could look after myself but mum just didn't see it that way. The working together didn't last very long as I was sent to another shop and there I found my independence.

At twenty I was a confident young woman just out of a painful relationship and having a drink in my local with my dearest friend when I spot the man of my dreams. They say that the way to a woman's heart is through laughter and Colin, Oh, did he make me laugh? We had our ups and downs but after eight years and many breakups and reconciliations we decided to get married. It was a hot August day, a beautiful sunny day, bride and groom nerves abundant and after the ceremony looking forward to a wonderful future. We weren't thinking of children immediately, we just wanted to enjoy each other for a while.

I fell pregnant within a few months and although it came as a shock we looked forward to having a child. I miscarried at three months and can't even begin to explain the emotions we both felt. We got through this difficult time and began planning again for our future. In 1991 we decided the time was right to try for another baby; it wasn't so easy this time around. I had been feeling unwell, my skin was itching, it got progressively worse and was accompanied by hot and cold sweats. I had no idea what was wrong nor did my GP and it took almost a year before out of desperation the doctor sent me for blood tests, which came back positive for an overactive thyroid gland. I was immediately referred to a endocrinologist and given medication.

We got back to planning for a baby. I ask you 'Are things ever that simple?' 'No!' We tried for a year but our dream wasn't coming true, despite Colin and I both feeling that we were ready. I had been working for Coral racing for three years as a telephonist when I found that I was pregnant. We wondered throughout the pregnancy what colour hair the baby would have and who the baby would look like. My father was auburn haired and my Mother-in-Law Joyce, who unfortunately I never got the opportunity to meet, also had auburn hair. I remember having a conversation with my Sister-in-Law Denise, we were chatting about the baby and she said, 'You know what, you're going to have a baby with ginger hair and freckles'. Of course, I didn't think she would be right. On March 5th 1994, at 4.33pm, Ryan began to enter the world. Colin arrived at the hospital soon after I went into labour and my wonderful cousin Gloria arrived at the hospital with sandwiches and refreshments also thinking she would have a long wait, but Ryan arrived eight hours after I started labour. Colin couldn't contain his excitement and rushed outside to tell Gloria and to phone the grandparents.

Colin's dad, Terry already had two beautiful granddaughters and he was overjoyed to have a grandson. My mum and dad were totally relieved that everything had gone well. Ryan had a wonderful head of red hair and a touch of jaundice. We settled down to a contented family life. We didn't plan for another child but to our surprise seventeen months later along came our second bundle of joy, Andrew. Andrew was a beautiful child, strawberry blood hair and the face of an angel. When we brought him home from hospital our family seemed complete. Andrew had trouble initially feeding and two days later he had to return and stay in hospital for a week. It was a very trying and worrying time for us all but when he came home, he took well to his feeds and we got back to some normality. Family life was good but tiring. We were adjusting to our new brood when something happened that shattered our whole lives.

At eighteen months Andrew received the MMR vaccine and five days afterwards he had his first bout of severe diarrhoea. A few weeks later he was vomiting and had developed a rash on his torso, which the GP suspected was measles; this I found alarming! There followed a vast array of medical complaints, eczema, conjunctivitis and tonsillitis. At this time diarrhoea became part of our everyday life with up to seven bowel movements a day. A referral was made to a pediatrician who requested tests for thyroid function, a stool test and one for coeliac disease; every test came back normal. As parents we were frightened and dismayed with our young son's health issues and it seemed even from the beginning that nobody had any answers.

Although the doctors were trying very hard to find the cause of Andrew's bowel condition we were becoming very frustrated. We noticed Andrew was not responding to us when we called his name; unbeknown to us he was showing signs of autism. A short stay in hospital followed, Andrew had developed glue ear and concern was growing that he may be having problems with his hearing. Grommets were fitted, there were no problems concerning Andrew's hearing, we were relieved but with relief came fear, fear of not knowing the reasons for Andrew's behaviour and the constant diarrhoea.

Andrew was referred by the audiologist to a consultant paediatrician, who looked over the coming year at Andrew's behaviour. In March of 2000 we were devastated to be told that Andrew was autistic. I won't talk about his autism now, it would be too emotionally draining.

The only optimistic aspect of Andrew's autism diagnosis was that we were assigned Gaye Picton as a health visitor. She was a wonderful lady, very caring in her approach to our situation, with unmatched knowledge. When she thought that we were ready, she asked us to look at details of autism traits. I don't know if she has any idea of how much she helped our family to understand Andrew's disability. She became a friend and will always have a special place in my heart.

Anyway, at the time Andrew's bowel condition was concerning us greatly. Our first thought was that the bowel condition came first, autism second, although we did feel that the two things could be connected. Andrew attended a nursery where we met other parents, in particular Matt and Justine, and their son Tom. Parents need to be in touch with parents who are going through the same problems because only they know what it is like to care for an autistic child who also has a bowel disorder. They need to be able to share their fears and feelings.

Everyday the nauseating smell of diarrhoea filled our house. I think that over time we began to get used to it. Tests and referrals followed, one after the other for Andrew, and then the problem of getting Andrew into a special educational needs school. We were sitting at home one day, exhausted by the ongoing appointments and referrals, when we heard a letter come through the letterbox. I remember saying to Colin, 'I hope it's not another bloody appointment', every letter that came through our door at that time was either a referral or an appointment. When we opened the letter, what did we find? Yes, another appointment. We had to take Andrew to see another consultant paediatrician; I had resigned myself to thinking that this was just another doctor, nothing was going to change. However, by the time the appointment came round I recall feeling excited.

A little hope had come back; this was the day, I felt, when Andrew was going to be helped? So I was carrying a great deal of emotion when we attended the appointment. I won't ever forget that day, we sat ourselves down opposite the doctor, Andrew took himself underneath her desk and sat at her feet, I found myself apologising for his behaviour, she said 'don't worry mum, I completely understand, I have a son with Asperger's syndrome'.

It was such a relief to talk to someone who understood autism and was also caring and compassionate. It turned out to be one of the best days of my life. We spoke about Andrew's medical history, it felt as if the only words that ever came out of my mouth were concerns for Andrew or interest in his medical records – I recall an occasion when somebody had remarked to me that they felt I liked the sound of my own voice, I didn't react but I wish now that I had because my voice is the only voice Andrew has and I make no apology for that.

I digress, back to the consultant's room... Then came the words that I had waited for so long to hear: 'How would you feel if I referred you to Doctor Andrew Wakefield at the Royal Free Hospital?' I sat and I cried like a baby, the doctor looked puzzled by my reaction and with a great deal of alarm on her face she said, 'Mum, whatever's the matter?' I knew of Doctor Wakefield's work and knew that the Royal Free Hospital was considered a centre of excellence for bowel conditions. I said 'Doctor, this is what I have been wishing for, for a very long time. I just know in my heart if Andrew attends this hospital they will find out what is wrong with him and they will treat him'. I could not really put my feelings into words as I left the hospital. Even thinking about it now as I write, the word euphoria comes to mind.

As the time came near for the appointment at the Royal Free, my mood became happier and the feeling of excitement became quite unbearable, although on the day inevitable trepidation joined my feelings. Entering the hospital, we could not get to the paediatric department quickly enough; I almost fell over myself in the rush. We sat in the chairs opposite the doctor, again we went through Andrew's medical history, but going through his medical history this time did not phase me at all; I was thinking that perhaps Andrew's journey was coming to an end. At last Andrew would get the treatment he so badly needed, or so I thought. It was felt that Andrew's bowel condition met the hospitals criteria for investigations: an endoscopy and a colonoscopy. I was a little disappointed when we didn't see doctor Wakefield in person. In fact, although Dr Wakefield was at the hospital then, we never did see him and shortly after that time he left for the United States. Andrew was admitted to the hospital on the 15th January 2002 and the procedures were to be carried out the next day. On the evening before the procedure I met a lovely lady called Carol, her daughter was at the hospital suffering the same problems as Andrew. We got talking and found out that we both had concerns about the MMR and MR vaccines; Carol told me that she supported a group called JABS.

I contacted JABS straight away and told them about my concerns that Andrew had been vaccine damaged. We prepared for the operations. I recall that the night of the 15th January we had to give Andrew medication to empty his bowel in preparation for the procedure. The day of the procedure we were asked if we minded if a biopsy was taken from Andrew for researching the condition, we readily agreed, it all went well and we took Andrew home that afternoon. We also did a urine and faeces test and waited anxiously for our next appointment, which was in May 2002. We were eager to find out the results, quite naively thinking that all the diagnostic questions would be answered and treatment forthcoming; we couldn't have been more wrong.

The doctor told us they had found enlarged lymph nodes and that this was very common in autistic children, again naively I asked if they had found any inflammation. The doctor said 'no' to this, even though 'enlarged lymph nodes' did constitute inflammation. The doctor then wanted to check Andrew's throat and rectum for bacteria. I found this strange as he had just had an endoscopy and colonoscopy, I suppose they could have been looking for infection after procedure, Klebsiella is known to be a bacteria caught from internal procedures, unfortunately this is one of the bacteria they found in Andrew's swabs. I was informed that the research doctor would call me with the results of these tests and in October of 2002 I was told that the tests showed Andrew had Klebsiella 5+, E Coli 1+ and Enterobacter Cloacae 5+ in the throat, and E Coli and Klebsiella in the rectum. The research doctor told me they had no idea why these bacteria were there. It was suggested that Andrew should start a course of three antibiotics but since the trouble at the Royal Free these studies were halted and Andrew has received no medical intervention for his inflammatory condition, nor six years later have the swabs been redone. I have questioned this on various occasions when attending the hospital but they have no answers, so I still don't know to this day if the bacteria remain. I was told that these bacteria were not dangerous.

I had thought our journey was coming to an end with our visit to the Royal Free. It was, however, only just beginning. Instead of an ending, there began many years of medication. The hospital had put Andrew's problems down to autism and constipation and began treating him for constipation; his first medications were Liquid Paraffin per day and Sodium Picosulphate at weekends.

In January of 2003 Andrew was again suspected of having measles, which had come as a surprise as it had already been suggested back in 1998; he recovered well from whatever the rash was. It had been suggested to us that we could try taking Andrew off cow's milk, so we tried rice milk; it was helpful, but only for six weeks. The diarrhoea did appear to be less but then returned. A gluten free diet was also suggested. I had my reservations about the diet, I was aware that you could only get the basic items on prescription, it wasn't successful for every child and could be very difficult to implement, although it has been said that some children can show remarkable change. You also had to be sure that every agency involved with the child would implement the diet strictly. The bowel condition was taking up a lot of our time and energy. Andrew had no control of his bowel movements, he could not tell us a motion was coming, so we would not be surprised on entering his room to find that incontinence had overtaken him and he had smeared faeces on to walls, bedding, carpets and his bedroom door. I recall many times when on liquid paraffin and sodium picosulphate, he would walk across the room with a bulging nappy and it would quite literally be running down his legs leaving a trail of diarrhoea. Although the hospital was treating Andrew for diarrhoea, what we were witnessing was overflow from a bowel impacted with hard faeces. The hospital's refusal to look at this impaction was linked to their unwillingness to consider Andrew's inflammatory bowel disorder. At some stages must have been quite prominent. Sometimes when Andrew's brother went to his room he would find that Andrew had smeared his bedclothes. It was certainly not an ideal situation for any of us to be living in.

Andrew was a very bland eater and would not try new foods easily; if he did not like the smell of certain foods he would not try them. He began to suffer with sickness and we had noticed on various occasions that his stomach would become distended. He also suffered with dry lips. What was of great concern was a strong change in his behaviour. Of course, Andrew could not tell us when he was unwell so he would show us in his behaviour; our only way of knowing was visually.

I spoke to other parents of autistic children who told me what I had suspected, that a change in behaviour was related to his bowel being impacted. We arranged with our local paediatrician that Andrew would attend the local hospital for X-rays. I was beginning, through experience, to learn that if a doctor felt Andrew's tummy and said it felt soft, that this was not always the case and on the majority of times I was right; more often than not, he was impacted. This was exactly what the X-ray showed. This situation was becoming quite unbearable for us, we felt utterly useless. There was nothing we could do to help him except to regulate his medication when we thought it appropriate.

Andrew had his first appointment at the Royal Free Hospital in 2002 and we had seen no real change in his condition. The question of diet was raised again; the questions I wanted to ask were about special diets, particularly their cost. Why would they suggest the diet if they felt that Andrew did not have a bowel condition? Did they want to put Andrew on a special diet for autism or his bowel condition? Would he be monitored? How would we deal with any withdrawal symptoms? None of this information was readily available.

By 2004 the hospital had decided to introduce Movicol[i] on a regular basis. Other medications didn't seem to be helping Andrew, so after another appointment we were told we may have to clear Andrew out at home with three to five sachets of this medication a day. We knew we would have to watch him like a hawk, we couldn't risk taking him out during this time for fear of accidents, the diarrhoea was falling out of him like water.

I can remember looking through correspondence from the hospital and coming across a letter that I found quite shocking; the procedures had been in January 2002. The letter referred to the results of Andrew's colonoscopy and endoscopy. The report stated that there was a focal increase in the lymphocytes, which I had been told, but what I was not told was that there was some chronic inflammation in the terminal ileum, in the small bowel. After the procedures were carried out, at the first appointment we were told there was no inflammation. At home we sat for quite a while trying to make sense of the letter, I think we must have read that letter many times, hoping that our thoughts were a mistake.

It seemed that I hadn't been told the truth about Andrew's condition. As a mother, deeply concerned for her son's wellbeing, I deserved some answers so I asked questions that weren't always entirely welcome. I recall a particular appointment when I put my concerns about the letter to our doctor and he said, 'I think this letter must have been sent out by mistake, we have looked at the histology reports and we have found no inflammation'. Then came the surprise, he asked me if I would like a cup of coffee. Now, what would a doctor be doing asking a mum in the middle of a clinic if she would like a cup of coffee? My reply was 'I don't want to keep you from your work'. 'No, No' he replied, 'The clinic isn't very busy this afternoon.' He left the room for what seemed like an eternity, returning after about ten minutes, which I remember thinking was an awfully long time to make a cup of coffee. He was quite relaxed and I felt somewhat uncomfortable. He wanted to chat about Andrew's brother and asked how he was getting on and if he had any problems. I went along with the conversation out of courtesy and when I left the room I remember thinking to myself 'Wouldn't it be a joy if all consultants invited you for a coffee and a chat?'

I wasn't going to be put off my mission, and believe me, right at that moment it felt like a mission to find out whether there was a problem with Andrew's bowel. Going by this letter there was a problem and we were going to find out about it and get treatment. So before we left the room I told him I wanted a senior consultant at the hospital to look again at Andrew's histology report and the biopsies from the procedures carried out in January 2002. He said he would speak to someone about my concerns but that I had nothing to worry about. That letter was beginning to feel like the burden of our lives and I wanted answers, not small talk, coffee and obscured words.

Another X-ray was carried out and this time Andrew wasn't badly impacted but still needed to be on one and a half sachets of Movicol per day to keep him regular. Another long journey home and the realisation that nothing was actually being done for Andrew; nothing was going to be done for him. I wrote to the Royal Free because it was exhausting going backwards and forwards to the hospital with Andrew, only to be sent home with medication on every visit. Andrew too found the visits difficult to cope with, we had to hope that we didn't get stuck in traffic because Andrew would become aggressive and frustrated and this would cause mounting stress to all of us. Because I had great respect for the hospital and its place in gastroenterology, I kept attending the appointments on a regular basis. However, I became more assertive with the doctors, my frustration was showing and the doctors were beginning to notice it.

Probably by this time the doctors were fighting amongst themselves and drawing straws to see who was unlucky enough to see me at Andrew's next appointment. I was never deterred; our son's health was our prime concern. In fact, knowing that our son had been suffering all these years only pushed us further into demanding answers.

Personally, I don't suffer fools easily but I do respect honesty. I might have got it wrong but aren't doctors supposed to help us when we are ill? Where was the help for Andrew? Looking back on this period now it seems that all the activities of the doctors at the Royal Free at this time must be considered in the light of what had happened to Dr Wakefield. Everyone was back peddling.

At one point, we thought we had received some news that would encourage the doctors to finally do something to help Andrew. Andrew had a condition known as Mild Acute Mucosal Inflammation. I had found a doctor at the hospital who had seen the biopsies so now I wondered why every time I attended with Andrew all the doctors continued to deny the fact that Andrew had inflammatory bowel disorder. I obviously didn't know whether this condition was serious, but it seemed that the hospital could only have known of it from the procedures carried out on Andrew, in January 2002.

Preparing for Andrew's next visit in April 2005 I was thinking that the appointment was going to be no different from previous ones. I was certainly not expecting the consultation to go as badly as it did. At first, it was all very calm and civilised with the usual questions being asked: How had Andrew been since the last visit? How many bowel movements were there per day? Was he eating OK? Everything you would expect the doctor to ask. I broached the subject of inflammation, I could see by the look on the doctor's face he was not best pleased with my approaching this subject, 'Look', he said 'we have had this conversation on three separate occasions and I have explained the situation to you'. I wasn't prepared to accept his response to me because I knew Andrew had a problem and I continued to reiterate my concerns again.

A welcome interlude came when Andrew decided a bowel movement was in order, I asked the doctor if he minded if I changed Andrew, 'of course not' he said. When I opened Andrew's nappy I drew the doctor attention to what filled it: 'Look at this diarrhoea, this is what Andrew and we have to deal with everyday'. I urged him to come forward and look; he didn't take up my offer. I think he felt his efforts weren't appreciated, he said, 'Look, it is quite obvious you have little trust in us and I think it would be best if we referred you back to local care'. For a moment I seemed to be lost for words. Once I had recovered my composure I responded, 'Are you chucking me out of the Royal Free?' He stood and stared at me for a few moments without attempting to answer. When I put the question to him again, he said he would see Andrew in a year and he called another doctor into the room because I questioned Andrew's care. I put it to him that a doctor who had left the hospital was convinced that children with autism and bowel conditions should be on appropriate medication, which in many cases should be anti-inflammatory medication. His response to this was that nobody believed this doctor. 'How normal is it' I asked 'that my child has been suffering with diarrhoea and constipation for seven years?' I am, if nothing else, persistent and asked again about Andrew's biopsies – I must have asked this question over many appointments – 'I want the biopsies looked at again by a senior gastroenterologist'. In fact, I had been asking for a year, but on this occasion I got the answer I had been waiting for: 'We have looked again for the second time and found small areas of inflammation', he did not say where, only that the inflammation did not require anti-inflammatory drugs.

So I had been given the answer I had been waiting for. In fact, the answer should have been given in May 2002 at the follow-up appointment, after the procedures. My hopes of medication had been dashed and the expression 'banging my head against a brick wall' came frequently to mind. I still wanted to know why Andrew did not require anti-inflammatory medication; the doctor said, 'The only time we would consider anti-inflammatory drugs would be if the child appeared to be losing weight or that child had constant diarrhoea'. My God, I thought, if Andrew wasn't getting constant diarrhoea, what would you call bowel movements between four and six times a day for six years? I was livid, but the doctor was quite adamant, Andrew's condition did not warrant any medication other than the constipation medication, i.e. laxatives and softeners, that he was being given.

Inevitably, parents with vaccine-damaged children experience the same life traumas that other people have to cope with. Sometimes these can throw up very pointed lessons about the nature of autism and your other children's lives. In October of 2004 my mother was taken into hospital. This wasn't unusual; hospital stays were becoming frequent with her breathing difficulties. She was a very ill but determined lady, that's maybe where I get my persistence from. My brother Richard who lived in Poland with his wife Dominika and my two beautiful nieces Zofia and Miya came over to England on business so we visited mum together.

I remember us on either side of her bed; she was having great difficulty breathing. She said to Richard, 'You have to get me out of here, I know I won't be coming home.' I remember sitting holding her hand, I felt so helpless, we both did. I reassured her that she would be coming home, she had to get better because Richard was coming over from Poland with the girls for Christmas and mum had not yet met Miya, his youngest, so it was important that she got well.

We had known that she had a small cancer in her lung and so we requested to see the doctor. I could tell he wasn't hopeful, he didn't commit himself; I suppose it depended on how strong she was, she had always been a fighter and never given up easily on any aspect of her life. We went back to her bedside, it was very difficult for us both to see her in pain, I could feel the tears falling from my face and Richard was quick to tell me to go outside, he didn't want her to see me cry, we said our goodbyes and left the ward. Stepping out of the ward gave us a great sense of relief; I don't think either of us could have sat there much longer watching her suffering.

She had been worried about her arms feeling very dry and the fact that her nails needed cutting. I rang the hospital to see how she was and a couple of days later, visited with moisturiser for her arms and scissors so I could cut her nails, she was now unable to do anything for herself. When I entered the ward she was sitting on a chair beside her bed, she was slouched over and looked very uncomfortable. I called the nurse and asked why she looked so uncomfortable, she replied that mum had wanted to sit in the chair; she wasn't able to sit straight, so I asked the nurse to help me put her back into bed. We put her into bed but couldn't get her to sit straight.

The next morning heading down the stairs at just past nine the phone rang, I knew it was the hospital: my mother had passed a few minutes ago. Throughout their lives, different people react differently to death. With the death of my mother I saw the difference in reaction between Andrew and Ryan. Because of his autism and lack of understanding Andrew appeared to be without feeling for his grans, he had not seen my mother on a regular basis because she could not walk and as much as she loved him, Andrew had no understanding of this love. Ryan, however, had formed a relationship with her and I could see that this was going to be a painful time.

When you have a child who is unwell, it doesn't matter what you are feeling at any given time, you try and put that aside to deal with your child's anxieties. I made sure that I was there for Ryan, I knew that there would be many questions and there were. If he wanted to talk about nanny or anything else he always knew that he could call me upstairs and we would have a little chat, he knew I would be there to reassure him and that I would understand and help him to understand.

I have mentioned my mother in my chapter because it is relevant to how it had an affect on our home life and how Ryan went on to perceive his brother and his brother's disability. Ryan's initial reaction to the loss of nanny wasn't telling, but the very next day he broke his little heart. After he finally settled down in bed, Andrew's circumstances and my mum's death filled my mind. I put myself on the settee in a foetal position, and sobbed until I could not sob anymore.

Andrew's illness remained unchanging through 2004 and 2005, with no new diagnoses and no breakthroughs in treatment. It was very difficult to watch him in pain after taking Movicol, it was obviously causing him some discomfort and these side effects were mentioned on the box; however, we had to continue to trust the doctors. We had to contact the hospital again in July of 2005 because his bowel movements were very watery, again we had to watch him quite closely because he had no control of his motions, the diarrhoea would come through so quickly, if you turned away for a second there would be a trail behind him. He would be sitting watching his videos and it would just fall away from him, his smearing would cover the walls, his bedclothes, carpets and his bedroom door. On this occasion we were told to stop the medication for two days, then to reintroduce it at one and a half sachets but only if he became constipated. At this time, we were also giving Andrew probiotics to try and promote a healthy gut.

Andrew would then go through phases of urinating, not always in the toilet; he would pass water wherever he felt the need: in the sink, behind a chair, in the living room or he would find a cup or a bowl and urinate into it. When he was passing bowel motions, he would bend over a chair, it seemed to give him some comfort. He still stands or bends over something when trying to release a bowel motion.

I often felt useless. Wasn't a mum supposed to be the one to relieve situations? I couldn't do so, I felt trapped in the constant medical merry go round, I had never been in the company of so many doctors in my life, it felt like there was an army of people behind Andrew pushing him from appointment to appointment. I often thought that we were all tired and I didn't want to play this game anymore. It had become like a game: mum, dad and Andrew would drive to the hospital, hoping to find a space – a nightmare. Get out of the car, get a firm hold of Andrew's hand, in case he decided to escape – a nightmare. Inside an unknown nurse would take height and weight. In to see doctor, aggravated persistent mother, many questions asked, some old answers, sent home with Movicol. Fearful that on the way home that we might get stuck in traffic. If there was no movement Andrew would become very distressed – nightmare.

I know that it's beggar belief but we have had many years of this. Reading about it now, I hope you can at least imagine how soul destroying it had become. I suppose if you are reading this you may be asking yourself why we kept at it? I'll tell you. My greatest hope was that the hospital would one day research autistic children with bowel conditions and treatment would become available, this thought kept us going; if there is one thing that can help us through our everyday lives it's hope. Hope has helped me to stay strong.

I learnt patience through having children, it is something we lose when our emotions take over and it is something that recently I have lost often. Another lesson I have learned over the last nine years is to be informed, especially while dealing with the medical establishment. I now regard myself as an informed parent, and I have had to be an educator. As Andrew's mother I know my son better than anybody; what was it that Dr Andrew Wakefield said? 'Always examine the patient and always listen to the parent'. This comment is always relevant.

We have now arrived in the year 2006 of Andrew's journey. I had the most wonderfully romantic notion in my head, that this year would be the year that everything that I had wanted for Andrew would fall into place. I had to be hopeful because the only other way was spiraling downwards and I wasn't going to spiral. So we tried to look forward, we said that 2006 would be a good year for us as a family. Our hopes were high until April.

Andrew woke on a Sunday morning yawning, and then started to cough. Knowing that Andrew had no speech, I was immediately tuned into his ways and any unusual behaviour. I think it was the yawning that had alerted me. I was right, within a few seconds after coughing he started to bring up bile. This episode passed quite quickly. We saw a doctor who said that Andrew had a virus, nine days afterwards he biled up and had sickness all day; this episode was worrying. Five days later he was biling while in respite; the staff were understandably concerned. Six days later he was sick twice and biled four times. I was not convinced of the doctor's opinion that this was a virus; it had started in April and continued into June. My gut feeling and my motherly instinct were telling me that the problem was in some way linked to Andrew's bowel condition.

At Andrew's next appointment at the hospital, a very welcome one, as the sickness and biling became more apparent, an X-ray was taken of Andrew's lower abdomen. I told the doctor that I was concerned Andrew may be impacted and that was possibly the reason for the sickness and biling. The doctor said he would call us with the results of the X-ray. My motherly instinct was right, Andrew was found to be impacted. I imagined that this was going to be a difficult time for us all, and so it proved. We had to clean out Andrew's bowel at home; this would consist of a regime of Movicol: day one had to be two sachets; days two, three and four were four sachets; days five, six and seven were six sachets, until I got to days eleven and twelve when I had to give him twelve sachets. This proved difficult because we could not take Andrew anywhere in case he had leakage. I had to make sure that Andrew did not have bitty diarrhoea, but unfortunately we got a fair bit of diarrhoea with undigested food and mucus.

In the middle of July, Andrew began to bile again. We were amazed; having just had Andrew on a regime of Movicol, how could he be impacted again so soon? I called the Royal Free for advice, their advice was bring the medication down to two sachets of Movicol and if this did not help they would see Andrew before his next appointment. Andrew was in respite for a few days and while there he did not have one bowel movement, but when he came home he had four, almost one after the other. It was very typical of Andrew not to open his bowels when not at home; it was also very worrying. The biling continued as did our frustration, who could we turn to, where were we to go to get help for Andrew?

During August 2006 Andrew biled up all day, I phoned the out-of-hours GP, he said to take Andrew to the local Accident and Emergency department. Andrew was seen quickly. The doctor, after examination, said it could be gastritis or gastroenteritis. We had to make him drink copious amounts of fluid and see if he could keep it down. An X-ray was taken of his abdomen and, as I suspected, he was impacted again. I had by now the experience to know, through Andrew's behaviour and through him biling on many occasions, that he could not keep any food or liquid down because he was so badly impacted.

We were given a specified dose of Movicol for Andrew to take. They were unsure about whether to admit him, but had decided that because he had settled down he could go home. Once home we gave him boiled water, which he could not keep down. We contacted the Royal Free the next day but no one returned the call for three days. I called again and spoke to a paediatrician; I was told that someone from the gastro team would call me. Once again we were told to give him Movicol, four sachets on the Thursday and four again on the Friday, then to bring it down to two. I could have screamed. I was told to take Andrew to the local hospital if there was no change.

Andrew continued to bile and we noticed very small bits in his diarrhoea that were black in colour. He also began again urinating in the strangest places. During a two-day stay in respite, he was again unwell, coughing, yawning, biling. We decided that enough was enough, I phoned the Royal Free and they agreed to bring Andrew's appointment forward three months. The appointment was memorable only for the fact that on the way up to the gastro-clinic I had this overwhelming feeling of déjà vu, somewhere in the parent-doctor conversation would come the word Movicol. I wasn't wrong; amazing, I thought to myself, I am now a qualified mind reader. However, a positive was on its way.

The consultant suggested a barium meal X-ray. Andrew's autism made any invasive test while awake impossible, how were we going to cope with Andrew's behaviour during the procedure? A suggestion was made to put Andrew on a milk free diet. We felt that there was now a little hope the barium meal may give some answers to Andrew's constant sickness, we always tried to remain hopeful when new ideas were suggested but inevitably we were to be brought down to earth with a huge thud.

The big day arrived on October 2006: the barium meal X-ray. Emotions were running high and answers were anticipated. We were on the north circular with Andrew being sick in the car on the way to the hospital. How much more would this child have to go through and how much more energy would we, his parents, have to find to help him get through this? We arrived, settled him onto the ward, and waited. What were we to expect? Would this be easy? Would Andrew be calm? No, because Andrew's fears and non-understanding did not allow for any procedure, we would be lucky if on seeing the dentist Andrew would allow him to look in his mouth and count his teeth. The nurse arrived with the tube, which had to go through his nose and into his stomach. I had a dilemma, I had a child lying on a hospital bed who could not tolerate any medical procedure and I had his dad, who could not bear to see Andrew in any kind of distress. I know Colin well enough to know that he would find it quite easy to tell the nurse to stop. I had to balance my feelings for both Colin and Andrew; I thank God for my determination and more than a little persistence.

I had to encourage both my son and his father through a traumatic time, Colin held the bottom half and I held the top half, Andrew struggled, cried and was in a great deal of distress, he was sick twice before the nurse came to his bedside. Andrew may have been a young lad of nine years of age, but he had great strength; two attempts had to be made to get the tube into his stomach because he was so distressed. To ease the upset I had said to Colin that this test might give us some answers. The tube was finally secured and we were taken to the procedure room where Andrew was sick again, having been so distressed he had worn himself out and was now very calm. On the way home Andrew was sick twice.

A few days after returning home we decided it might be a good idea to get Andrew tested for milk allergy. I was told that the test would only show up an immediate allergy; the test was done but came back as negative. We then received a letter from the Royal Free concerning the barium meal X-ray, it was noted in the letter that no malnutrition was found.

At the end of 2006, Colin and I sat down and talked about what we might do next. We began giving Andrew soya milk; this made a remarkable difference to the sickness but no difference in the bowel condition. One of the doctors at the Royal Free had said that being impacted could be the cause of Andrew's sickness. Well, excuse me, but I had been saying the same thing for months. ARRRRGGGHHH!!!!! However, I am only his mother. A hospital X-ray had again shown impaction. We had to put Andrew on Docosote[ii] twice a week with Movicol, and if there was too much diarrhoea, to take the Movicol down to a certain amount.

Unfortunately, on January 19th 2007, the same scenario began again: coughing, yawning and biling, but if Andrew was impacted we were to expect this. The question was, why was all the medication not getting rid of the impaction. At this time Andrew had been on Movicol for nearly two years and with various other constipation medications since three years of age. They had always treated the constipation, but not the diarrhoea or overflow. The doctors, however, were not looking at the cause of the problem, just the symptoms. While in respite he appeared to be lethargic and in pain, his glands were swollen and considerable diarrhoea followed. The next day, large watery diarrhoea, a sore dry mouth, coughing and a temperature. When would this end?

Movicol was causing Andrew to experience spasms of pain in his stomach, the higher the dose the worse the pain. It was very hard to see Andrew in pain from the medication, we wondered if a more mild form of medication might be better. We put Andrew on Lactolose[iii] to try and ease the constipation. I remember quite vividly sitting uncomfortably across from the consultant at our next appointment waiting for the next hammer blow to fall. I was not disappointed: 'You are just going to have to manage his constipation with medication'. So responsibility was now given to us, his parents.

I recall Colin saying to the consultant: 'With all due respect doctor, we have been attending the Royal Free for many years with Andrew and all you seem to do is send him home with constipation medication, perhaps we should stop coming'. I jumped in at this point and said 'No, no'. I wanted Andrew to continue under the care of the Royal Free in the hope that further research may be done to assess children with bowel conditions; maybe one day the Royal Free would take responsibility for diagnosing and treating this condition. We were given a further appointment. Despite our constant hard work and resilience, we felt broken; it seemed that this was how it was going to be and that there was nowhere else we could turn. I did not think it could get any worse; how wrong could I be?

In April of 2007, another bout of sickness from Andrew led us back again to the local accident and emergency department and sure enough, mother's intuition, call it what you will, Andrew was impacted again. Once more Movicol was advised, to come back in the event of any more sickness. It seems quite remarkable that a young lad of ten years of age would have to suffer a medication for so many years and this fact simply emphasised that there was obviously something seriously wrong with his bowel. No more tests were offered and no help, it seemed medically neglectful to allow a child with a bowel condition to live by means of constipation medication and not want to investigate the condition.

I had originally had great respect for the gastroenterology team at the Royal Free but as the years rolled on and the regime there changed that respect dwindled away. How, I wondered, could they leave my son to suffer as they had done, what was stopping them from researching the bowel condition? Where could I go now? I was already at a centre of excellence. It was surely not ethical for a child to go through his young life from three to eleven on medication, while suffering from inflammation of the small bowel, that went untreated. If as the NHS maintains, every child matters, why is Andrew being left to suffer like this?

By the end of 2007 Andrew's episodes of sickness had been greatly reduced but the diarrhoea and constipation were still ongoing. It seemed that all of our efforts to get the doctors to take

Andrew's primary condition seriously were to no avail. The journeys to the Royal Free had becoming tedious and unproductive; it had become an effort to make them. There were many times over the eight years when we were worn down, that we could have accepted the superficial view of doctors at the Royal Free but what would have been the point of this? As parents, we are tuned in to our children, I know when they are ill, sad, frustrated and in pain. What purpose would I fulfill as a parent if I weren't aware of my children's needs?

In January 2008, Andrew had to be brought home from respite, he was sick. We kept him off school and I contacted the Royal Free once again, for advice. As on other occasions, I have to apologise for sounding like a broken record, his sickness was due to him being impacted once again, etc. The hospital called back advising one sachet of Movicol and Lactolose and keeping a diary until the next appointment. So off we set again in February 2008, with the diary I had kept. I was desperately hoping for a little interest. My intention was, as it had been for the last eight years, to make the doctor listen to my concerns; that was always my intention – to make them listen.

From the way the consultation was going I wasn't even hitting first base. The doctor examined Andrew and requested an X-ray. X-ray done and back to the doctor. After a short discussion I expressed my views on the medication, it was no longer acceptable to us that Andrew be put on more medication. The doctor lit up the X-ray, and mum was proved right again, Andrew was so badly impacted that they suggest he either come in for a cleansing prep or we embark on another regime of Movicol. By this time I was almost literally climbing the walls, my frustration was obvious to see, I grabbed Andrew's notes and said I'd had enough of the Royal Free and would take my son to America where there were doctors who would help him.

The doctor grabbed the notes back and said 'no, sorry, you can't take them, they are hospital property.' She attempted to calm me down and informed me that a new study was underway to look at why autistic children had slow bowel mobility; I asked if this research would be put into a medical journal? 'Yes' she replied, 'but not for a while'. I proceeded with my questions and told her that I had now lost all my faith in the Royal Free, she wanted to get another consultant to talk to me before we made that decision.

The doctor returned with the consultant who seemed concerned that we wanted to leave the Royal Free; but not unduly concerned. His laid back approach was almost uncaring in respect of us feeling unheard. I saw a letter on the desk in Andrew's file, which I should have received but had not. It was written by a consultant who had just left the Royal Free. It said 'we cannot be sure of the condition of Andrew's bowel at the moment because no tests have been carried out since 2002', which shows how interested they had been. At the same appointment I broached the fact that I had proof of inflammation in a letter from the Royal Free following Andrew's colonoscopy and endoscopy.

I was told that the biopsies showed superficial inflammation and told again that this problem required no drugs, my interpretation of superficial is that the inflamed area is affected on the surface; superficial or otherwise is still inflammation. They were treating this condition not with anti-inflammatory drugs, but with medication for constipation. I suggested that maybe because Andrew's bowel hadn't been investigated since 2001, that further investigations were necessary, my suggestion wasn't welcomed, the consultant's thoughts on the subject were clear. The hospital was not happy to perform such an invasive test because there was a risk of a perforated bowel and also a risk with general anaesthetic. I asked what the procedure would be if a child was admitted and clearly needed these procedures, the reply was that they would only perform *if it was necessary*.

The consultant was concerned regarding Andrew being impacted, but not concerned enough to help him it seemed. Even if Andrew had been admitted for a cleansing of the bowel, we would still have to manage him with medication after the procedure. With the problems Andrew has with his bowel, he would no doubt be impacted again; this would just be an ongoing situation. We felt the time had come to walk away from the Royal Free. I felt that they were probably relieved too; they would no longer have to fight the questioning that had become a major part of our visits.

As we walked out of the doors away from the hospital, I was overcome with relief, our journey to get Andrew treated at the Royal Free had come to an end after seven years. What, if anything, could the Royal Free have done for Andrew? Well, he was never offered a scan, which would have given a clearer picture of his bowel and its condition. He was never offered a marker test – it's a procedure where you have to eat pieces of plastic and then have an X-ray; the plastic pieces would show up in the X-ray if there were a problem. These non-invasive tests were never offered, so my feeling is that the doctors at the Royal Free declined to help Andrew. I do often wonder if Andrew had been a child with no signs of autism, would their attitude to him have been different?

If I could sum up the caring nature of those I had met at the Royal Free, it would be by reflecting on the following consultation in early 2008. I was at that time deeply concerned that for seven years Andrew had been on some kind of laxative or other and I made my feelings known to the particular consultant who attended. I questioned the fact that Andrew was now so reliant on laxatives that he could not open his bowel normally, he told me that Andrew needed to be on this medication. I questioned this again wanting only to put my very valid point across, his reply was quite sharp and I felt uncaring, he said: 'take it or leave it, that is what I have told you to do.' What response could I possibly give to such an uncaring remark? In retrospect I had wasted seven years of Andrew's life attending a hospital of great standing that wouldn't or couldn't treat my son's condition.

✤ ✤ ✤

Now Andrew is in the second phase of his journey for treatment and we don't intend to give up. What have I learnt in these seven years, if anything? I have learnt to be informed, to trust my gut feelings, to be assertive, this I have to be. As I remarked at the beginning of the chapter, Andrew has only my voice to speak for his needs. Never let anybody tell you that they know what is best for your child. Be happy to take advice and support where offered – by God you need all the advice and support you can get – but never be afraid to ask questions. Autism, and in this case its preceding bowel condition, is a complex disability that is difficult to diagnose.

You will only know by the sounds that a child makes, i.e., eeeeeee, or a behaviour that is characteristic of autism, such as hand flapping or spinning, no eye contact or a distant look in the eyes, as if they are looking straight through you. As one behaviour diminishes another can take its place. Behaviours can go and then return; I could never be an expert on autism, I haven't got the time, it is hard enough just keeping Andrew safe. I do learn from Andrew every day of his young life and I have learnt that his brother Ryan has missed a great deal of attention from his parents, because autism is such a needy disability.

You have to deal with autism twenty-four hours a day. I can't have a lunch break; I don't have the time to allow for that luxury. It breaks my heart to hear Ryan suggesting that we walk away from Andrew's problems, obviously so that he might have more attention himself. Ryan has often battled with me; it frustrates him that he cannot have a normal brother relationship. Andrew can't communicate verbally, so in some respects it is as if Ryan is an only child. As much as we try to accommodate for the loss of that special relationship between two brothers, it is the relationship between parents and son that has suffered. Ryan has given up so much to allow Andrew's needs to be met.

Andrew has been showing signs of early puberty and I know through various conversations that puberty in an autistic child can begin at an early age. The trouble is that Ryan is also hitting puberty and even though Ryan is two years and five months older than Andrew it was Andrew that was showing the first early signs. Having to deal with two boys who are experiencing changes in their bodies and all that comes with those changes is no easy feat. With Ryan it was a case of answering his questions as frankly as age would allow and reading up on the computer for further information, but how the hell was I going to explain puberty to an autistic child who could not speak and had limited understanding? A near impossibility. I signed the word 'no' to him whenever he showed signs of inappropriate behaviour. As I had said previously, behaviours can come and go and change. Andrew would try to straddle his TV; he became quite obsessive but was discouraged at every opportunity. He is a very sensory child, he liked to wriggle up and down on the leather material, but would often do this when he was nude.

At one point he would not touch any fruit. But even at these times, when things seem hopeless, there can be sudden breakthroughs. For six years I had been trying to get him to eat fruit. He was watching the Jungle Book on the television, his biggest obsession – he has always loved to fast forward and rewind videos, this hasn't changed since he was about five years of age. He was watching the part of the film where the monkeys are eating bananas. He brought us into the living room to unpeel one of our bananas and to our amazement started to eat it. We were amazed but happy, and he has since then always liked bananas.

If your reading this and thinking, 'My God. So, big deal. He ate a banana', you've missed the point; it really is a big deal. To encourage an autistic child to try any type of food can be a battle, because of the sensory aspect of autism. If my son does not like the feel or the smell of a particular food he will just throw it away, if you had been in our living room at that very moment when he took his first taste of a banana, you would have thought we were all raving bonkers. We were jumping up and down laughing and clapping our hands; I think I almost squeezed the life out of the poor child. What an amazing moment.

With all that wonderful, positive advance, also came the worry. If Andrew could copy something he saw on a DVD, we would have to be constantly aware of what he was watching. Andrew had no sense of danger or fear. He could easily attempt to copy something that was dangerous. We are always trying to be one step ahead of Andrew, which has not been easy at any time, we have to keep all doors and windows locked, because Andrew is what I call 'an escaper' and given the opportunity would run away. We would leave his fan light window open when he went to bed and when we woke up in the morning there would be an array of items in the front garden: books, soaking wet nappies, toys and perhaps a sleeping bag half draped from the window.

He would throw out items quite randomly – from faeces to toast. You would find items in the strangest of places. I would wake up in the morning exhausted from the night before, move the chair to hoover and find crisps, rice cakes, chicken nuggets, books, pencils, underpants and pooh, amongst other things. Andrew could surprise us with some normality and then lose it in seconds, he is very capable on the computer and likes us to put 'You Tube' into the search engine, he proceeds to type in the word 'teletubbies' and watches all the clips. He will then take himself into the kitchen, find a cup and urinate into it. As his parents, we can often be proud and disappointed at the same time. It is quite an education to see what he is both capable and incapable of.

Nothing for Andrew can be out of place, everything has to be straight, he will straighten chairs if they are sitting at an angle, books must be straight, the kitchen mat has to be straight. He will not get into bed until he has performed a bedtime routine that consists of the bathroom door being in alignment to the wall, he insists that I pull the toilet chain and put the toilet seat up, then he puts his hands behind his ears, does a little dance in my bedroom, switches my bedroom light on and off, blinks the amount of times he has switched my light on, then tries to jump into his bed before he has turned my light back on. I tuck him into bed, attempt to leave the room, he jumps out of bed then has another little play with the light switch and tries again to beat the light, then he will settle into bed. He has a temperature control problem and once in bed will remove his pyjamas; we once allowed him to walk into the garden completely naked in the snow, he jumped onto his trampoline and began jumping, as if it were summer.

Andrew has some understanding and will find a way of telling you what he wants, he communicates with his pecs pictures,[iv] but will take you to the kitchen if he is hungry and he will give you his cup if he wants a drink. Andrew has, since this all began, drunk copious amounts of fluid. He became very bland in his eating habits, preferring rice cakes to any other food. His etch-a-sketcher is a great source of fun to him, but he wants me to write words for him at the most unusual times. If I am having a lay down he will often come and wake me up just so that I can write a word for him, or even in the toilet: he will come and find me.

I was one of over a thousand parents who took to the high court in the hope of gaining recognition that my son had been damaged by the MMR vaccine. After legal aid was denied in the ten-year old case, ten parents of vaccine-damaged children formed the MMR10. Jennifer Horne-Roberts, the barrister, was resilient in her quest for justice for all the children and parents, and in particular for the MMR10, who she guided through the Royal Courts of Justice. We were denied justice and went on to the European Court of Human Rights (ECHR) but to no avail. As with other parents, I was asked by the court to state the difference between my son's case and the other lead cases. This was something that I could not do because no information about the lead cases had been made available to me.

The reason I mention the court case is because in my Answer to Lord Justice Leveson on this very question I added some of my feelings. It was something I had thought long and hard about and I wanted to be as clear as I could about how Andrew's disability could affect him in later life. Below is part of my response to Justice Leveson's question.

I am never going to get back that normal growing boy that I had before the MMR vaccination. I fear he will never be able to go to work, drive a car, get married and have children of his own. Something I was told many years ago: if an autistic child does not speak by the age of eight then it is very unlikely that he ever will. And do you know what really hurts, is that he will never be able to say 'I love you Mum' and even more painful for myself and Colin is that he will never be able to understand how much we love him.

What then is the future for Andrew? Now as he reaches his teenage years it is almost impossible to envisage him any other way than the way he is. This is Andrew. However, so often I think that this is Andrew in relation to me; who will Andrew be when I am no more?

Endnotes

i. **Movicol** (Mov-ik-ol) is a medicine which is used in constipation and faecal impaction. Movicol contains macrogol 3350/potassium chloride/sodium bicarbonate/sodium chloride. It is supplied by Norgine Pharmaceuticals Limited.

ii. **Docosote** is given to make stools softer and easier to pass. It is used to treat constipation due to hard stools, in painful anorectal conditions such as hemorrhoids, and for people who should avoid straining during bowel movements.

iii. **Lactolose** – Medication to soften faeces.

iv. **Pecs Pictures** – Picture Exchange Communication System (PECS) is a form of augmentative and alternative communication (AAC) that uses pictures instead of words to help children communicate. PECS was designed especially for children with autism who have delays in speech development.

CHAPTER SIX

Jodie's Story

The first year of Jodie's life was full of joy. She was so lovable, yet so full of mischief, and together with her big sister Candice there was never a dull moment. At her Christening Jodie blew a raspberry every time the Vicar tried to speak. The families present were in stitches, although the Vicar did not appear amused.

Less than two months after her first birthday our lives changed dramatically forever. On 17th May 1993 we received a card to attend for the MMR vaccination and after much thought we proceeded to have this done. On arrival at the Health Centre we were ushered into the waiting room. Jodie's name was called and Pat carried Jodie in for the jab. It seemed like less than a minute when I heard a high-pitched scream, which made my blood run cold. I realised the scream was from Jodie and rushed to the room just as Pat came out. Pat said that the syringe was already made up and the nurse was very rough. I looked at Jodie, pale and shivering and looking as if she was in shock and all the time screaming, a scream like I had never heard before.

Although Jodie had previously had a very good appetite, now we were only able to coax her to drink. All previous abilities like the beginning of her speech disappeared and her appearance became like that of a zombie. She seemed oblivious to everyone as if we did not exist. We made numerous trips and calls to the surgery; they were all in vain as help was non-existent. Despite the fact that Jodie was soon keeping us busy 24 hours a day we were unable to obtain financial help. We tried the doctor one last time for help in August 1994.

After being told by a GP to shut her in her bedroom and let her cry it out, we blew our top. We phoned the health visitor and warned her to visit or we would contact the police. When the Health Visitor did arrive she agreed there were very obvious problems with Jodie and it was agreed that she needed urgent diagnostic assessment. At this time Jodie was not eating, had lost speech and eye contact and was clearly in extreme pain. She was not sleeping and appeared to be lost in her own little world.

Unable to leave Jodie and work, mortgage arrears had built up and we were facing eviction from our home. We decided to contact the Disability Living Allowance department to explain our situation and to enquire whether financial assistance could be obtained. The DLA department sent a Dr Ritchie to our house to examine Jodie to see if she qualified for help. The doctor was convinced that Jodie was entitled to the allowance, and from 1994 she was awarded the highest rate. Alas, by then the mortgage arrears were too high and in Febraury 1995 we lost our home.

We were given an appointment for Jodie's assessment at our local hospital in January 1995 under a Dr Christine Smalley, who suggested that Jodie should be in full-time care as she would never know even her own family; we refused this suggestion. An appointment was then made for Jodie to attend Wordsworth House – a day nursery where her behaviour could be supervised. We were invited to attend a meeting to discuss Jodie with seven female doctors involved with the children who had special needs attending the nursery. In the event, Pat had damaged her back and I attended alone.

I was shocked by the lack of knowledge displayed by these doctors. One suggested that Jodie be put on Ritalin, without listening to the details of Jodie's problems. All the doctors were adamant that bowel and digestive problems, for which there was no treatment, were an inevitable part of Jodie's autism.

In June 1995, when Jodie was only three years old, she began attending three days a week at Ridgeway House, a school for children with Severe Learning Disability. In November of the same year we were allocated a three-bed roomed house, which meant a moved back to the area we had been evicted from. At this time we also began seeing a new consultant, who felt that Jodie needed an MRI scan; his view was that Jodie was not autistic. After the scan was carried out in January 1996, we were told that it showed no abnormalities.

Soon after this we discovered Salterns School, a school for children with Severe Learning Disabilities; it was near to our new home, and we successfully applied for Jodie to change schools. For a while this seemed to be a vast improvement. We spent much less time attending appointments, as it was much easier to get to the school. The school was also aware that I often took Jodie out for a car drive in the night when she was unable to sleep and when she was tired, they allowed Jodie to rest during the day.

Life continued in this fashion and in July 1997 we were approached by a parent who was very interested in the pattern of Jodie's behaviour. She introduced herself as Julie Baugh, and so began a series of conversations that the school clearly disapproved of. Julie told us that her son had been normal until he was given the MMR vaccination. We listened in awe to the similarities between Jodie and Mrs Baugh's son, particularly with respect to how they had regressed after the vaccination.

While the medical advice we were receiving at that time amounted to being advised to let Jodie suck on a peppermint when she suffered colic, Julie told us the problem needed expert input and the only real experts were at the Royal Free Hospital in London. We were given the contact details of Dr Andrew Wakefield, one of the few doctors with the courage to investigate the children's problems.

When we spoke to Dr Wakefield he suggested that Jodie's problems may amount to something more serious than colic and he advised us to contact our GP and request a referral to the clinical team at the Royal Free. When we contacted our GP, Dr Greenland, she stressed that she would need to see Jodie before she could advise referral, but after seeing her, she agreed to it. At this time Jodie had not eaten any cooked food since her vaccination and was little more than a skeleton.

In December 1997 we kept an appointment with a local consultant who stated that Jodie had much improved. In January 1998 we saw Professor Walker-Smith at the Royal Free Hospital, who immediately gave Jodie an X-ray. Shocked by her condition, he refused any further treatment until her blocked bowels were cleared. He also stated that she was different from the other children he had seen previously and that her problems were more severe.

A urine sample was· taken from Jodie and sent to Sunderland University for testing after which we were contacted by Mr Paul Shattock, who said that there were some unexplained differences in Jodie's urine sample, when compared with other children with autism whose samples he had analysed. At this stage Mr Shattock asked us to provide the batch number associated with Jodie's MMR vaccine.

When we approached the local clinic, we were told that on 17th May 1993 Jodie had been given the diphtheria-pertussis-tetanus (DPT) jab. We immediately contacted Jodie's GP, who said she had also had the MMR and to go back for details. The records showed that Jodie had been given one vaccination containing two multiple vaccines each of which had three constituent parts and one single polio vaccine mixed in – seven vaccines in all. We were not aware that the DPT had been added to the MMR as we had refused consent for these, which was recorded. We had just been turned down by the Vaccine Damage Payments Unit (VDPU) and appealed against this decision citing this latest information and were invited to attend the appeal and let doctors assess her damage.

When asked what evidence we were taking we replied, Jodie and proof of her higher rate DLA. Our appeal and the award were turned down because they would not accept that MMR causes autism. Our MP and a health minister took up the case. They argued no one had mentioned Jodie's other serious medical problems or the other vaccines. Our MP stated to most people, including John Denham, the Health Minister at the time, that there was no doubt Jodie was vaccine damaged. He also questioned whether the unit was acting properly. Sadly after questioning the actions in parliament, he gave up the fight. One small thing missed was a statement from the VDPU, which said that owing to the problems in this case, they might need to alter the way that they make decisions.

We got so frustrated as time went by that we eventually went to the police and asked them to take an assault charge out against Dr Allison Hill, the person who ordered the vaccine cocktail. We believed that the moment the skin had been pierced by vaccines we had refused, then an assault had taken place. A child protection inspector agreed, but warned us politics would stop him from finishing the case. The case was examined and put to the Crown Prosecution Service. They in turn contacted Dr Elliman of Great Ormond St. for a report. His decision was the DPT and Polio were administered but not the MMR.

Our complaint was that we had not given permission for these vaccines and the refusal was in writing and on record. The MMR and its batch number were clearly on record. At the same time we were pressing Alexander Harris solicitors for our MMR case to be changed to a consumer protection one as the MMR was contaminated with other vaccines. They refused and also ignored our written request to change solicitors. They too tried to make Jodie's case an MMR case, ignoring all other factors. No one else would help.

We complained to the GMC who surprisingly agreed the act was unprofessional; unfortunately they said that even if the doctor had signed consent she could not be blamed if the nurse who gave the jab acted incorrectly. We were shocked at the way the doctor seemed to be able to avoid responsibility for giving consent despite our refusal for the other four vaccines to be administered.

We had a new problem, when, in April 2000, the new consultant refused to look at Jodie. Pat quietly told him we would not go until he did. He said he had no experience of autism or the type of problems that Jodie had. Jodie's behaviour had changed little from the day of the vaccination; she continued to scream in agony, vomiting her food and needing many car rides to quieten her down. In June 2004 the local hospital agreed to admit her to an annexe to see if they could identify the problems.

Jodie was given a stomach X-ray, which showed an object, although not in her stomach. This was ignored and the doctor ordered Jodie to have a feeding tube inserted. She fought them. Clearly there was a problem. When the tube was in Jodie pulled it out. I refused to let them reinsert the tube. We asked for an X-ray as her sickness increased. When they had inserted the tube they had pushed down a dimmer light cap she had swallowed. She was sedated and the cap removed. The radiologist was not happy and a further search found two 2p pieces.

Also in 2004, Brian Deer was on the scene making a film for Channel 4. He contacted us to try and get permission to film the X-ray being taken and also asked to film Jodie at school; both requests were refused.

After many more digestive problems a fundoplication operation was suggested. This is a process where a band is fitted to prevent acid reflux entering the oesophagus. By this time huge ulcers had formed that could not be left untreated. I mentioned to the doctors her bowel problems that the hospital had never looked at. A colonoscopy was carried out and the pathology report confirmed exactly what Dr Wakefield had described with respect to the bowel problems. After the operation we were told Jodie could not possibly be sick in the future because the acid could not return past the band.

Also a Professor Warner confirmed the problems were all linked to an allergic reaction of long standing. However, all allergy tests taken were normal. We asked for mercury levels to be tested, but the hospital was unable to do this test. We noticed that Jodie's fits were getting worse. We were ordered to increase the dosage of Lamitrogine. We almost lost her when she began fitting continuously even in hospital. I complained that the dose of tablets was too high at double the maximum daily dose for an adult. The dosage was halved and the fits eased.

Ever since the vaccination Jodie had suffered so much, and the pain would never go away. When the group MMR litigation was stopped in 2003 we raised the issue individually of negligence in the administration of seven vaccines in one syringe, this despite a refusal. If we had known anything else was being added we would not have shown up at the clinic.

With Dr Fletcher and help from Keith and Jenny Horne-Roberts we managed to obtain legal funding and we arranged for a local solicitor to act for us. Not surprisingly any chance of a break-through was being held back by the Legal Services Commission and the Special Case Unit. We were told not to communicate with anyone connected with the MMR litigation or funding would be stopped. The expert for us complied with every stipulation and simply asked if Jodie could be mercury tested. Our funding was stopped and we are now awaiting an appeal date.

In 2007 Jodie's problems continued and she was still toe walking and had become unsteady on her feet. The sickness was almost continuous and the fits were causing us much worry. On one occasion she collapsed and went under the water whilst bathing. Pat was with her luckily as she insisted Jodie could not be alone. We were told that everything known had been tried and failed. An appointment with a neurologist led to Jodie being given a second MRI. A condition was discovered which had been missed in the 1996 MRI. On Dec 3rd 2007 Jodie was admitted for an operative procedure to correct a 'Chiari' malformation. This involves lifting the brain and tonsils back into position.

Following the operation Jodie has spoken odd words like mum, hello and dad, which was the last word she spoke on the day she was destroyed by the illegal vaccination. She has been seen kicking a ball, cuddling and kissing family, walking on occasions flat-footed and attempting to sing. The sickness that used to be continuous has now become a rarity. She is also much more alert and aware. We wonder if this condition had been picked up earlier could life for her have been better. Jodie is now happy with one drive in the evening and Pat and I have rarely missed a night's sleep. The life-threatening convulsions are also far less frequent and not so severe. Since writing this chapter we have found that Jodie has a mitochondrial disorder and this has made us aware of the real need to test children before vaccination.

We have no doubt that Jodie was left disabled by a combination of vaccines that has not and never will be tested for safety. This illegal concoction was deliberately mixed in one syringe and it destroyed our daughter. We will never give up our fight to obtain justice for Jodie.

CHAPTER SEVEN

Futures for Billy

'He doesn't look very well', the nurse said as I proudly presented my 12 month-old son for his MMR vaccination.

'He's not', I replied, 'He's on antibiotics for another ear infection.'

'Bring him back in a month's time, but don't leave it any later. Children like Billy who suffer from ear infections could burst an ear drum or even go deaf if they catch measles ... bring him back in a month.'

I marched off with Billy's 'red book' neatly tucked under my arm. Yes, I'd be back in a month's time, exactly a month's time, there was no way I would allow my son to be made deaf by measles!

I look back at this now and I can't believe how I behaved. What was I doing? My mother brought me up on homeopathy and nettle soup; had I learnt nothing? I was now obsessed with being the perfect mother, the mother that ticked all the right boxes in the little red book that came when the health visitor gave your baby his first check-up.

❊ ❊ ❊

Jon and I met in 1988 in The Peak Health Club in Cadogan Place, London. Jon was the manager of the club and I was working as a presenter for a programme covering 'What's on in London?' I had to interview Jon about what it takes to be a fitness instructor. I still have the interview and I still laugh when I watch it.

After five years of living together on the 'golden strip', Fulham Road in London, in a flat that quickly became known as 'the all night café' – everyone and anyone would turn up at anytime – Jon left The Peak and set up as a fitness and health consultant and I ran around presenting, acting and body doubling for Sophie Ward and Charlotte Rampling. Life was fun.

Jon asked me to marry him one evening in 1992 on Wandsworth Bridge. I had told him once that when I was a drama student and working evening shifts in The Ship pub, I would walk over that bridge and if I couldn't make my mind up about something by the time I reached the other side I had to go with the last thought and that would be my decision. That's where we became engaged. After we were married we carried on living in our 'all night café'.

Nothing changed until I became pregnant with Bella, I carried on working until I was unable to hide my bump and then I had to stop. One Sunday, while heavily pregnant we visited friends in Hampton, Middlesex. My pregnant friend and I heaved our way around Bushy Park, I'll never forget that day; it was beautiful. Jon and I came away from there knowing that this was the place we were going to live.

We moved to a pretty three bed-roomed terraced house in Teddington, Middlesex and Bella was born on the third of January 1995. Easy pregnancy; easy birth. Bella was a bright bubbly baby. I was always going to go back to work so when Bella was two weeks old, my agent called me up with a casting in central London. Great, Jon looked after Bella, and off I set to London. I was fine until I tried to park the car; the space wasn't even small; I couldn't park it. I tried so many times. In the end I called Jon in tears.

'Come home darling, Bella and I miss you', he said.

I called my agent and she said, 'Go and have your babies and come back to work when you're done.' That's when I decided to become the 'perfect' mother. Bella was a star and it was all very easy.

When Bella was only six months old, I realised I was pregnant again. Apart from a course of antibiotics for a tooth infection and a reported 'hole' in the placenta that was 'nothing to worry about and very common', the pregnancy went smoothly. Billy was born on April 30th 1996; again an easy birth.

I didn't breast feed Billy for long; there was no excuse. I was running around after Bella who was 18 months old and 'a bit of breastfeeding' to me was better than none; he went straight onto SMA for hungrier babies as advised by my doctor friends. Billy only lasted four months on the bottle before we had to give him a cup with a lid, he used to suck the teat so hard that within seconds the teat would be vacuumed back into the bottle; this happened every time.

The health visitor insisted that because Billy was so hungry we should start him early on solids. So as soon as Billy sat up at five months, I started feeding him lovely little 'gluten' sticks. I gave them to him everywhere, in the supermarket trolley, in the car at home, at playgroup. Billy was happy and strong. At two, three, and four months Billy had his DPT vaccinations. All was fine until he started a nasty cough at five months.

'He needs some antibiotics', said Jon one morning.

'You're right', I said and sped down to the doctors.

In Billy's first year he had six courses of antibiotics for ear infections and chesty coughs. When the doctor told me to 'come back if he doesn't get any better', I did. They knew best and I wanted to be a perfect mother. He flew through his hearing test, nine-month check and all other baby clinic tests. He played with his sister, after chasing her in his baby walker he would pin her against a wall. They would giggle hysterically.

At 11 months Billy had a nasty case of chicken pox. Bella also caught it and I remember bathing them both in oatmeal together – apparently it eases the itching. Billy had a worse case, but he was on antibiotics so we knew he'd be OK.

It's becoming harder to write this, knowing what we know now.

So, just after Billy's first birthday I took him for his MMR; only to be told that he didn't look well enough to have it. A month later, to the day – I had actually marked it on a calendar – I was back at the doctor's surgery. Billy had just finished yet another course of amoxicillin. He had taken so many that he was starting to vomit as soon as they were given to him. I couldn't give it to him anymore. Jon would do it because, like me, Jon believed that 'doctors know best'. Billy wasn't any better than before he started the course, so the nurse said, 'He looks like the type of child that is always going to be chesty and coldy. Most boys are.'

So on the 30th May 1997 at 13 months old, Billy had the MMR.

That night Billy developed a high fever, we gave him Calpol and put him to sleep in his cot with his beloved drinking cup of milk; he was now on cow's milk straight from a carton, slightly warmed. The next day he was restless, he cried a lot and maintained a fairly high temperature. That evening I went to check on him and he was lying in his cot shaking uncontrollably. He seemed cold. I grabbed a blanket and wrapped him tightly and held him close. Later I found this was the wrong thing to do.

My sister, Rosie raced over to sit with Bella while Jon and I dashed to Kingston Hospital. In the car I held him tighter and tighter, Jon kept talking to him, 'It's OK son, we'll get you some help.'

'He needs a massive course of antibiotics, he's probably had a reaction to his jab, it's quite common. In future don't wrap him up; you should have stripped him off and let him cool down', said the hospital doctor.

We watched our little boy sitting on the examination table, shaking, his teeth chattering. His cheeks, tummy, tops of his arms and legs were scarlet. Another young doctor came in and gave him a jab of yet more antibiotics. 'Take him back to the doctors if he is still like this in 48 hours', they said.

Well, guess what, he was, and we were prescribed a 6-week course of antibiotics 'to really blast everything out'. Billy was vomiting so much on the antibiotics now; he couldn't even drink his milk without projectile vomiting.

'What are you doing?' my mother said one day, 'Try homeopathy, it worked for all of you.'

I didn't listen, Jon's family were doctors and doctors knew best.

Billy deteriorated fast; he lost the few words that he had. Within a week he started to reject most foods, he only wanted Weetabix, milk, apples and his bread sticks. We tried to encourage him to eat vegetables, meat, and all the foods he used to love so much. He would throw his head back against the chair, banging it repetitively and screaming this new high pitch scream. He lost a lot of weight and eventually his hair started to fall out. But the very worst part of all of this was his diarrhoea. It was frightening; it was liquid and endless; it seeped through any nappy and into everything.

I took him back to the doctor.

'Does he eat lots of apples?' he asked.

'Yes, he loves them', I replied.

'Good. Don't worry, it's perfectly normal, just toddler diarrhoea, keep him hydrated.'

So I did, but it made no difference. Bella was starting nursery and Billy was sick. Even though Jon and I didn't say it, we knew something was badly wrong with Billy.

As the months went by he became increasingly withdrawn, his high pitch scream was never ending, his head banging continued day and night. His tummy was swollen, yet he carried no weight. He drank gallons of milk and watched Spot the Dog videos all day. But worst of all he didn't seem to know Bella or us, he simply ignored us. By this time I was pregnant again.

'He's deaf', Jon's father, a GP from America, said to us one day.

'You need to get him checked out.'

Within weeks Billy was at an ENT specialist. A month later he was taken to hospital for a grommet operation. We were told, 'If your son does not have this operation his eardrums are likely to burst'. He was rushed through the system as an 'emergency'. I'll never forget that day; they couldn't get him to 'go under' with gas and air. I sat with him in my arms; they seeped the gas lightly above his head, so as to not frighten him. The next thing I knew I was going under too and was 'helped' out by a nurse. I remember them picking up my screaming Billy and holding him down. He eventually went under; they said they had never seen a child take so long to go under.

What annoys me to this day is that straight after the operation they came to tell me that because Billy's adenoids were so large they had taken those out too. They didn't ever seek permission and we still feel that it was a completely unnecessary operation.

When Billy was 18 months old, the health visitor turned up for his routine check. After asking Billy to 'Brush Dolly's hair', 'Point to his nose', and 'Pick up a book', it was blatantly obvious that Billy had a serious problem.

'I'm going to refer him; he is showing strong signs of autism', she said. Then having told me to wait, and not to worry, she left.

All I could think about was how I was going to tell Jon. Jon had always wanted a son and always wanted a 'Billy'. We used to talk for hours over Long Island iced tea in the 'Goat and Boots' on the Fulham Road, about the cricket, football and rugby games to which Jon would take Billy. Billy was Jon's dream and somehow right at that moment I felt he was a dream I had somehow ruined.

These thoughts quickly turned to anger. This can't be right. My Billy who was so strong, so happy, chubby, gorgeous, bright ... everything a parent could ask for. Now this. Why? Why? Why?

Trying to digest this new information, I had to pick up Bella from nursery; I scooped Billy up, screaming because I had interrupted his precious Spot video. We were early so I took him to Bushy Park opposite the nursery. Billy ran and ran. I stood at the entrance to the park and watched him, he clearly had no idea I was there; he didn't care; he never looked round; he just ran and ran. A rage ran through me like none I've known before, and before I knew it I was running faster than ever, shouting his name over and again, seeing no response, not even a head turn.

I grabbed him, turned him to me, and held his face in my hands, 'Where's Mummy?' I yelled, 'Where's Mummy? Look at me, Billy, what's happened to you?'

I was shaking him, I was out of control, but I couldn't stop. Billy showed no response. When I eventually let go, he turned and ran just as before in his own world, utterly separate from me.

When I eventually got him into the car, the only place I could contain him safely, I sat listening to his screaming. I stared straight ahead willing myself to cry or feel something that would make me feel better. But instead I just felt a massive anger, so strong, so unlike anything I have ever felt before. I was rooted to the spot unable to move. I just remember this burning anger, anger that I have never felt since and hope I never do again.

We went through the rigmarole of doctors and psychologists and eventually we got our diagnosis. Severe autism with severe speech, language and behavioural delay. The National Autistic Society sent us a depressing list of books to read. We looked up autism in the library and it told us that it was the most severe form of mental illness with no cure and most, if not all those affected, will be institutionalised.

Jon and I cried every night for six months listening to Billy banging his head, crying or screaming his now familiar high-pitched scream. Our friends and family irritated us; we answered the phone to no one.

Helpful comments such as, 'They must have got that wrong', 'No, he's too young', 'He'll grow out of it', or 'Well, it's not our side of the family…' just made us feel worse. Jon and I didn't discuss Billy with each other; it was too painful. There was nothing out there and no one that could help us.

I remember when a family member had a miscarriage at 12 weeks; the family rang around with updates on her health and suggestions about what we could and should do to make everything better for them. I lost it after the millionth conversation and said shockingly, 'Well, I'm sorry for her, but guess what … I would give anything right now to swoop Billy's situation with her. Yes, let's all plant a tree for her baby, let's all write letters, but my situation isn't going to go away and from where I'm standing it's going to get a whole lot worse. So, please don't talk to me about her miscarriage anymore – at least she has an ending to hers. What about my son? What's going to happen to him? Me? Jon? What? What? What?'

Even now that isn't easy to write and people reading this might rightly be horrified, but the pain and loss we experienced then, with no help, was too much to bear. How can a child develop normally and then so suddenly decline?

Billy was now so difficult to handle that we couldn't go anywhere. If we didn't turn right outside the front door he freaked. We couldn't take him shopping, to get new shoes, eat out. Nothing except the 'turn right' outside the door route. On one occasion I attempted to take Billy to a local playgroup. We were asked to leave within an hour. Billy kept banging the kitchen door over and over again, another of the repetitive and on-going things he did day and night. I was told to find a more suitable playgroup.

One day a newspaper cutting came through our door from a neighbour who had seen me struggling with Billy: 'Gluten and Casein Free Diet could help children with Autism'.

This was Billy's only diet: bread, Weetabix and gallons of milk. What the hell was he going to eat now? Jon wasn't convinced and having talked to his 'doctor family' and friends who told him that it could actually be dangerous to take Billy off such essential nutrients, he really wasn't keen. I did it anyway. We had nothing to lose, Billy was a living nightmare and Jon and I were at our wits end. I fast became an expert in reading food labels, making gluten-free bread and baking anything that Billy might eat without the criminal gluten or casein ingredients.

Toby was born on the 14th April 1998 just before Billy's second birthday. It was an easy birth; he was handed to me straight away.

'Open your eyes Polly, he's OK, he's gorgeous', said Jon.

An earlier scan had indicated that Toby was too small so I had convinced myself I was going to give birth to a thumbnail of a baby. Toby weighed 8lb 3oz and Jon was right, he was perfect. Exhausted from an all night labour, I soon fell asleep. I woke up three hours later to find a nurse handing me Toby wrapped snugly in a blanket. 'We let you sleep', she said, 'Don't worry, we looked after him … oh, and here's his certificate of vaccination!' I was handed a certificate to say that Toby in his first few hours of life had been given the TB vaccination.

So, I had a newborn baby, a two year old with severe autism and a three and a half year old daughter who needed to play with her Barbie doll constantly. Jon was working all hours to make ends meet. I ran around with a double buggy and Bella running as fast as her little legs would carry her to keep up. Billy was still massively obsessive about 'turning right' outside the front door, so most days it took an awful long time to get anywhere.

The difference I saw in Billy after taking the gluten and casein from his diet was huge but we were still far from having an easy life. He stopped vomiting, he started to acknowledge Jon and me; by that I mean we had occasional eye contact when we called his name. His diarrhoea calmed down, not water anymore but more like the diarrhoea that you would expect from a child with a stomach bug. Now, I realise this was unacceptable, but when you are living with it day and night and no one can help you, you begin to accept all these factors as 'autism'.

We quickly realised we needed more space and having made almost double on our little house, we moved to Hampton to a bigger house with a good sized garden.

Jon came back from work one day, stepped over Billy as he always did with his usual greeting of, 'Hi son, Daddy's back'. There was no response as normal and I, as usual, was ready with a glass of wine, ready to move the subject on.

That day, Jon was excited. He told me about a woman in America called Victoria Beck that had given her son a pig hormone called secretin and had seen amazing results. Secretin stimulates the pancreas to release digestive enzymes; that's all we knew and that was good enough for us. Jon could get this from his father in the States; so all we had to do now was to get someone to administer it. I hadn't seen Jon so happy in ages. He was adamant that we tried this, as he said:

'We have nothing to lose, Billy can't carry on like this.'

Before I knew it, we were in London with the only doctor in the UK that seemed prepared to risk giving Billy the secretin injection. Dr David O'Connell knew little about autism but told us that for science to move on, things had to be tried. The *Tonight with Trevor MacDonald* documentary team followed us and filmed everything we did.

It might seem odd that it was only now in the summer of 1999, that we had our first experience with the taboo subject of 'MMR'. We did a general interview about Billy and his little life up to that time and Jon talked about Billy's decline after the MMR vaccination. None of this was shown; it was all cut ... not mentioned.

After the secretin, Billy did the largest stool ever (think cow pat and double it). We saw a really dramatic change in our son: eye contact better; tummy less swollen; and, most magical of all, speech – not much, just counting to ten – but we heard his voice. What happened after that was surreal and it all happened so fast.

London Weekend Television (LWT) said then, and still says now, that the programme brought the highest rating for a programme on the *Tonight with Trevor MacDonald* show. We were personally inundated by literally thousands of emails from parents desperate for help. Help? How could *we* help?

What followed from that first public foray into treatment was to change our lives. Jon went into massive research mode: why was

Billy doing so well on the secretin? He rang everyone whose name and telephone number he could get hold of. He found that, far from us being alone, there was a whole community out there, concerned with and working on the problem of vaccine-induced autism. Jon puts most of his early help down to Bernie Rimland, Paul Shattock, Rosemary Waring, Paul Reichelt and Rosemary Kessick. It was then that we first started to hear the name of Dr Andrew Wakefield and his research.

The other consequence of our appearance on the programme was that mountains of emails flooded in daily. What was I supposed to do with them? I couldn't ignore them nor could I answer them. One evening my wonderful brother Jamie came over for a drink; we sat in the garden chatting and I showed him the files of emails and letters we had received.

'That's easy, Polly, you know what you have to do – set up a magazine and let everyone help each other. If there is no one out there you are going to have to do this yourself and you'll get help with Billy too. If anyone can do it Polly, you can.'

It was then that Jon walked out into the garden.

'I was just showing Jamie the autism files we've got', I said.

'There's your name too', said Jamie, 'I bet every parent of a child with autism has an autism file.'

I spent the next week sifting through the mountains of emails. Most wanted help; a few offered words of advice. I contacted parents that had stories of treatments that had or hadn't worked; they were all keen to write.

My brother set up a website, my sister worked out some sort of subscription system. I met a designer and sourced a printer. Jon and I rang a few companies and begged them to advertise, it wasn't hard; everyone was so supportive.

In the autumn of 1999 *The Autism File* was launched with the help of my brother Jamie and my sister Rosie. Jon threw himself into researching treatments and diagnostic testing. He constantly asked, 'Why?' I suddenly had a husband who was enthused and happy. His life, he said, was now dedicated to Billy and others like him. He also started talking medical gobbledygook but I didn't mind that, his feet were still firmly on the ground, his life now based on trying to help Billy and other children like him.

Through *The Autism File* we started reporting on tests that we did with Billy and others; parents wrote in with their stories and experiences, people that we hadn't known existed. We began to realise we weren't on our own and we started to learn so much from others. Jon quickly worked out that Billy's problems were gut related and after his first Defeat Autism Now! (DAN!) Conference in 2000, he came back on a mighty mission.

'We can do this, we can help Billy', he said.

He buried his head in research and theories and started writing it all down for each issue of *The Autism File*. Meanwhile, I collected every story I could from parents and professionals and printed them.

In the first issue in September 1999 I printed a letter from a man called Garry Maher; the letter was titled 'Big Cover-Up?' It was about how the DPT and MMR vaccination were damaging our children. I also printed two more in that first issue titled 'MMR Vaccination' and 'Autism and MMR'. They were both written by equally angry parents who wanted to know why the Government were still insistent on using the vaccination when so many children were being damaged by it.

This was my first experience, as an editor, of what happens to you when you publicly speak out against the MMR vaccination. We received a couple of letters from anonymous writers warning us that we would not stay in print if we carried on publishing such dangerous claims.

Jon was stuck in the world of diagnostic testing and was busy testing Billy, in fact all of us, for everything imaginable. We used all our savings and started to borrow money in the hope of getting an understanding of Billy's illness.

It was difficult, of course, to keep away from our GP, with whom we obviously wanted to share our information. Jon went to see him, armed with test results to try and get a viral antibody test conducted on the NHS. All I can remember is that less than an hour later, he came flying through the door with a face like thunder and an unprintable statement about the GP.

That evening I picked up the phone to hear our GP at the other end of the line. The following conversation took place.

'Can I speak to Mrs Tommey?' he said.

'Speaking', I said.

'It's about your husband, Jonathan.'

'What's the matter?'

'I think he may need some psychiatric help.'

'Why?'

'He asked for unnecessary tests on your son and when I explained that we couldn't possibly authorise any tests on a child that has a behavioural disorder Jonathan slammed his fist down on my table and messed my papers up.'

'Why are you talking to me about all of this, I thought patients had a confidentiality agreement with their GPs?' I asked.

'In my opinion he needs help. He thinks he's going to recover his child and that Billy was somehow damaged by MMR. This has been proven to be ridiculous and parents sadly are using this to make themselves feel better', he said.

'Billy was damaged by the MMR and my husband is right. Our son needs these tests; we are already seeing improvement', I said.

'I can see we are going to get no further with this conversation, but please be careful what you print in your magazine as you will cause a lot of families more pain with your unfounded accusations.' And with that he put the phone down.

In Issue 3 of *The Autism File* published in the year 2000, Jon wrote an article titled: 'Is Billy another Victim of the MMR Vaccine?' Here is an extract:

> The biggest breakthrough we have found since my report in the last issue is that Billy has a high reading of antibodies to measles. Dr Singh found Billy to have a high antibody to measles reading of 6.3 in comparison to a reading of 3.15 for the normal control reading. This is double the value ... Why did this not show up in his earlier viral antibody test conducted here in London two months earlier where the results showed negative? This could indicate an active measles infection. Dr Andrew Wakefield at The Royal Free found a number of children with autism with gut related disorders have a measles virus present in the dendritic cells of the colon ... and so it goes on.

The phones went wild, mostly supportive, but a few odd calls and cancelled subscriptions. One GP told us that we were a danger to other families with autism and that he would be taking this further; did we not know that 'Dr Wakefield was in it for the money' and we were all buying into it?

That just made me so angry. We were not 'following' Dr Wakefield anyway. We were living the situation for real, this really happened to our son and we wanted some answers. All Dr Wakefield was doing was listening to parents and trying to understand the problem.

The issues went on; the stories about vaccine damage grew. I tried to keep a balanced view in the magazine, but too many were writing in with the same stories. We quickly realised that 'shouting too loud' about Billy's decline was going to get us nowhere; and fast too. None of the big autism organisations wanted to be associated with parents who were perceived as 'hysterical'.

One leading autism organisation which was also 'shouting out' about MMR and the damage done told us that we were new parents and what did we know about autism? We were told to leave the 'shouting' to the professionals. We soon realised that there was competition between the autism organisations; something I won't tolerate and people who now read my regular 'Polly's Piece' in *The Autism File* will know that I feel very strongly that only by working together will we get the answers we so badly need. There is neither room nor time for rivalry and competition in the autism world.

Our advertisers didn't like it, some readers didn't like it. As far as we could see there was no benefit to writing or talking about what happened to Billy to anyone, very few wanted to listen or be associated with it. In 2001 we made an appointment for Billy to be seen at the Royal Free Hospital, we waited in the waiting room with Billy for two hours. Billy freaked, and Jon and I couldn't cope. We left with Jon saying, 'We'll do this ourselves'.

In 2002 Jon signed up for a three-year degree in Clinical Nutrition, a subject much neglected by the medical profession; he was determined to help other children with autism.

This was a financially hard time for us. I took a job as a drama teacher at Bella's school and between us we just about kept the magazine going. It was a tough three years. We moved again into a beautiful wreck of a house that we planned to 'do up' some time in the future. With Jon off mixing with course mates and me having to cope with three children on my own, in a 'new' house, I felt isolated and under pressure. Needless to say we came through those difficult days.

We still had to be 'careful' about how we wrote about the MMR. We quickly realised that if we were too outspoken about it then doors closed, advertisers pulled out and subscribers were frightened off. One woman, a well-known figure in the autism world, who I won't name, rang me after the first day of the GMC hearing.

'I want to pull my article out of your next issue', she said, 'I saw you on television at the opening of the GMC hearing, you know, the one with Dr Wakefield ... well I won't be associated with bad science.'

'It wasn't me', I replied, 'Sadly I couldn't attend as I was on a plane coming back from America.'

'I have it on good authority that it was you and I won't be associated with people or magazines that support this nonsense.'

I first met Andrew Wakefield after I interviewed him in 2006 for the magazine and gave everyone a small insight into what was going on at that time. As soon as we went to print, all hell broke loose and we had a barrage of abusive phone calls. Most were of the same ilk, 'Wakefield's supporters will never win'; 'Carry on as you are and your magazine will be finished'. Sometimes they were quite frightening, but our good friend Paul Shattock reassured us that we would always come up against this stuff. He insisted these 'creatures in the woodwork' were everywhere and we shouldn't let them get us down.

The calls from parents into the office – then, and still today a bedroom – were getting more desperate, day by day. Ann Jones, a friend I couldn't live without, who is the back bone of the magazine, Jon and I were answering numerous calls and emails from parents who couldn't get help either from their GPs or schools, or funding for biomedical treatments or educational help in any area. The sheer desperation from some was heartbreaking. Many we couldn't answer, but there was always someone out there, mostly a parent, that could. The magazine was working.

One day a man rang me from the M1 motorway. He wanted to commit suicide, his son was damaged and he couldn't help him. He didn't have the money to pay for treatments or the energy to carry on. No support was coming from anywhere. I talked to him for over an hour and at the end of our conversation he promised me that he would go back to his son. The bottom line, I told him, is that no-one else was going to fight for their son like his parents; they can't, it's a love thing and it's hard, really hard, but we can't just give up. I said, 'If you commit suicide, then what? They win and that can't happen. We are a team, we have to lean on each other and learn from each other and then we'll get the answers.'

I recognised next that certain members of mine and Jon's family, certain friends and perhaps worst of all people that work within the autism world started warning me. The warnings were diverse:

'Polly, I've just read the paper and Dr Wakefield's work is unproven. The MMR is safe and you have to accept that you were wrong. It might have felt and looked to you that Billy was affected by this jab, but really so many studies have been done on this and they all say the same thing. It's OK to be cross and need to blame something, we are all cross too. So, come on, try and move on and talk about all the other wonderful things that are going on in the autism world.'

'Polly, it's all a load of rubbish, we are doctors and I'm sorry but you'll just have to accept that this is propaganda made up by a doctor that wants publicity and you are falling for it.'

'Polly, come on … my children have all had the MMR and they are fine, I really think you should just accept Billy for who he is.'

'Polly, be very careful what you say, try and step down a bit from this, otherwise you are seriously going to affect your charity. Now, you do want Billy to have a future and build one for others, don't you?'

'Polly, I am also a mother of a child that was potentially damaged by the MMR, but I have learnt to keep my mouth shut and so should you. I'm afraid that if you carry on like this, then I won't be able to work with you.'

The list goes on and on, and it still does. Every dinner party we get invited to, I check to see if any GPs are there. Jon and I have lost friends over these parties. It's always the same old thing: the doctors say it's a load of rubbish and we tell them the way it is. Jon is particularly good at this as he often blinds them with stuff they quite obviously know nothing about. They always finish with the same old patronising line about how Jon and I should 'Get out more and try and accept that the MMR is safe'. We have also lost a few close friends through our refusal to back down on this.

We've fallen out with family members, mainly on Jon's side, as they are GPs who refuse to listen or even try to understand. This particularly hurts Jon who cannot understand why anyone who knew Billy before and saw what happened to him could believe 'the media' over what really happened.

The more we spoke to parents and professionals in the autism world the more we learnt and without realising it, we were changing; our lives were changing. We could not tolerate 'friends' that didn't understand or support what we were beginning to see. Through our contact with readers of the magazine, it was a much bigger and more serious problem than just Billy and a few others; there were a great many more than we could have imagined, most too frightened to speak out.

❖ ❖ ❖

So where are we now? Jon is running his clinic helping children and adults with autism to improve their health and lives; he is also working closely with doctors from around the world to set up The Wellness Centre associated with The Autism Trust, here in the UK. This will be a place where all families and people with autism can get help in any area of treatments including biomedical, alternative and educational. How I wish we had had access to such a place when Billy was so sick.

The Autism File is now worldwide with Spanish and US editors, and we retail in many countries. It's still an ongoing battle and as I write I am thinking about how to replace one of our main sponsors; one that has just pulled out over my recent reporting on the GMC hearing and controversial interview with David Kirby on his recent visit to the UK. Will we stay in print? I hope so, as *The Autism File* is an important 'voice' for autism. I have to keep saying to myself that what will happen will happen, but I will not be bullied into keeping quiet over something so serious, much to the frustration and warning of many around me who still constantly advise me to keep quiet for the magazine and The Trust's sake.

I gave up my job as a drama teacher. I had enjoyed putting on plays and not thinking about autism for short periods but I had to begin working full time for the magazine. We sold our 'done up' wreck of a house and downgraded to a similar smaller wreck and invested in new phone lines, proper computers and a bigger bedroom office. Ann and I work flat out with Jon in between his ever-mounting clinic work.

Billy is doing really well. He speaks, which is something I am so grateful for; it's not great at times but it's brilliant at other times. He twisted his ankle at school yesterday and when I asked him what happened he said:

'The stairs did it Mummy.'

'The stairs did what Billy?'

'They tripped Billy up; I need to go to hospital!'

So, we haven't exactly got typical speech for a 12 year old, but through the work I do I am all too aware how very lucky we all are to hear Billy's voice at all. Billy doesn't respond well to 'interventions and educational therapies', in fact he hates them; we have tried so many. 'Exercises are for school', he always yells throwing a wobbly every time. Maybe he's right. Billy is a very happy boy who now has high functioning autism.

There are people out there that try and encourage us to 'push' Billy more, but somehow I feel that with Jon keeping a check on his wellbeing, Billy talking and happy, maybe things should be left as they are. We nearly live like a typical family with Billy, although it's hard for Toby, who is now 10. He says he wishes Billy didn't have autism; he wants a brother to play football for more than 10 minutes without him wandering off with no explanation. We are very fortunate that Billy has done so well on his biomedical treatments, goes to a good school, and generally has progressed as he has.

We now share the greatest worry for all parents with children like Billy: what is going to happen when we, his parents, are no longer around? It's almost too painful a question to address even in our minds. So, we have set up The Autism Trust with the help of Oliver Jones (our Chairman) to build futures for Billy and others like him that need ongoing support in developing their skills and fulfilling their potential, but above all to build a place where they will be safe and happy. We owe that as an absolute minimum to these children whose lives should have been so very different.

I hear of so many families with children like Billy that haven't had such good results, many can't afford treatment, many haven't the energy or the time, few have support and so many are tired; tired of fighting the doctors, the legal system, the educational system, their families; everything is a constant battle to fight for your child's rights. Parents feel guilty but they shouldn't have to.

Help should be free and readily available, but it's not, and the real battle to get the Government and the medical profession to act on behalf of vaccine damaged children rather than against them, has, I fear, only just begun.

Perhaps I should have made clear something earlier in this chapter; I am not against vaccination. My daughter had everything and is bright and fine. From the work that I do and the people I speak to, I know only one thing for sure: There is a subset of children that simply should not have had vaccinations at the time that they did or indeed ever. I cannot and will not accept that sufficiently comprehensive studies have been carried out on the MMR yet and that it is 'totally safe'. This is simply not true. My son and thousands of others like him are living proof of this.

Why the denial? What is so important that the truth is being kept from new parents and more children get damaged every day as a result? If we are to continue vaccinating at the rate we are with no prior screening to test for a compromised immune system, to look at genetic predisposition, mitochondrial dysfunction and the child's medical history, then the number of autistic and vaccine damaged children will continue to grow and the personal and social problems related to their health care will become a time-bomb. The problem has nothing to do with Dr Wakefield; he is just a part of the solution.

What began as a medical problem has become a political issue because of the intransigence of health officials, the Department of Health and the interests of the pharmaceutical companies. Parents are getting angrier and the politicians are heading into a storm the scale of which they don't realise. Our numbers are growing daily; enough is enough and, in this case, enough is far too much.

To the 'powers that be' that make and enforce these vaccinations I would like to say it doesn't have to be like this. No one is saying that you should stop the vaccination programme, but even if one child is damaged then that's one child too many. No money is worth a child's life and that child's potential. When it's your child that is damaged by something that is preventable then nothing is more devastating.

If a 'social contract' exists between the Government and the people and if everyone agrees that vaccination is necessary, then the Government has to massively increase safety testing and research on vaccines. It has to institute testing for vulnerable children in every GP's surgery. It has to stop denying the existence of any vaccine damage and make adequate financial and social provision for any of the small number of children who might still be affected.

I simply speak as an informed, passionate and caring mother, who has seen her precious child's future snatched from him by expedience and production-line health treatment. That just can't be right in any decent, caring and developed society.

CHAPTER EIGHT

Disgusterous!

When Jan and I married in 1980, we both agreed we had three things in common. We both loved beer (real ale, none of this new fangled imported lager stuff), live jazz (especially the trad jazz scene around the south London circuit of Young's Brewery public houses) and thirdly, curries. We had a standing order table every Friday night at our favourite restaurant for over three years. Beer, Jazz and Curries: a good basis on which to start any long-term relationship!

For many years, Jan commuted from Kent to London in her career in the Ministry of Defence (MOD). The early 80's were exciting times to be in Whitehall. Post punk, post miners, new age romantics, this was a period of rapid change. My career in food manufacturing was progressing moderately whilst Jan's career accelerated in the MOD and took her to a three-year posting in No 10 Downing Street, to the Prime Minister's Private office. I should stress at this point, this was a Civil Service appointment and not a political appointment. From humble beginnings, Jan found herself working with a very select few, providing a back office function of information gathering on all the major events of the day, which were briefed firstly to a team of four Principle Private secretaries and then on to the PM of the day.

During the first three months of Jan's appointment to Downing Street she witnessed at very close quarters the end of the Jim

Callaghan era, when he lost the vote of 'no confidence' in the House, and the beginning of the Margaret Thatcher era. Thatcherism had arrived. It was not unusual during those early days of her term in office to see stalwarts of the Tory party, the Tory grandee's coming out of the PM's private office, ashen faced and speechless from the grilling they had just encountered. It was clear from the start that she was 'the iron lady' long before the term was publicly attributed to her. Many of the old guard in the party were not to be seen twelve months later: the Thatcher revolution had begun.

Our daughter Elizabeth arrived in 1988. Were we proud parents? You bet we were! In May 1990 our son Thomas arrived. He was a big lad weighing in at a very healthy 9lb 8 oz, Jan being a rather petite five foot two inches. All seemed well during the first few months with just one exception. Thomas's head circumference was growing quicker than normal, so at six weeks a scan was arranged at Great Ormond Street to ensure there was no evidence of hydrocephalus or 'water on the brain'. All clear, and the rapid growth was just put down to a large baby, a small Mum and the babies head just regaining its normal size after birth.

As a consequence of this event, Thomas was formally reviewed and monitored at three monthly intervals by a Consultant Paediatrician at the Kent and Canterbury Hospital. Each assessment passed without issues arising, and at nine months we were formally told that Thomas's development was ahead of the norms on all counts. At nine months he was already cruising around the furniture, and at 12 months we recall how he stole the show at a family wedding. Lizzie, by now a very polite three-year old, was doing her sisterly duties by introducing Thomas to family and guests at the wedding. No sooner was Thomas introduced when he took control of the gathering. Laughing, giggling, clapping hands and wholesale eye contact was the order of the day and Thomas already knew how to grab an audience from his delightful sister!

At 13 months, his records reported 'advanced in his development', he had double sounds and was standing up. The only concern noted on his medical records was his persistent cough.

Between Lizzie and Thomas the MMR vaccine arrived, or as it was marketed then 'the triple vaccine'. We were pleased; only one shot so less grief for all. As for side effects, we were the sort of people who had never read a product leaflet in our life, and certainly no one had any discussions with us about risks. No one asked us about Thomas's continuous chest infections over the previous months or the bout of chicken pox a few weeks earlier. There was no need for us to raise these points because anyway the doctor had this all in his medical notes.

Thomas had his triple jab on 12th June at age 13 months. Supplied by Meriux Immravax, Batch no D1400. The impact was not immediate, but over the next two weeks Thomas started to lose his spark. He just slowed down, slept a lot more, and started to get grumpier. Another wedding, two months after the triple jab, turned out to be quite the opposite of the previous one. Thomas virtually slept through the whole event. He made no attempt to 'grab the audience' as he had done before. I especially remember when the disco started up. Thomas's pram was next to the speakers, and the music came on suddenly and loudly. I went over to remove him from close proximity to the speakers and was very surprised that he had not woken; he was out for the count.

Something was clearly wrong, we gave ourselves the usual re-assurances: growing phase, typical boy, don't worry he will soon be babbling ten to the dozen. My career was on the move, literally, and we were in the midst of planning a relocation from Kent to Dorset. We felt we needed to push for more medical investigations, but saw no point in starting something in Kent that we could not see through. Better, we thought, to wait until we were settled in Dorset. Who knows, we told ourselves, by then this phase will probably have passed us by. We were probably just over anxious parents and anyway, why concern our families when our move from the region was enough to worry about.

Contact with our new doctor in Yetminster, Dorset, came immediately after our move, as was a referral to Dorset General Hospital. The company that I had joined, indeed invested into, ran into serious cash flow problems the month I arrived. We were a long way from home. Suddenly these were worrying times. Dr Barker, Consultant Paediatrician at Dorset General Hospital moved assessments along at a brisk pace, starting with an EEG and culminating with an MRI scan at Weymouth General Hospital. This was to be the first (of many) general anaesthetics for an MRI scan, and with regret, Jan had to deal with this one on her own. Picture this: a grubby waiting room, with most of the furniture damaged and broken, no children's ward and Thomas is booked onto an adult ward. In the bed opposite was a large woman. On second glance, not a large woman but a Les Dawson type transvestite complete with plastic earrings and gaudy jewellery. Jan describes it as a scene from Clockwork Orange. Returning to the ward, Thomas was still sedated from the anaesthetic and now the transvestite was cruising up and down the ward. Jan could not get out of the hospital quickly enough. On leaving the hospital, Thomas vomited violently, covering Jan in bile. Jan had to remove her trousers in the car park before driving some 30 miles home in her underwear.

This was the first of many low points and we became frightened. What follows are two parallel stories, tracking the medical and educational aspects of the next fifteen years.

The Medical Story

The letter arrived… *'Please, come in to discuss the recent assessments'*. Thomas was now just three years old. A relatively minor abnormality had been found in the EEG. *What are you saying: has he got brain damage?* Well, yes, you could say that. *Is there anything that can be done?* Well maybe a trial treatment of drugs, but not sure if it will help. He might have autistic features.

Devastated, we left the consulting room. Dr Barker held me back as Jan tried to escort Thomas out of the room. *Two bits of personal advice Mr Crean: firstly only one in five marriages survive the stress of a mentally handicapped child and secondly, if I were you, it might be best for Mrs Crean if she were to have another baby.* That was it. Signed off, might try a drug trial that may not work, stick together and pro-create to keep Jan busy with another baby. The impact on us was hard to describe.

We went back to Dr Barker saying we wanted a referral. *No point,* we were told. Not good enough we said. But he has some sort of brain damage, and all we have had is an EEG. We need some detailed scans of the brain to find out what is going on, a neurological review. *Well, maybe, perhaps, OK, but not before a drug trial* we were told *and the Paediatric Neurologist, Dr Kennedy from Southampton does not see any referrals until the outcome of a drug programme is completed.* Busy man obviously, and we had to wait six months. Tegretol was prescribed and stepped up to maximum dosage of 500mg per day.

Repeatedly we reported that Tegretol was having no positive effect, that it simply dulled all his senses and he became much more aggressive. As an aside, we wrote to Ciba Geigy, the makers of Tegretol, asking for more details on its effects. Three letters and several phone calls resulted in no responses over a six-month period. The referral to Dr Kennedy finally came through nine months later, in March 1994. Thomas was by now almost four years old.

'Language development disorder' was the conclusion, probably related to the macrocephaly (the large head). *Come off Tegretol,* we were told, *there is no track record for Tegretol resolving these types of problems, Thomas's development will be down to education, good luck with the education.*

We were speechless. We concluded that the prescribing of Tegretol was a stalling mechanism, a pre-condition to see a Consultant Neurologist. We felt our confidence and trust had been bluntly abused. We asked our Consultant Paediatrician for a second opinion. Clearly Dr Barker was getting embarrassed with our persistence, and our challenges of her colleague, Dr Kennedy, but by now we did not care about her feelings. At this precise moment in time, our trust was lost.

We did not get a second referral, so we went privately to Manchester and saw a second Consultant Paediatric Neurologist. This was the first of many long journeys to overnight hotels. General questions and answers followed over a thirty-minute consultation. The outcome: *Good chap, Kennedy, new his father well, we went to the same medical college, sure his opinion is right and good luck with the education. Oh, and do give Dr Kennedy my personal regards when you see him next.*

It was a long, lonely and silent drive back from Manchester to Yetminster. Jan cried silently and in desperation. I tried to concentrate on the road, not knowing where we were going to go next. That was it: signed off by the neurologists at a stroke and we had nowhere else to go. No follow-ups, no further investigations as to what might be wrong with the brain, no guidance, no direction medically at all. Just a referral to the Maudsley to confirm his lack of communication and confirm the autistic label.

It just did not fit. Thomas was so loving to his Mother yet he would often bite and hit his long suffering and loving sister Lizzie. Thomas would regularly hit me if there was any attempt to interrupt him watching repeated viewings of 'The Shoe People', 'Postman Pat' or 'Rosie and Jim'. Thomas would actively engage in eye contact with Jan but not with us: he was being selective, he could make choices, but he had no language to support him.

Lorna Wing implies in the opening paragraphs of one of her books on autism '*when you are told that your child is autistic you will not accept it'*. So that was it, we were in denial. As parents we had missed the early signals of what was to be known as the 'onset of autism'. We simply felt this was claptrap, a catch-all approach to something that was much more complex than a single label definition which starts with parental denial.

We were not going to be told we were in denial about Thomas's early development. We had the medical records to prove it: 'advanced in his development'. At one year of age, we all went to Portugal for a holiday on Thomas's first birthday. He was enthralled by the plane and was making all sorts of engine type noises. By his second birthday, he did not even react to a plane flying low overhead.

Neither Jan or I could accept that there was to be no further medical investigation. Neurologically, *'relatively minor abnormalities with the EEG'* (June 1993) was all we were being given. A drug trial was being proposed. All too grey. How could the specialists know what the remedy was to be unless we had a clear and full understanding of the condition of the brain structure? One EEG was simply not enough. And what was the cause of this *'minor abnormality'*? Was the cause still there, would it continue to make the minor abnormalities progressive, could it become a *'major abnormality'*? For me, I had to know the condition of the brain <u>and</u> the cause. Cause, condition and cure, to us it was that simple. If we knew the first two, cause and condition, then to my simple mind we could logically develop a strategy towards a cure.

Jan already had a clear view on the cause. Something had changed and gone dramatically wrong at around 14 months, at around the time of the triple jab.

I should explain that over the next two-year period, we actively fought against the autistic label for a number of reasons. Firstly there was evidence of an EEG abnormality; was this the cause of his language loss and behavioural problems rather than autism? Secondly we knew the autistic label closed off medical involvement in Thomas: we had been told clearly by the medics that his progress was all down to education. Thirdly, and importantly, Jan had now seen several schools for autistic children and was deeply depressed at the lack of intervention with the children. If the autistic label stuck, Thomas would be consigned to such a school.

Finally there were so many other things that were going wrong with Thomas. Things that were not included in the definitions of autism that we had researched. Why did Thomas keep falling over: even Dr Barker at Dorset General had noticed him 'dropping' in the consultation room. Why did he perspire so much at night, and often sleep for very long periods. What about the excessive drinking of apple juice and Ribena (a concentrate bottle could easily go in just two days). Why did Thomas gorge on certain foods, breaded products especially: it would not be unusual for Thomas to consume five packets of crisps in one go. What about the grey eyes, the pot belly and the explosive poos? We were not prepared to let Thomas be written off neurologically, with an autistic label that we believed did not fit all of these other aspects of his condition.

I remember coming home from a two-week business trip to the States. I arrived to find Jan in the hall, trying to wipe excrement off the walls of the stair well. Thomas had not made it upstairs and had one of his many 'explosions'. None of this fitted the autistic label. The Maudsley had said autism, and Lorna Wing told us in her essential book on autism that as parents we were probably in denial. The neurologists had shown no interest: good luck with the education, next please! Sure Thomas had some autistic tendencies but we were certain that there was something else involved. Surely more investigations could be done. No one was listening to us anymore; we were lost in the wilderness.

Whilst Jan was clear about causation, I was more circumspect at that time. I wanted to go back over the large head debate. Dr Kennedy and Dr Barker had described Thomas neurologically as having 'macrocephaly with language delay'. Was the large head the cause of the problem? Consultations with legal medical specialists resulted in a review of the scans at six weeks from Great Ormond Street Hospital (GOS). They found no problems with the scans or the birth itself, and furthermore this had been confirmed by Dr Appleyard Consultant Paediatrician, at 13 months – *'advanced in his development'*.

A very good former colleague of mine, Rene Wijers from Holland, had sensed that things were very wrong from our long distance conversations. So he came to visit us in Yetminster. Rene was one of the few that had kept in contact over the years. He was a passionate European and with me being a fully paid up member of the 'Euro Sceptic – Save the Pound – God Save the Queen' party, our discussions were always lively! Rene heard our tales of consultations, about labels and the negative impact of the wrong label, and about second opinions and the old boys network. Immediately he wanted to help and furthermore he saw a possible answer to break the second opinion/old boy network problem. He also recognised that he had a potential opportunity to score valuable points in the debate about the benefits of little Englanders being in Europe!

From our home, he rang his neighbour in Holland, a local doctor, seeking the name of a local paediatrician. Rene then rang this person who put him in contact with somebody in Utrecht, considered to be the expert in the field of paediatric neurology. Within just one hour, Rene had made four calls and got all the way to Prof Onno van Nieuwenhuizen, Head of Child Neurology at University Hospital Utrecht, and enquired if he would provide a second opinion! What's more, Rene had made a consultation appointment for us for the following week! My newly found 'European Brother' had opened a door for us, and at last we felt we had a ray of light.

The following week, in November 1994, we all travelled by ferry to Holland and stayed with Rene and his lovely wife Lon. Off we went for our 10 am appointment expecting nothing more than a

30-minute consultation. What a hospital! We checked in at reception and we were issued with swipe cards rather like credit cards. We were given a clear route map of where to go in this huge building and the card was to allow us specific access through specific access barriers. The swipe card allowed us as patients to get free coffee from the vending machines and there was even a high quality shopping mall for patients and staff alike. All a very far cry from the broken chairs of Weymouth General!

Prof Van Nieuwenhuizen is a very tall man (6ft 4inch), thin, a kind of 'Gerald Scarfe' type character. He has a formidable presence, even when sat down behind his desk. Peering over his half rimmed glasses he glared, *Tell me, just why have you come all this way and what do you want to know from me.* We were caught off guard by this frank and direct question. None of the usual stuff about tell me the story from the beginning, how was the pregnancy, etc. etc. that we had been through so many times before. Why do they all do this, why don't they spend ten minutes and read the notes instead of wasting ten minutes and more of valuable consultation time?

We understand you are an expert in your field, we replied, *and we would like to know if we should continue to ask for more investigations into our son's brain damage. We want to know this because we believe that if we know more about the type of brain damage, then perhaps this can help us to better know what we can do as parents to help our son's potential.*

OK, he replied, we will *make that our objective* for the day, and we were immediately despatched out of his office by his assistant. We had expected a consultation of just half an hour and that would be it. We were whisked off by clinicians to a series of assessments lasting the whole day. Speech and language assessments, hearing tests, occupational therapy assessments and a full EEG were all performed during our one day visit, all conducted in English and not a Les Dawson look alike in sight!

At 4pm we returned to Prof Van Nieuwenhuizen. *'You asked me if there should be further investigations to your son's brain. The answer is yes. You suggested that this information might help you to develop your son, and I agree it could help you. The EEG is not normal, you need a place where there is 'higher maths', and I believe you have a right to know what is happening in there. He is not classically autistic. I joined the play session and I could make eye contact with him. His large head is not related to his language delay. I have a very large head, but that is because I have a very large brain. I will send you my report shortly and my recommendations, and put you in contact with the appropriate people'.*

We were speechless. There *was* something else; he would not say precisely what because more investigations were necessary. We were right to pursue these questions, and we felt vindicated in taking this trip to Holland. What would our existing medical team say: we had gone privately outside the system. Would we be black listed? Who cares, we were getting directions, opinions that gave us the encouragement to find out what was really going on. Thomas was now four and a half and what happened next was probably the most bizarre event in our journey so far.

One evening, shortly after our trip to Holland, a cautious caller rang, introducing himself as Dr Neville from Great Ormond Street Hospital (GOS). He carefully enquired about Thomas, checking if we had moved from Kent to Dorset and had we previously been to GOS when Thomas was six weeks old? All points confirmed, an appointment was duly made to see Dr Neville. In fact Dr Neville turned out to be Prof. Brian Neville, head of Paediatric Neurology at GOS. He had met Prof. Van Nieuwenhuizen the previous week at a European Conference in Tel Aviv. They had discussed Thomas's visit to Utrecht. What an ironic situation! First we had the old-boys-network appearing to work against us in the UK and now we were getting introductions at the highest level due to a Super League Euro Conference Network! Perhaps this European thing was not so bad after all!

At our first meeting, I expressed our intrigue as to why Prof Neville had called us directly to make the appointment. When he had been told of Thomas's case, Prof Neville came back to check the records at GOS for Thomas's initial visit when he was six weeks old. It appears the somehow Thomas's records had been marked DECEASED, hence the cautious call from Prof. Neville to check the ground and to be sure that this was the same Thomas Crean. A personal touch that we came to learn over the years was a mark of the man.

Our visit to GOS was to be the first of many, many more with more scans than we care to remember. Somehow the quest for knowledge helped us to overcome the dread of pinning Thomas down whilst an anaesthetist tried to sedate him. God, how I hated this process. Pin down was the only way we could get Thomas under control for EEG, MRI, SPECT scans and angiograms. It took seven grown men to hold him down on one occasion. I would hug Thomas staying close to his face so he could clearly see me, someone he could trust, trying to re-assure those petrified eyes, as finally he gave way to the anaesthetic. Jan could not bear to be in the sedation room and waited outside, and I cried like a baby after each and every one of those events. Surely the scientists and engineers can come up with a better delivery method for sedation, some method that does not rely on pinning the patient down?

But we were getting somewhere. Professor Neville's team at The Wolfson Centre at GOS repeated the tests conducted in Holland and with the benefit of an MRI told us something new. The EEG abnormality, as it had always been called since age two, was in fact temporal lobe epilepsy. Thomas had substantial epilepsy and later we were to learn that there was lesion damage indicating evidence of haemorrhaging. 'Star Wars' was Prof Neville's description of what was going on inside Thomas's head. The multi-disciplinary team under Prof Neville were studying the effects of 'onset epilepsy' and Thomas met all the criteria. The epilepsy affected areas directly related to communication and to the receptive hearing channels. We had a clear cause for the 'drops', the jerks, the absences, the hot sweats at night. Thomas did not have grand mal seizures, the only type of epilepsy we knew, but he had several other types of seizures, sub clinical, temporal lobe, drop seizures, myclonic jerks, etc.

With hindsight, we still do not know why the epilepsy diagnosis was not reached when he was two years old in Dorset and Southampton. There were only ever references to 'EEG abnormality' and 'macrocephaly' in relation to Thomas's neurology in two years of discussion. Were they afraid of the consequences of applying a label of epilepsy?

We had a new label, Llandau-Kleffner Syndrome (LKS): 'acquired aphasia' or, put more simply, onset epilepsy leading to an acquired loss of language. This 'label' changed everything for us. We did not know what was causing the eating/drinking/ diarrhoea: GOS were only interested in 'head issues'. No matter for now, our view was simple enough. The brain was the most important thing and far more important than the gut, and that seemed logical enough. We had lost so much time, time now to catch up, press on, let's deal with the epilepsy and so we did. A series of drug trials followed with mixed success.

With good support from the GOS team we willingly entered into new trials with high dose corticosteroids. This was experimental stuff but we were willing to try and sure enough, we had some breakthroughs. One of several trials proved particularly successful. Jan had noticed that in assessments with speech therapists when word games were being used, Thomas appeared to be very disruptive by picking up the letters and words and throwing them up in the air. To others, this seemed destructive. However, Jan recognised this activity as a mimic action from a Postman Pat video. So Jan started cutting up words and encouraged him to throw them in the air and then let him re-assemble the words. Just like Postman Pat! At last, a medical intervention that improved Thomas's ability to interact, and we discovered that written words were a key to Thomas's attempts to communicate.

Prof Brian Neville led a very talented team at GOS. The team had won significant funding to research relationships between epilepsy and functional disorder such as loss of language, sight, etc. We recognised that we had arrived there at the right time. Janet Lees, Paediatric Speech Therapist, and Victoria Burch, Paediatric Neuro-Psychologist, were two of this very talented team who gave us so much support at a practical and realistic level. Janet Lees heard the Postman Pat letters story and introduced Jan to the concept of *Language through Reading*. Janet provided fantastic advice and support above and beyond the call of duty. This advice was to have a profound effect on Jan's work with Thomas – more on this later.

At this time in 1995, we were in the early days of new concepts for education in autism such as Lovass, Son Rise, The Wisconsin Project, Higashi, TEACHH and others. Most of these strategies seemed to come to the UK from the US, most appeared to be non-directive approaches and none of them seemed quite right for Thomas. This is not to say that these schemes were flawed, rather that in our opinion we were looking for a more word-based and directive approach. To be fair there was also the underlying factor in that we had resisted the autistic label for so long that we had an inbuilt natural resistance to autistic concepts and educational strategies for autism in general.

Victoria Birch helped us to understand Thomas's behaviour and introduced us to concepts such as *replacing bad behaviour with good behaviour*. Simplicity itself to say, incredibly difficult to attain. Ignore the bad stuff, reward the good stuff, create a reward culture. To understand Thomas's aggression towards me was simplicity itself, but only once Victoria had helped us understand what was actually happening. We all knew that Thomas had a great love for his Mum, Jan. So why should I be surprised if after a two week business trip, Thomas would hit and kick me upon my return? *What did you do when you came home?* Tell Jan all about my trip of course and catch up with Jan's events. *Where was Thomas when this was happening?* Sat nearby watching Dad talking to Mum. *You have just broken into his exclusive relationship with his Mum!* Well, yes, when you look at it like that then I suppose Thomas might feel excluded.

So that was why he hit out at me when I came home. I was breaking his personal and continuous link with his Mum! Once I understood this, I would return home and immediately bring myself to Thomas and focus fully on him. The hitting and kicking stopped immediately. Replacing bad behaviour with good behaviour. Simple when you know how: what an understatement!

We began to understand the power of networking to satisfy our need for more information, and we became directly involved in the LKS parent support group, appropriately named FOLKS (Friends of Llandau Kleffner Syndrome). This group was actively encouraged by the Great Ormond Street team who were big enough to realise that they too could learn a great deal from a collective group of parents.

The medics were listening to us, at least on the brain stuff. We had an agenda, there were things that we could do. Until this time we had felt powerless, rudderless. But what about the tummy stuff? And what had caused the epilepsy and the haemorrhaging? I had discounted the large head issue. Jan had always suspected the MMR vaccine, but nobody wanted to discuss this as a possibility. GPs – we went through four in as many years – consultants, clinicians and neurologists, local and national and even Professors simply did not want to discuss causation. In any event Jan refused the booster jabs in 1994: her mind was made up already. Having closed down the possibility of the large head being a possible cause, I now agreed with Jan. Vaccine damage was the likely cause, so no more vaccines. Full stop.

Quietly Jan started to deal with the gut stuff. It came to a head at Christmas 1995 when Thomas was almost five. At our Christmas lunch Thomas chose only to eat chicken nuggets, Alpha bites, banana and tomato sauce. That was it, the last straw. All breaded products went from the freezer, and gluten and dairy free came in. We had heard about Paul Shattock's work in Sunderland, so we did the urine tests and, yes, there was intolerance to gluten and casein proteins. We started to read the literature, proteins, peptides, leaking gut, etc. Whilst consultants debated the merits of the *autistic continuum* we were discussing the *MMR continuum*, starting with mercury, leaking gut, prions in the blood stream, etc.

We realised that this approach – gluten and dairy free – was not in the frame of reference for our supportive medical and clinical team at GOS, for whom we remain always grateful. We just got on with it quietly ourselves, trying to avoid confrontation for fear that the support we were getting would be turned off if we as parents were seen as *troublesome*. We have spoken to many other parents since who have the same fear of the NHS reaction to parental views on causation.

Privately, our GP at that time supported our work on diet and gave us prescriptions for gluten free bread, then over £3 a loaf and then, in 1995, inedible. We also developed some very simple logic to support our view on the effect of the triple vaccine. One concept went along these lines: *If someone had three shots of whisky they might feel drunk. If they had one shot each of whisky, gin and rum, all in the same glass, they would very likely be sick. So it may be with a triple vaccine.* We developed these comparisons in an attempt to describe to others what might be happening to Thomas. For what little we knew of the science behind the debate, we simply felt we would be un-convincing. Hence a simple analogy or two.

The press coverage on the possibilities of MMR and autism links began to appear. Jackie Fletcher (JABS) was asking why no one was investigating our children, autism was on the rise. North London and Californian studies both said so. Una Glenn, Brenda O'Reilly and Rosemary Kessick (AiA) were deep into the science and the links between vaccine, bowel damage and autism. I remember well the AiA conference in Solihull in October 1997: the speaker list was outstanding. I am sure it has been said before, and it should be said again, but all parents owe a debt of thanks for all the work and all the pressures undertaken by Jackie, Rosemary and their respective teams. They put in a huge effort to keep the subject in the press, and in so doing, gave so many other parents the albeit 'cold' comfort that they were not alone.

By late 1997 we knew the diet was having a positive effect. We asked our supportive GP for a referral to The Royal Free Hospital. It took us almost a year to get the appointment with Prof Walker Smith in December 1998. He and Dr. Simon Murch reviewed Thomas's X Ray, at age 8, the first that Thomas had received. *Thomas was heavily impacted 'gross loading of the whole colon', he was 'overflowing presenting as diarrhoea'.* We were told *the base of his rectum was solidly impacted, the mass being similar to the size of a newborn baby's head. This boy was in pain, it appears to be his normal condition and he does not have the language to complain of the pain.*

We were in stunned silence, we did not hear the rest of the meeting and when we left the consultation, Jan burst into tears. Like so many other parents, Jan asked herself why had we let this go one for so long, why had we not pushed harder when we knew it was not right and all the other what ifs…

Liquid paraffin and Picolax followed (laxatives and stimulants). Initially we were not offered a colonoscopy. Like the brain issues and the quest for more investigations, I pushed for the colonoscopy. I wanted to know what was going on inside, what was the condition of the gut. Eventually a year later at the end of 1999, Thomas had a full ileo-colonoscopy. Subsequently measles virus was detected in biopsy samples taken from his bowel, confirmed by Prof O'Leary and the team at Coombe Hospital Dublin.

Thomas has been off anti epileptic drugs for some years now, although there is still some anecdotal evidence of activity. For the last 10 years Thomas has been on medication for his bowel and has been on Picolax all of that time. Picolax acts as a a pre-medical stimulant to empty the bowel. As parents, we tried it, but wouldn't necessarily recommend it; *Liquid-dynorod* would be a better name. The explosive effect is something else!

We can routinely see Thomas's behaviour changing and when it gets to the point where he gets so agitated that he starts fiddling with the collars of other people's shirts and blouses, we all know he needs Picolaxing. Given Thomas's severe shortage of language, he occasionally makes up with his own words. On taking Picolax he will grimace, contort and pronounce **DISGUSTEROUS!** This great new word needs no definition, and forms part of our family vocabulary for anything that tastes, well... disgusterous. It appears that Thomas will need to stay on this regime for life.

I would ask the Chief Medical Officer to try disgusterous Picolax and he would understand our view that this should not be the only option for a decongested life and that there should be more investigations into causation, condition and alternative cures. Somehow I think we all know the answer to that one!

The Education Story

Education was an entirely separate matter. By the time Thomas was four, we had chosen to leave the special needs nursery at Yeovil. Jan was becoming very uncomfortable with the staff attempts to try to include Thomas in busy language based activities. Thomas had lost almost all his language, making phonetic sounds only, and was clearly noise sensitive. These language-based sessions simply distressed him. In time Thomas was 'asked to leave' two other nurseries. The first, our village Montessori nursery – where Thomas had bitten several other pupils – and then a local Preparatory school which had a Pre-prep nursery. It soon became clear that Thomas was an embarrassment. To be fair, Thomas should not have been at either establishment. We were still desperately hoping that just as 'the lights had gone out' so perhaps with the right stimulation they might just start to come back on again, and we could all live happily ever after!

The pressure on our home life was increasing dramatically. Constant fights to get up the ladder of hospital appointments, trying to understand their hierarchies through eight different hospitals in the UK and Holland and all the necessary documentation took so much time. Coupled with my continuous travel to the US, Australia, NZ and throughout Europe with my work, we were becoming exhausted and beginning to run on empty.

We were also increasingly conscious of the impact that Thomas was having on Jan's ability to give time to Lizzie, our daughter. We compensated for this by enrolling her as a day pupil in the local Prep school. This educational choice had the clear advantage of giving Lizzie a full agenda from 8am to 5.45pm Monday to Friday and a half-day on Saturday at school. This was an expense we could not easily afford. Jan had given up her 'return to work' plans mid-way through her degree to retrain to become a teacher. We knew we were likely to remain a single income family for some time.

We were both becoming increasingly concerned about educational provision for Thomas. We were referred for an assessment to a new autistic start up unit at Wimborne in Dorset. In the class that Thomas was expected to attend was a very autistic youngster, around 12 years of age, still having to suffer nappies. Thomas was just five and Jan already knew that Thomas was very visually receptive. As Jan put it at that time, surround Thomas with a few autistic children and very quickly he would learn to mimic the behaviour of others and would quickly become the most autistic in the group. This was not the right school for him.

At this time we did not think critically about conventional autism or the educational provision, we just did not believe that such provision was right for Thomas. As described earlier, there were a lot of relatively new educational concepts coming on the scene, many of them non interventional. We did not want passive play and non-directive therapy. We did not even want expensive solutions that we had read about such as Son Rise or Lovass. Nor did we believe that Makaton or PECS were especially relevant to Thomas. What was the point of trying to generate language through play when this boy did not want to play? By this time, aged five, we knew that the written word and *language through reading* were ways to reach Thomas and we strongly believed that pragmatic interventional strategies were essential for Thomas's development. But to the educationalists, what did we know, we were only the parents.

In respect of speech and language therapy (SLT), we were getting consultation and advice on strategy at the macro level from the inspirational Janet Lees at GOS. What we needed was SLT delivery at a local level. However, our local SLT service wanted to start by fully re-assessing Thomas themselves all over again. No recognition for the work, reports and recommendations already undertaken at GOS; it was so frustrating. Not only was there no suitable school for Thomas to go to, there was also a complete gulf in regard to our views on strategy for Thomas and those of the educationalists and SLT service. We felt we were banging our heads against a brick wall. The crunch came when we asked through our GP for SLT support for Thomas locally; the request was rejected. The Head of SLT for Dorset carefully explained that the resource was very scarce and had to be focussed where it could have most effect. In her opinion, this was not a good use of resource and anyway there seemed little point, as Thomas showed no real signs of speech!

For Jan this was the last straw and her reaction was immediate and decisive. Her position was now unequivocal: *I know that there is a way into Thomas and if no one else will do it the way I feel it should be done, the way that GOS were supporting and advising me on, then I will do it myself.* That was Jan's view, and there was no further discussion, stop the duplicitous and independent assessments, stop pleading to be heard, stop all the meetings and the theories; it was time for delivery and for action. Home education loomed, or as it is called 'education otherwise' (taken from the legal term in The Education Act that 'all children are entitled to an education at school *or otherwise*'.

We decided that for this to work we would have to re-organise, reduce our costs and scale down our expenditure. Our four bedroom executive house on the pristine cul-de-sac would have to go. We needed a different kind of space, away from tut-tuting neighbours, where we would feel less inhibited as a family. We put the house on the market just as I was heading off for another two-week business trip to Australia. The property market was in the doldrums and nothing might happen for months.

On landing in Melbourne, the first voice mail was from Jan: 'we have had an offer for the house, what should I do?' Take it, we agreed and by the time I returned home from down under, contracts were ready to be exchanged. Just one problem: we had nowhere to go!

We decided to rent as an interim move, but all I could find was a semi derelict bungalow on the edge of the Beaminster valley, a lovely private location deep in Dorset and next to a huge donkey sanctuary. No matter, only short term says I, but I do remember the *'Oh my God, what have I done'* moment as I desperately tried to repaint the interior and scrape the fungicidal mushrooms sprouting all around the shower cubicle the week-end before we moved in!

Jan set to work with gusto. 'Post it' notes were everywhere, covered with large words and letters. White boards and pin boards took over from where pictures would be on the walls. On the one hand, euphoria that we had no neighbours and that we were getting on with delivery to Thomas and not just talking about it. On the other hand, we were isolated, literally, and very much on our own. Anything could happen and the future was very uncertain.

On any journey, you follow the signposts, and you can turn left, right, go straight ahead or even do a U turn. There were no signposts on this journey. Gut instinct, tempered by fear of getting it wrong were our only guide. I quit my commercial job soon after

Jan started home education. It was a huge decision, and I was able to take a local job for a dairy processing and cheese business. I was lucky enough to meet Phil Cook who ran Coombe Farm. He recognised that there was a mutual opportunity for me to bring my commercial experience to his organisation in return for me being at home at night and most importantly giving us the benefit of living in a spacious farmhouse on the estate. East Leaze Farm became our home and the perfect setting for Jan to develop home education plans for Thomas.

My salary almost halved and we struggled to stay afloat financially, but we managed to maintain our priority to keep Lizzie at her Prep School as a day pupil. Lizzie loved it at Perrott Hill School and we knew it was only a substitute for the time that Jan could not give to her due to the pressures of caring for and educating Thomas. We were just trying to juggle all the balls as best we could. Holidays and other luxuries went by the by, but we were so grateful for the space provided by our farmhouse and the folk at Coombe Farm. It is with humility that we thank Phil Cook and Nancy Ralph, trustees of The Warren Trust, which owns Coombe Farm, for their quiet, discreet and unquestioning manner in which they supported us over several crucial years.

Somehow Jan built a 'home education team' of several local volunteers around herself and Thomas. In all, the period of home education lasted over four years and many good things happened on the way. We met Mary Manning-Thomas who was a retired speech therapist who gave Jan so much encouragement. It does not matter if you have to repeat a word 999 times she said, because maybe on the thousandth time he will get it. Do not give up, do not be afraid, invade his space when you want to and always do what you feel to be naturally right.

Others locally were generous with their time in providing a regular slot in Thomas's 'school' diary. It was surprising how much people are willing to help, provided you are brave enough to ask, and you can handle rejections on the way. Janet Lees and

Victoria Birch from GOS also went above and beyond the call of duty during this time. Within their remit, they had the ability to visit specialist schools. Recognising that Thomas was being educated at home, they decided that he was in a school, albeit a school for one. On several occasions over the years, they came all the way down to Somerset to give Jan really practical support in delivering educational strategies to Thomas.

By the age of eight, Thomas was speaking in a very limited manner. Thomas's behaviour was slowly becoming more manageable, but in fact we had become more isolated as time went by. We were well and truly *'educating otherwise'*, well and truly outside the system. We knew that at some point Thomas needed to re-enter the educational system, and indeed it was necessary if he was going to develop socially. We started to look at schools again, and made contact with the local Educational Psychologist, Nigel Armistead. He complimented Jan's work with Thomas and promised to do his best to prepare the right Statement of Educational Need for Thomas, in order to get him into the right school and promised to support our application and our preference for a specialist placement.

We probably visited 25 schools over a two-year period from The Isle of Wight to Mansfield and everywhere in between. Several assessments took place, some over several days. All bar one ended in rejection and a refusal to offer a placement for Thomas. Finally we elected for St. Elizabeth's in Much Haddam Hertfordshire, an epilepsy based school that could handle elements of autistic tendencies. Most importantly, they had high levels of speech therapy available on-site and a full medical team for medicine control and monitoring. A request was made to our Local Education Authority (LEA) and it was rejected. The LEA proposed a local moderate learning disability (MLD) school, in a class of fourteen and with no experience of LKS and without a 'one to one' speech therapy support. We would have to go to tribunal.

The Tribunal process in education is fundamentally flawed. Firstly, LEA's almost always employ solicitors to argue their case for them. You are obliged to match firepower, so you need to employ a very specialist lawyer to represent your case. However, there is no legal aid for educational tribunals, it is not a 'means tested' matter, there simply is none. Even if you win a Tribunal, you have no right to have your costs paid by the LEA; you have to pay your own costs. This in itself puts most parents off the Tribunal process and even when parents do represent themselves, they have to carefully brief themselves up on the whole process of litigation. You then have to commission independent reports to counter those of the LEA. You often have to use your own initiatives to find suitable and independent specialists in areas such as SLT, educational psychologists, occupational therapists and the like. You have to commission these reports at your own cost in order to support you claim that the LEA's specialists have come to the wrong conclusion about school placement in your child's Statement of Educational Need; such reports become the basis for your appeal to a Tribunal.

So for many, the cost of employing a lawyer and other specialists, and/or the fear of managing a complex process oneself deters most from taking up an appeal to a Tribunal. The net effect is to deter the majority of this minority group of families with special educational needs from using the Tribunal process; this was surely not what the Tribunal process was intended to do?

In our case we were also naive in believing that the LEA Educational Psychologist, Nigel Armistead, would not act against us at the Tribunal. He had visited St Elizabeth's ostensibly, we believed, to understand and support our preferred choice. At our Tribunal he did an about turn, arguing that following his visit to St Elizabeth's, he now believed the local MLD school could, with his personal support, learn the skills necessary to support Thomas's education and import these skills to the local school, for delivery to Thomas!

We lost our Tribunal for three reasons. Firstly our Barrister, one of the leading specialists in the field, lost the Tribunal panel with an overly complex argument. Secondly, the tribunal took the view that as Thomas had not attended the local school, we could not demonstrate that they would not be able to meet his needs. Finally, the promises made by the LEA Educational Psychologist convinced them that Thomas would be fine at the local Moderate Learning Difficulty (MLD) school. This was galling in the extreme. If Thomas was to move on from home education, we had no choice but to send Thomas to the local MLD school.

There were also two prevailing political pressures in education circles at that time, namely the principles of 'in county' and 'inclusion'. These doctrines also surrounded our fight for the right education or Thomas.

For those not familiar with the Statement process, the essential factor is the naming of a school that is to be the provider for your child's education. Since education budgets moved from the Department of Education to the hands of the County Local Education Authority it is now also a matter of the County's budgetary control. The LEA's priority is to keep their own county schools full, and therefore they seek to place as many children as possible 'in county'. A request for a school such as St Elizabeth's in Hertfordshire was deemed to be an 'out of County' provision and as such Somerset would have to pay St Elizabeth's for the privilege. The consequence is that the doctrine of 'in county' has created an internal market for special needs education delivery with each county trying to meet *all* variety of special needs within its own borders. The result is that this policy creates diluted specialization at best and duplication in neighbouring counties at worst; crazy but true.

We were also caught up in the 'big experiment' of that time, the mid/late 90's: the concept of 'inclusion'. All children were, and still are, encouraged to attend main stream schools and additional support is intended to be provided for children with special needs.

Inclusion may be right for many children with special needs but for some, such as Thomas, inclusion in an inappropriate environment amounts to exclusion.

For many, the policies of 'inclusion' and 'in county' were seen as a poor guise for closing a raft of special schools around the country and reducing costs.

We came to the view that we had to win the placement of our choice, based on several factors. Firstly, that Thomas had been assessed and declined from many specialist schools meant that he had very specialist needs. Secondly that he had only been accepted at St Elizabeth's and they were a highly selective and specialist school. We even had the written support for our choice from the team at GOS who were perhaps the most knowledgeable in the country. This team had very specific awareness of the available educational provision for children like Thomas on a national basis and in many cases had direct links with these schools. Finally Jan's opinion as his teacher for four years had to count for something.

Thomas was at Fairmead (a local moderate learning difficulty school) at that time and we would have to wait at least another year before we could seek another Tribunal. Given our last experience, we felt that there was a high risk that the LEA would simply acknowledge that Fairmead was not working, and recommend another 'in county' placement. We had visited all the local LEA options in the Somerset region and felt that none were appropriate.

Throughout the legal process our solicitor Robert Love (a specialist in the field of educational tribunals) gave us frank advice. His patience with us and our many 'what if' questions was admirable!

In the end we came to the dangerous decision to appeal the Tribunal's decision on the grounds that 'their decision was perverse' in the face of the facts before the Tribunal. This meant we were going for a Judicial Review of the Tribunal's decision. Put simply, to over-turn the Tribunal's decision, we had to make a claim that the Tribunal had come to the wrong conclusion, and we were seeking to have their decision quashed. To do this we had to hire a new barrister and a QC. This was another one of those '*Oh, my God, what have we done*' moments. If we lost the Judicial Review at the Royal Courts of Justice in London, we would have to stand the full costs of the LEA! We ran the risk of being bankrupted. Do we turn left, turn right? We believed we were right so the only direction we knew was straight on, the only direction we could follow.

On the 10th November 2000 the day came for our hearing in the Royal Courts of Justice, our case, Crean vs. Somerset, was scheduled for a half day hearing. Justice John Sullivan, in his opening address said that he found it to be a contradiction to be hearing an appeal about a boy who hardly communicated for which there was over 650 pages of written evidence! The paper mountain surrounding our case sat before him on the bench. He advised the Clerk of the Court that scheduled half day allocated would be insufficient for a full hearing, and to re-schedule the court diary to make two days available.

At last, we felt Justice Sullivan was going to allow our legal team the time to go the extra mile in presenting the facts of our case and explaining why the Tribunal got it wrong. The arguments flew over a two-day period and the hearing went from heart-sinking pessimism to soaring optimism; it was a roller coaster but to our immense relief we won.

Our appeal against the original Tribunal decision had been upheld. The LEA had claimed that their school, Fairmead at Yeovil, was 'on the learning curve' to meet Thomas's needs. However, Justice Sullivan ruled that the Tribunal failed to establish where they were on the learning curve. Furthermore, Justice Sullivan found that the Tribunal failed to address the substantial evidence submitted by us for experienced specialist speech and language therapy and occupational therapy to be delivered to Thomas. Any LEA named school has to be able to have the required skills and resources in house at the time of the placement. It was not sufficient to promise to 'import the skills and learn as we go' (our words) as Somerset had intended. Therefore the Tribunal decision was deemed perverse in the face of the facts.

The case of Crean vs. Somerset has established the principles that an LEA named school cannot simply claim to be 'on the learning curve' of complex needs and that expert evidence for the need for specialist provisions such as speech or occupational therapy must be addressed by the Tribunal and the LEA. We have since learnt that other lawyers have cited this ruling to win their cases.

We were now referred back to a new Tribunal, in effect for a rematch. In fact, all the Royal Courts judgement had done was quash the original decision, and the Court does not have the power to change the name of the school. Therefore we had to start again to build a new Tribunal hearing.

By now Thomas was ten yeas old. At Parents' Day at Fairmead, we would go through the motions of congratulating the school on the work being done. We would ask to make copies of his work, claiming that we wanted to replicate their work at home as a form of homework for Thomas. In fact, what we were doing was building up a portfolio of his work to demonstrate that Thomas's work was in fact deteriorating. Imagine, Jan had spent over four years progressing Thomas's development and we had to hold our quarter, watching and logging his regression. It is one thing to watch your child stand still in education, but quite something else to watch them go backwards.

Given our first Tribunal hearing, and an overly complicated presentation of the facts, we decide to change our team, with the exception of our very patient solicitor Robert Love. We used an excellent Educational Psychologist, Ruth Birnbaum, Janet Lees from GOS and the late Principal of St Elizabeth's, Clair Walker who all supported us at the Tribunal. We faced the old foes from Somerset but this time we won. Thomas was to go to St Elizabeth's. The whole legal process took over three years, the paperwork just ballooned and the file system just got bigger and bigger. In the two-year period to March 2001, the whole process cost us over £35,000.

The Holiday Story

During the late 1990's, we were increasingly aware of the legal developments around the MMR vaccine. Indeed we spent time with Alexander Harris and Co, who were preparing the cases for the families.

In parallel, the pressures of home education and our own legal battle for education were taking their toll. Do we concentrate on a case for compensation or the educational case for school provision? We did not have the energy to do both, so a conscious decision had to be made. We took the personal view that with all the weight of the drugs companies and the might of the Government machine – with the Department of Health as its mouthpiece – compensation was at best a long way off and probably unlikely.

We took the decision to concentrate on what we believed was most likely to directly influence Thomas now, the legal battle for education, and we let the MMR debate slip quietly into the background of our personal agendas. By 2001, when Thomas was eleven, we had lost the first Tribunal, won the Appeal to the Royal Courts of Justice and won a second Tribunal. We were exhausted and very poor. It was time to get my income back on track and try to catch up lost ground. A big job came up in Lincolnshire, and we took the chance for a new start. Ironically this meant that Lincolnshire had to take up the schooling cost for Thomas and Somerset got away scot-free! We just had to move on and leave the old 'war wounds' behind.

Over the years we had attended many conferences and become tired of specialists *talking about* it but *not delivering it*. We met very few who seemed passionate about delivering services at the point of need. We had learnt early on that divorce is exceptionally high in families where there is a child with special needs, with only one family in five staying together for more than five years. So why is there so little effort being made to support the whole family?

Holidays were rare and when they did occur they were very stressful. We had been reduced to taking remote cottages on our own, away from others in order that we avoid the glares at our son's behaviour. All we wanted was to be treated as a regular family, aspirational, who like doing nice things without having to apologise.

It seemed crystal clear to us that good holidays are a small but very important component in helping keep families together. After all, holiday times are the most time that Dads spend with their children. If the holiday experience was not a good one, even one of dread, then that did not auger well for the whole family's ability to pull together. In fact, we believed that bad holiday experiences could have a very negative effect, potentially eroding family energy and weakening their collective strength. This seemed all wrong to us and there was a clear need that was not being met.

What if we could provide such a resource for families like ours that we had met on this road? We were convinced there was a need, and so when we moved to Lincolnshire and bought Westfield Farm we bought it with such a project in mind. 'Farm' was a bit of an exaggeration really. Originally over 500 acres (a proper farm!), the previous owners had sold off parcels of land over the years until there was just 25 acres left. In this part of the world this is more of a large garden than a farm. Either way, farm or garden, the important thing was that it was completely private and had a lovely set of derelict barns and outbuildings.

It took several years to pluck up the courage to start our own holiday business. During 2005 and 2006, a handful of great people gave us tremendous support, helping us to prepare business plans with which we were able to raise the funding and mortgages. A grant appeal to Defra was prepared and promptly rejected. We prepared an appeal (we were now experts at these appeals!) – and eventually our grant was approved under the heading 'Social inclusion in the rural economy'. This heading was one of eight headings under which one could apply for partial grant funding. We found out later that ours was the first application that had been made under this heading in the five years that the scheme had been running.

We opened late and over budget in the late spring of 2007 and The Thomas Centre was now ready to receive guests. We now have three houses and three bungalows all independently accredited to 4 four star and five star status. We do not exclude anyone, but we do specifically market to the autistic, epileptic and communication impaired groups under the strap line 'A unique holiday park for the *whole* family or group with communication impaired children or adults'. The emphasis is on the *whole* family or the *whole* group. Disabled activity centres are fine, but they clearly focus on the disabled member of the group. In our experience this is 'not very cool' for siblings and other youngsters in the party, and hence our focus on the whole family or group.

The aspiration for our project is to provide first class facilities that meet some of the expectations of each member of the family or group. On site we have a wide range of regular facilities, which can be accessed and enjoyed by all. We are not a charity, this is a business that is clearly meeting a need that we believe is not being adequately met, and we are mortgaged forever! Our aim is to somehow clear the debt, and that this can become our full time occupation, a place where Thomas can work within the limits of his abilities. Naturally, I do the lottery every week!

Jan runs the business with her sister Val. It is a full time occupation, as with any service business and with six properties, 26 beds and eight bathrooms or wet rooms on site. There are also extensive grounds to be maintained and we employ other staff on a part time basis. Lizzie, our daughter, currently studying to become a teacher in Geography in Birmingham, provides all kinds of holiday support and in particular oversees the development of our web site.

Conferences, meetings and discussions are all fine, but we prefer delivery at the point of need. We wish to treat people as we would wish to be treated ourselves in the belief that when we do, people respect what is being provided and will look after those facilities as they would look after their own. We believe strongly that a good holiday is an essential part of good family life.

We are not on a personal crusade, nor are we on a mission. Quite simply we are trying to take a holistic approach to provide first class holiday facilities for families and groups with children like ours. We are also trying to develop a family business, with the possibility that it can provide a place of work for Thomas and maybe, who knows, others in the future. We have just finished our second summer season and the response has been tremendous, and we have had some lovely experiences. One mother of three, upon finishing her family's private session in our indoor heated swimming pool, came over to Jan, hugged her and burst into tears. 'Thank you for allowing me the chance to swim with my son for the first time' she said. 'He can't cope with the noise of a public pool so we don't go, and haven't been for over four years.'

For our own personal survival we are 'trying to replace bad behaviour with good behaviour', to block out the bad memories of the past and to concentrate on good memories. By comparison with many that we have met we are very lucky with Thomas. I know that I could not take Thomas to Twickenham and discuss the tactics of an international game of rugby with him, nor could I take him to Glastonbury and dance and sing to Mr Brightside by The Killers. Both of these things I have enjoyed doing with Lizzie. However, as a family we have done so much more than we ever thought we could have done with Thomas. For example, after four years of attending the annual Spitfire Prom at Belton House (a combination of Last Night of the Proms, Proms in the Park and sprinkled with rampant patriotism as the Spitfires fly over to the orchestra playing the Dambusters theme tune) Thomas now really enjoys the event. Therefore we can replace bad memories with good memories, celebrate what we can do rather than grieve over what we cannot do.

Hopefully The Thomas Centre may provide many other families with the chance to relax, recuperate and have some good holiday experiences to remember.

To sum up, some very personal closing thoughts on our experiences.

On education

Firstly in relation to battles over education, there are a number of things to be considered. To other parents we would say this: for you the best educational provision is the least that your child deserves but for the Local Education Authority (LEA) your child's school placement is simply a budgetary matter. Immediately prior to the appeal to the Tribunals and the Appeal to the Royal Courts of Justice, I met with John Freeman, Deputy Director for Education for Somerset, and with Michael Jennings, Director of Education for Somerset. I pleaded with them not to proceed with the defence of their position in the face of all the specialist evidence supporting our case (and this was substantial). We faced massive costs and possible bankruptcy, I explained. Their replies were simple: Prof Neville (GOS) and his team's opinion on educational placement had no relevance, they are medics, we are educationalists, we know what is right in education. So much for multi-disciplinary reviews!

The cost of a placement at St Elizabeth's at that time was approaching £50,000 per annum. Given that Thomas's placement would last around 10 years it was made quite clear to me that the LEA were happy to fund Somerset LEA legal fees each and every year as they had a budget to manage. We were trying to develop Thomas to the point where he might not have to be in institutional or residential care for life and here Directorates of Education were primarily concerned about this year's budget. So much for the concept of whole life education and whole life costs.

If you do decide to 'educate otherwise' and educate at home, then the longer this continues the harder it is get back into the system. This is also as much about the fact that the longer you are your child's teacher the more you will know about their needs and the harder you will find it to accept compromises and second best positions for a school placement. Remember that the LEA Educational Psychologist has a mortgage to pay and is employed by the LEA. Do not rely on them to support your position (even when they tell you they will), if your position is going to cost the LEA money.

Your case officer at the LEA is trying to manage a budget. Even if, privately, they think your choice is right, no case officer will develop their career by recommending an option that will cost the LEA a lot of money. Therefore LEA personnel will gladly abrogate the decision to a Tribunal. In many cases they know that parents do not have the ability to take on such an action. If parents do take the LEA to Tribunal then any conclusion is then not the decision of the LEA personnel. They are simply complying with the Courts and by this simple mechanic, careers stay intact.

Understand in detail the importance of each part of the Statement for your child. This is crucial.

If you do employ a lawyer or barrister, make sure you can understand them and that they appear logical in their analysis of the argument. If you do not understand them (and you know the case better than anyone) do not expect a Tribunal panel to understand the argument presented by your lawyer. Do not be afraid to change advisors if you are not comfortable, you are paying.

Keep some money in the pot for extra quantities of alcohol, you will need it to steady the nerves! Seven years later we have no regrets that we chose to fight for the right for appropriate educational provision. We do regret that we were forced to have the fight in the first place. Through home education, where Jan did such a stalwart job, and latterly at St Elizabeth's, Thomas has progressed beyond our expectations. He will always need support and still has huge limitations in many basic communication skills. However, he is happy, has a great sense of humour, desperately wants to make others happy and has the potential to learn simple work routines by rote.

On the MMR vaccine

On a broader front, for a moment leave aside the politics and the controversy around the MMR. Imagine that thalidomide type deformities were an 'onset condition' as autism is now so described. There would be full investigations into causation. In such an example as thalidomide, a cause was found. As we all know, mental disorders do not command the same attention as physical deformities, so there is no public clamour to push for investigation. There is also the sneaking suspicion held by some that autism has a genetic factor and there is an hereditary element. On-lookers often look at the near hysterical parents and, of course, their hereditary theory is immediately (if privately) confirmed. No need for individual investigations then, it's probably down to the parents anyway!

Why are there not automatic individual investigations into each child's full condition in an attempt to find causation when there are clear groups of children with such similar conditions and a clear upward trend of incidents? Not all thalidomide deformities were exactly the same, but they all had a common theme to them. The only investigation our son has had was when we pushed and pushed. We are lucky, we have a voice and the energy to use it. Many do not. We also know that we still do not have the full picture and are never likely to do so.

It is not sufficient to look at 'herd statistics' and 'epidemiological studies' and use these to justify why there is no need for individual analysis. Our children are individual children with individual case histories but with so many common characteristics. Apart from the Royal Free investigations by Messrs Wakefield, Murch and Walker-Smith, there has been no attempt to look at our group of children where bowel performance and autistic features are jointly presented.

During the late 1990's my career was in the dairy sector of the food industry. We did not rely on 'epidemiological studies' to justify ignoring the BSE crisis. Dairy farmers were monitoring their herd individually and on a daily basis, looking out for signs and pro-actively testing. The national herd had never been so scrutinised.

The cattle could not tell us how they felt. Nor can our children. Yet we give our cattle more observation than our children. The dairy industry took collective action to investigate all potential causes of BSE and made major changes to the feed supply chains. In so doing, the disease has been brought under control. Our collective medical establishment has taken no such comparable action to investigate cause, and simply and crudely relied on statistics. A strange set of values. A very strange set of values.

On 'brosters'

The term 'sibling' is used extensively by professionals. Ask a sibling what they think of the term and generally they hate it. Rather like 'maiden', 'spinster', 'bachelor', or 'widow/widower', these terms seem to suggest a person with something missing in their life. The term 'sibling' appears derogatory, and implies that there is something missing from their life, that they, the sibling are also in some way handicapped.

Lizzie, Thomas's older sister, hates the term sibling. She feels it neutralises her as a person and I think she has a point. Perhaps we should develop a new word for siblings, a 'disgusterous' type word. How about 'Brosters' or 'Sisbros'?

Fear of what the future will hold has been well documented by others and we all try to protect our 'Brosters' from the pressures that life will bring on them. However, we all have to accept that we are all the sum of our genetic map and our own life experiences. On this basis, there is no getting away from the pressures that will affect brosters.

And finally

The traumatic effect that the MMR has had on our son, the consequential epilepsy, the haemorrhaging and the chronic damage to the bowel are matters of fact in our mind. The massive communication deficit, the gross motor weaknesses and the ongoing bowel sensitivities are, in our opinion, part of this train of events. We have had to learn how to join up personal strategies for each of these separate elements of our son's condition as we have gone along this road, in order to maximise the potential for Thomas. We have had to learn how to rationalise events and to exercise choice along the way and we have made mistakes. We know Thomas can learn visually and by rote. He can follow basic and repetitive tasks, and he can increasingly express a view on what he prefers to do.

While the GMC trial of Andrew Wakefield, Simon Murch and John Walker-Smith endeavours to have them struck off the medical register, who will investigate how the measles virus got into our son's bowel, and what caused such a catastrophic chain reaction of events? What are the relationships between all these separate elements of his condition? Will the GMC put as much energy into finding causation for our children's condition as they are doing in bring these gentlemen to book?

I think we all know the answers to these three questions.

Contributors

Jan and Richard Crean started life from modest hard working backgrounds, growing up on the same council estate in Kent. Jan went into the Civil Service and eventually into the support team of 10 Downing Street during Mrs Thatcher's early years. Richard has worked in various sectors of the food industry and ended up running some of the largest food production plants in the UK. The sudden changes in their son's development led to huge changes in their careers. Jan now manages The Thomas Centre, a unique holiday park providing five star facilities for families and adults with a range of communication impairment and specifically autism.

Heather Edwards has been married to Nick for 18 years. They have three children: Aaron 17, Josh 15 and Jodie 12. They live in Gosport, Hampshire. While most of Heather's life is taken up caring for Josh, she and Nick are also Portsmouth football fans and when they first started their chapter over a year ago they were looking forward to the 2008 FA Cup final on the 17th May between Portsmouth and Cardiff. A year later they are still very happy that Portsmouth beat Cardiff 1.0.

Celia Forrest is a single parent to Adam, a vaccine damaged child, and a full time carer for him. She has not been able to work since Adam was born. Previously she was a senior executive in sales and marketing for a major computer manufacturer, now she finds herself campaigning mainly in the area of special needs education for children with ASD.

Deborah Heather jumped at the opportunity to write about Andrew, her vaccine damaged son, despite being unsure of her writing abilities. After the case of over one thousand parents against the vaccine manufacturers collapsed, legal aid having been denied, Deborah became part of the MMR10, that continued to fight the case through the European Court of Human Rights and when this action failed, she dedicated herself to campaigning. Like other parents, she has struggled to bring up an autistic child, while fighting various departments and hospitals that won't or can't treat these children.

Barbara Loe Fisher is co-founder and president of a US nonprofit organisation founded in 1982 by parents of vaccine injured children known today as the National Vaccine Information Center. She co-authored with Harris Coulter *DPT: A Shot in the Dark*. This 1985 book put the vaccine risk issue on the map in the U.S and was the first published reference associating vaccines with autism. Barbara now writes and campaigns about how the vaccine safety and informed consent movement she helped launch in the early 1980's has impacted on public knowledge about vaccination and health. The National Vaccine Information Center organises the most informed vaccine web site in the world: http:// www. NVIC.org/. National Vaccine Information Center, 407 Church Street, Suite H, Vienna, VA 22180, Phone: 703-938-0342, Fax: 703-938-5768. Email: contactNVIC@gmail.com

Bill and Pat Marchant: Bill worked for the Ford Motor Co for 25 years and was a Manufacturing Specialist trained to find and repair both electrical and mechanical faults in Transit Vans. He then joind up with Pat to work an office cleaning franchise. They had both been previously married. Jodie, who has ASD, is their only child of six to have MMR; she is also their only child with any problems. They are now both full-time carers.

Iris and Derek Noakes: Iris was about to start school when WWII began and Derek is 77 this year! They met at Shell and married in 1956. Iris was a Bromley girl and Derek hailed from Bexleyheath, so cycling over to court her was not too much of a problem. They have lived in the same house since 1959 and their children, Deborah and Graham, were born in that house. Now, happily for both of them, they live quite close to their families. Their daughter Deborah has a vaccine damaged ASD son and she wrote a chapter in the first volume of *Silenced Witnesses*.

Dr Carol Stott has a BSc Hons in Psychology and a PhD from the University of Cambridge, following which she gained an MSc in Epidemiology from the London School of Hygiene and Tropical Medicine. She is a Chartered Psychologist and member of the British Psychological Society. She spent 13 years at the University of Cambridge, Department of Psychiatry, carrying out research into genotype-phenotype associations in developmental disorder and with the University of Cambridge Autism Research Centre investigating the population frequency of Autism Spectrum Disorders. She is now a Senior Research Associate to Dr Andrew Wakefield at Thoughtful House Center for Children in Austin, Texas. Dr Stott recently joined the *Autism File* Magazine as Scientific Editor and acts as a diagnostic and psychometric consultant to The Autism Clinic.

Polly Tommey is a mother dealing with autism. She is also the founder and Editor-in-Chief of *The Autism File*, now the leading retail magazine on autism in the UK, USA & Canada, with a current issue circulation of over 40,000 copies. Polly is also the founder of The Autism Trust, a UK registered charity that focuses on building an inspiring and sustainable future for children with autism in the UK after they leave full time education. Polly is a sector expert in the media. She is currently directing an investigative television documentary on autism and she presents a regular radio programme: Autism Issues From Around the World on Autism One Radio. She is married to Jonathan Tommey who runs The Autism Clinic and they have three children, one of whom has autism.

Martin Walker has an MA and he is a campaigner and author of eight books. Four of his most recent books are about ties to industry and conflict of interests in medicine. Eight of his most recent essays, mainly about vaccination and the Wakefield affair, have been published in *Medical Veritas*, April 2009 (www.Medical Veritas.com). He has attended almost every day of the Fitness to Practice Hearing that has tried Dr Wakefield, Professor Murch and Professor Walker-Smith; his accounts of the hearing are at www.cryshame.com. He has been a member of the Cry Shame Advisory Group and is editor and publisher of both *Silenced Witnesses* books. His web site is www.slingshotpublications.com.

About The Autism File

The Autism File is now the leading retail magazine on autism in the UK, USA & Canada, with a current issue circulation of over 40,000 copies. It is linked to The Autism Trust, a UK registered charity that focuses on building an inspiring and sustainable future for children with autism in the UK after they leave full time education. www.autismfile.com

About CryShame

CryShame is a campaigning group, co-founded by a number of UK parents and professionals who are concerned about the catastrophic rise in autism spectrum disorders and the potential link with environmental toxins – particularly MMR and thimerosal containing vaccines. The immediate mission for CryShame is to support Professor Simon Murch, Dr Andrew Wakefield and Professor John Walker-Smith as they stand accused before the General Medical Council of the UK. CryShame additionally supports the democratic rights of scientists and medical practitioners to engage in valid research and to publish relevant findings without fear of prejudice or attack.

About Slingshot Publications

Silenced Witnesses vol. II is a Slingshot Publications initiative produced with *The Autism File*. Slingshot Publications also produced the first volume of *Silenced Witnesses* with CryShame. www.slingshotpublications.com

Bibliography and other Popular Materials

Books about vaccine damage by parents

Coulter, Harris L. and Fisher, Barbara Loe. *DPT: A shot in the dark*. Harcourt Brace Jovanovich, USA, 1985.

Fox, Rosemary. *Helen's Story*. John Blake, London, 2006.

Grant, Marge. *A Stolen Life*. Precautionary Books, USA, 2005.

Silenced Witnesses. The Parents' Story: The denial of vaccine damage by government, corporations and the media. Written by the parents. Edited by Martin J Walker. Slingshot Publications, London, 2008.

An introduction to academic papers

Baron-Cohen S., Scott F.J., Allison C., Williams J., Bolton P. Matthews F.E., Brayne C. Prevalence of autism-spectrum conditions: UK school-based population study. *The British Journal of Psychiatry* (2009) 194, 500–509. DOI: 10.1192/BJP.BP.108.059345.

Galiatsatos P., Gologan A., Lamoureux E. Autistic enterocolitis: Fact or fiction? *Can J Gastroenterol* Vol 23 No 2 February 2009.

Genuis, S.J., Bouchard, T.P. Celiac Disease Presenting as Autism. *Journal of Child Neurology*, electronic pre-publication paper June 29 2009.

González L., et al. Endoscopic and histological characteristics of the digestive mucosa in autistic children with gastro-intestinal symptoms: A preliminary report. *GEN Suplemento Especial de Pediatria* 2005. 1: p. 41-47.

Hertz-Picciotto I., Lora Delwiche L. The Rise in Autism and the Role of Age at Diagnosis. *Epidemiology* (2009) 20, (1) DOI: 10.1097/EDE.0b013e3181902d15.

Mamone-Capria M. Preface to Series of Essays by Martin J Walker. *Medical Veritas*, 2009; 6(1): 2025.

Poling J.S., Frye R.E., Shoffner J., Zimmerman A.W. Developmental regression and mitochondrial dysfunction in a child with autism. *Journal of Child Neurology*, 2006;21:170-172.

Thrower David. Regressive Autism, Ileal-Lymphoid Nodular Hyperplasia, Measles virus and MMR vaccine. Available as a pdf: http://www.vaproject.org/thrower/mmr-briefing-20070430.htm

Wakefield A.J., et al. Inflammatory Bowel Disease Study Group, Royal Free Hospital, London. Ileal-lymphoid-nodular hyperplasia, non-specific colitis, and pervasive developmental disorder in children. *Lancet* (1998), 351(9103): pp637-641.

Wakefield Andrew J., Montgomery Scott M. Measles, Mumps, Rubella Vaccine: Through a glass, darkly. *Adverse Drug Reactions* 2000,19(4) 1-19.

Wakefield A.J., Blaxill M., Ryland A.J., Daniel Hollenbeck D., Johnson J., Moody J.D., Stott C.M. Response to Dr. Ari Brown and the Immunization Action Coalition. *Medical Veritas* 6 (2009) 6:1907-1924.

Walker M.J. Uncomfortable Science and Enemies of the People. *Medical Veritas*, 2009; 6(1): 2061-2066.

Walker M.J. An Interest in Conflict? The 'conflict of interest' policy of the General Medical Council and the fitness to practice hearing of Dr Andrew Wakefield, Professor Walker-Smith, and Professor Simon Murch. *Medical Veritas*, 2009; 6(1): 2067-2076.

Walker M.J. The Complainant - Brian Deer, the ABPI, Medico-Legal Investigations, and Dr Andrew Wakefield. *Medical Veritas*, 2009; 6(1): 2077-2092.

Walker M.J. An Open Letter to Brian Deer Rebutting His Article - 'Families duped by a sad smearmaster of MMR fabrication and hatred'. *Medical Veritas*, 2009; 6(1): 2093-2105.

Walker M.J. To Encourage the Others. *Medical Veritas*, 2009; 6(1): 2113-2124.

Walker M.J. The Urabe Farrago - A Recent Historical Example of Corporations and Governments Hiding Vaccine Damage for the Greater Good. *Medical Veritas*, 2009; 6(1): 2125-2146.

Welch M.G., et al. Brain effects of chronic IBD in areas abnormal in autism and treatment by single neuropeptides secretin and oxytocin. *J Mol Neurosci*, 2005. 25(3): p. 259-74.

Contemporary books about immunisation

Halvorsen, Dr Richard. *The Truth About Vaccines: How we are used as guinea pigs without knowing it*. Gibson Square, London, 2007.

Jepson, Bryan. *Changing the Course of Autism*. First Sentient Publications, USA, 2007.

Kirby, David. *Evidence of Harm: Mercury in vaccines and the autism epidemic, a medical controversy*. St. Martin's Press, New York, 2006.

Miller, Neil Z. *Vaccines, Autism and Childhood Disorders: Crucial data that could save your child's life*. New Atlantean Press, New Mexico, 2003.

Newspaper articles

Beck, Sally. 'Can You Ever Cure Autism? This Mum Believes Her Sons Have Recovered.' *Daily Mirror*, March 2 2009.

Campbell, Denis. 'I Told the Truth all Along'. *The Observer*, July 8 2007.

Ellis, Rachel and others. A series of articles: 'New Campaign for Vaccine Damaged Children'. *Daily Express*, May 2000.

Phillips, Melanie. A series of articles: 'MMR: the Truth'. *Daily Mail*, March 2003.

Roberts, Yvonne. 'A Shot in the Dark'. *The Sunday Times Magazine*, December 17 1995.

Sandall, Roberts. 'MMR RIP?'. *The Sunday Times*, December 14 2003.

Other material

Blakemore-Brown, Lisa. *Reweaving the Autistic Tapestry: Autism, Asperger Syndrome and ADHD*. Jessica Kingsley Publishers, London and Philadelphia, 2002.

Golding, Alan. *Selective Hearing: Brian Deer and the GMC.* 2009. www.cryshame.com

Hear the Silence (Screenplay: Timothy Prager. Director: Tim Fywell. Producer: Adrian Bate). Broadcast by Channel 5, December 15 2003.

Lathe, Richard. *Autism, Brain and Environment.* Jessica Kingsley Publishers, London and Philadelphia, 2006.

Mills, Heather. 'Report on MMR: The story so far: a comprehensive review of the MMR vaccination and autism controversy'. *Private Eye*, May 2002.

Walker, Martin J. Continuous contemporaneous account of the GMC Hearing on Dr Wakefield, Prof. Walker-Smith and Prof. Murch from July 2007. www.cryshame.com.

Walker, Martin J. *Brave New World of Zero Risk.* Slingshot Publications, 2006. www.slingshotpublications.com.

Walker M.J. Vaccine Damage Denial and the British Press. *The Autism File,* issue 30, 2009.

Court Decisions

In the United States Court of Federal Claims: Office Of Special Masters No. 02-0738V. Filed: 20 July 2007; Bailey Banks, by his father Kenneth Banks.

A federal vaccine injury program court concluded in November 2007 that Hannah Poling's underlying illness, that had predisposed her to symptoms of autism, was 'significantly aggravated' by vaccinations.

Websites

The Autism File magazine: www.autismfile.com

CryShame: www.cryshame.com

Slingshot Publications: www.slingshotpublications.com

Thoughtful House; Research, Treatment and Education Information: http://www.thoughtfulhouse.org

www.fourteenstudies.com

Facebook Pages – Autism File magazine

Autism File: Magazine – www.facebook.com/autismfile

Autism File: Mothers Campaign –
www.facebook.com/autismfile.mothers

Autism File: Brothers and Sisters Online –
www.facebook.com/autismfile.sibs

Autism File: Dr Wakefield's Work Must Continue –
www.facebook.com/autismfile.wakefield

Autism File: Science –
www.facebook.com/autismfile.science

Names Index

G

H

I

J

K

L

M

N

Nash, Jeremy, 115–7, 119–21, 124, 126, 135.
Neville, Dr Brian, 237–8, 240, 259.
Nieuwenhuizen, Prof Onno van, 235–7.
Noakes, Derek, 34, 266–7.
   See Chapter Three *Our Children's Children.*
Noakes, Iris, 33–4, 113–27, 130–1, 135, 266–7.

O

O'Connell, Dr David, 85, 126, 213.
O'Leary, Dr John, 158–9, 243.
O'Reilly, Brenda, 242.

P

Pegg, Michael, 8–9.
Picton, Gaye, 168.
Pilger, John, 10.
Poling, Hannah, 4, 274.
Pugh, Dr David, 89–90.

R

Reid, John, 2, 22.
Rimland, Dr Bernard, 66–7.

S

Salisbury, Prof. David, 1–2, 8–9, 133.
Savage, Prof. Wendy, 25–6.
Shattock, Paul, 156, 198, 214, 219, 242.
Shipman, Dr Harold, 23.
Spencer, Herbert, 67.
Stephenson, Juliet, 128.
Stott, Dr Carol, 1, 4, 29, 267, 272.

T

Taylor, Dr Brent, 133.
Thompson, Damian, 131.
Thompson, Dr Mike, 155.
Tommey, Bella, 204–6, 208–9, 212, 218.
Tommey, Billy, 37, 126.
   See Chapter Seven *Futures for Billy.*
Tommey, Jonathan, 204–23, 267.
Tommey, Polly, 10, 37, 267.
   See Chapter Seven *Futures for Billy.*
Tommey, Toby, 211–2, 223.

W

Wakefield, Dr Andrew, 1–3, 5–9, 11–2, 14–23, 25–8, 36, 39n, 64–7, 86, 98, 102, 106, 108, 110n, 129, 131–2, 134, 136–7, 152–5, 158–9, 162–3, 169–70, 175, 181, 197–8, 200, 214, 217, 219–20, 224, 262–3, 267, 272, 274–5.
Walker, Martin John, 1, 4, 11, 40n, 268, 271–2, 274.
Walker-Smith, Prof. John, 1, 3, 7, 9, 11, 16, 21, 110n, 152, 155, 198, 243, 262–3, 268–9, 272, 274.
Warner, Prof, 201.
Wijers, Rene, 38, 235.
Wing, Lorna, 232, 234.

Z

Zuckermann, Prof. Arie, 8–9.

Subjects Index

A

Abdominal pain, 20, 22, 83, 91–2, 96, 107, 118, 150–3, 155–7, 179, 185, 243.
ABPI, *see* Association of the British Pharmaceutical Industry.
Adam, 139–163.
Allergies, 56, 58, 63, 85, 88, 110, 151, 201.
   medications, 58.
   milk, 45, 56, 58, 184.
   peanut, 42.
   pollen, 58.
   vaccines, 58.
Allergy Induced Autism (AIA), 151, 242.
American Academy of Pediatrics, 52.
   Committee on Infectious Diseases, 66.
Anorectal manometry, 85, 109.
Antibiotics, 42, 46, 58, 61–2, 75, 78, 94, 116, 171, 203, 205–7.
Arthritis,
   acute, 54.
   chronic, 54, 62.
   rheumatoid, 58.
ASD, *see* Autism Spectrum Disorders.
Asperger's syndrome, 65, 169, 273.
   See also Autism Spectrum Disorders.
Association of the British Pharmaceutical Industry (ABPI), 2, 4, 29, 272.
Asthma, 42, 44, 56, 60, 110n.
Auditory Integration Training (AIT), 127, 135.

Autism, 6, 13, 33–4, 38, 42, 44, 55, 56, 61, 66, 69–70, 79, 83–5, 108–9, 118, 122, 130, 132, 134, 137, 144, 150–1, 153, 157–8, 161, 168–9, 177–8, 183, 189–91, 194n, 197–8, 200, 209–13, 217–8, 222–3, 233–4, 240, 242, 245, 265, 269, 271–2, 274.
   community, 4, 10, 36, 135, 218–22, 232.
   gastro–intestinal disorders and, 12–3, 15, 17, 65, 102, 108, 155, 158, 171, 173, 176, 183, 190, 217, 242, 271, 273.
   charities, 8, 161, 163n, 221, 267, 269.
   MMR and, 4–6, 12–5, 17, 21, 64, 67–9, 84, 102, 108, 131, 134–5, 198–9, 215, 242, 261, 274.
   regressive, 2, 12, 32, 56–7, 66, 69–70, 84, 272–3.
   vaccines and, 4, 33–4, 37, 55–7, 63, 66–7, 69–71, 131, 134, 137, 163n, 214, 242, 266, 273.
   See also Autism Spectrum Disorders.
Autism File, The, 37, 138n, 214–215, 217–8, 222, 267, 269, 274–5.
Autism Research Institute (ARI), 66, 126.
Autism Research Unit, University of Sunderland, 156.
Autism Spectrum Disorders (ASD), 4, 33, 38, 68, 101–2, 124, 126, 134, 161–2, 265–7, 269, 271.
   See also Asperger's syndrome.
Autism Trust, 10, 222–3, 267, 269.